Beyond Business Analytics

Eliezer Geisler

Beyond Business Analytics

The Foundations of Behavioral Perspective Theory

palgrave
macmillan

Eliezer Geisler
Illinois Institute of Technology
Chicago, IL, USA

ISBN 978-3-030-43717-6 ISBN 978-3-030-43718-3 (eBook)
https://doi.org/10.1007/978-3-030-43718-3

This Palgrave Macmillan imprint is published by the registered company Springer Nature Switzerland AG
The registered company address is: Gewerbestrasse 11, 6330 Cham, Switzerland

For Hani

Preface

The genesis of this book can be traced to my doctoral dissertation, several decades ago. At that time, I was awarded a research grant from the National Aeronautics and Space Administration (NASA). This was in the late 1970s. The race to the moon had already been concluded and with it the United States had won a great victory over the Soviet Union. President Kennedy's wish to land a man on the moon and bring him back before the decade of the 1960s is out had been accomplished. The American public's interest in space was beginning to wane. Congress started to inquire whether additional funding should be given to NASA, and more importantly, what was the revised mission of the agency, now that the race to the moon had been completed.

NASA was an organization in a state of flux and change. The managers of the agency wanted to know how to measure, perhaps even quantify these changes, so, as one of them put it succinctly: "we'll know what we are dealing with, so that we can make reasonable decisions." My task, as specified in my research grant, was to propose a system which would help NASA managers to monitor the process of transition they were facing, from space explorations to a more "earthly-oriented" research and development effort. This revised focus would then help NASA's government officials to make better decisions here on earth.

My doctoral dissertation was titled: "An Empirical Study of a Proposed System for Monitoring Organizational Change in a Federal R&D Laboratory." Empirically, to make the study more feasible. I concentrated on one of the five NASA regional laboratories. The director of the laboratory and his team of scientists, engineers, and managers, were graciously highly cooperative, thus making my experience at the laboratory very productive as well as enjoyable.

Since then, over the years, I conducted research in a large number of R&D and technological organizations, in the United States, Europe, and South America. I had interviewed and routinely interacted with a substantial number of scientists, engineers, departmental managers, and directors of these worldwide organizations.

During my graduate studies, I was very fortunate to receive intellectual inputs from several faculty members of Northwestern University, in particular my dissertation advisor professor Michael Radnor; and the members of my doctoral committee: professors Albert Rubenstein, Charles Thompson, Robert Boruch, and Haskel Benishay. With their guidance, I was able to find several salient attributes of the decision-makers in these organizations, and identify some interesting aspects of their processes of making these decisions. Most importantly, I was able to construct a system for the monitoring and measuring of these processes.

At the same time, I was constantly wondering: "what is being done with all the data/information that was being collected in these target organizations?" Some of the data was used to analyze the decision processes, but much of the data was just collected, classified, and stored, without a clear mandate for the implementation or usage by the decision-makers. It was also abundantly clear to me that this phenomenon was also occurring in all the organizations I was studying. Their managers routinely collected vast amounts of data, from the various divisions and functions of the organization. Also, interestingly, highly respected organizational behavior scholars at the time encouraged the collection of such data, usually as an instrument for strategic planning.

As discussed later in this book, the managers of these firms collected information on the functions, the processes and the activities of their financial system, their product or service acquisition of resources, the outputs and marketing effort of their product or service, their interactions with external organizations, and other data/information of the internal processes of their organization. In all these organizations I encountered the phenomenon of massive data acquisition and accumulation. Every organization was essentially mired in vast amounts of data/information. One manager compared this to the pile of municipal garbage. One has to sift through the entire pile to find a desired object.

For me it was comparable to an episode in AD 1209, when Pope Innocent III decided to deal with the sect of the Cathars who lived in the French town of Beziers and were Christians but had rejected the papal authority, and thus were considered by the Pope to be heretics. The Pope sent an army, led by the French nobleman Simon de Monfort, to conquer and destroy the Cathars. De Monfort ordered the citizens of Beziers to deliver to him the Cathars. The citizens refused. Accompanied by the Pope's representative, a monk named Arnaud Amalric, Simon the Monfort then attacked the town, killing about 20 thousand people, and then proceeded to burn the town.

When asked how should they distinguish between Catholic and Cathar, Amalric famously said: "Kill them all, God will recognize his own."

In a similar mode, managers assemble great quantities of data and then proceed to sort through the data in order to identify and to extract the desired individual data items. The idea is to have at the manager's disposal a large set of data, with the underlying assumption that within this mass of raw data there exists the desired piece of information.

I also sadly discovered that most, if not all, of these organizations lacked a formal system for the utilization of this mass of data/information they had collected in the process they used in making decisions, most importantly, strategic decisions. This was a peculiar phenomenon.

Organizational behavior scholars have long advocated and encouraged the managers of business firms to collect, store, and possibly to utilize this mass of data/information. At the same time these scholars were reluctant to construct a system of implementation of such data and their utilization in making decisions, nor to offer a feasible way of how to effectively utilize such data. This was the situation across organizations of all types, sizes, functions, and managerial strategies, whereby an insurmountable schism had been opened between the acquisition of data/information, and their possible usage in the firm's decision-making processes.

This book proposes a potential solution, in the form of the Behavioral Perspective Theory (BPT). This innovative theory advances the idea that the behavior of decision-makers should be designed to take into account the objective of the ultimate perspective of the organization: why are we making these decisions, and how do these decisions impact the ultimate goals of the organizations? That is, the decision made by organizational members are based not only on the qualitative and the quantitative attributes of the problem for which a decision is warranted, but also on the intellectual space between this problem and the ultimate goals (perspectives) of the organization. How decisions made in lower levels of the organizational hierarchy eventually affect the higher levels of the organization, through a process of "continuous clustering," by which the variables or dimensions of lower levels of the hierarchy are assembled into coherent higher-level constructs, which then they are clustered to allow them to reach the point where they impact the ultimate goals, or perspective, of the organization.

Chicago, USA Eliezer Geisler

Contents

CHAPTER 1

The Notion of Business Analytics

Business Analytics (BA) is a novel method, or set of methods, designed to collect, assemble, analyze, and interpret data for a better understanding of organizations, business firms, public entities, and other human enterprises (Braunstein 1974; Davenport and Harris 2007). The key question that emerges in this context: How is this done (Agor 1986; Bannister and Griffith 1986; Chen et al. 2012; Kaufman and Kirsch 2014)?

What is Business Analytics?

The notion of business analytics has been variously defined as the "skills, technologies, and practices for continuous iterative exploration and investigation of past business performance to gain insight and drive business planning" (Beller and Barnett 2009). Simplified, business analytics is a summary notion of the analyses we are able to perform on the skills, technologies, and practices of the organization. This analysis seeks answers to the question: What are the methods and techniques that the organization employs to function, to compete, and to move ahead?

One of these practices employs: (1) the collection of certain data; (2) the analysis of this data; and (3) the conclusions derived from this analysis. This means that business analytics is the theoretical space as well as the practice of collecting specific data, then analyzing it, and finally

E. Geisler, *Beyond Business Analytics*,
https://doi.org/10.1007/978-3-030-43718-3_1

reaching conclusions that may seamlessly serve as inputs to decision-making by managers (Janssen et al. 2017; Kiron et al. 2013; Laurson and Thorlund 2010).

Another definition of business analytics can be found in the popular website of *Techopedia*. This definition states:

> *Business Analytics (BA) refers to all the methods and techniques that are used by an organization to measure performance. Business analytics are made up of statistical methods that can be applied to a specific project, process, or product. Business analytics can also be used to evaluate an entire company. Business analytics are performed in order to identify weaknesses in existing processes and highlight meaningful data that will help an organization prepare for future growth and future challenges.* (Dahl 1963; Davenport et al. 2013; Drucker 1988; Fox and Tversky 1995)

Yet another simple way of describing business analytics is to consider it as a compilation of information from various and sundry sources assembled by a decision-maker, but without a specific model where this information may be inserted and without a pre-established set of criteria that would guide the information thus obtained into a given architecture of managerial decision context (Cosentino 2015; Geisler 2002; Ghosh and Scott 2011; Leavitt 1975).

In this manner, business managers collect data and store it in various organizational "containers" or systems. In some instances, these managers possess a systematic instrument that enables them to assign a given storage location to a piece or set or quantity of information. In other instances, this information is merely stored in a general system, together with other adscititious bunches of information.

A key factor in the usefulness of these storage systems is the ability of the manager to *retrieve* a given item of information whenever the need arises for such action. This means that analytics involves a set of organizational actions, among them (1) the selection of items of information for storage, (2) the criteria for storage and retrieval of these items of information, and (3) the ability of the manager to apply the information thus retrieved as input to a decision-making process (Nutt 1990; Schroeck et al. 2012; Siegel 2013; Taylor et al. 2014).

The aforementioned descriptions of business analytics are limited to the institutional activities of collecting data and organizing the data into the storage facilities of the organization. Such storing means that the data is "on the shelf" for the use of members of the organization when they have the need to make decisions, hence to mobilize such data off the shelf and into service as inputs to the decision-making process (Nutt 1990; Rockart and DeLong 1988; Wang et al. 2016).

However, the descriptions do not extend beyond the activities and do not go into the space of the decision-making act itself as it is exercised by the decision-maker. That is, in the description of business analytics we have the mere information, but not its application, implementation, or incorporation into the cognitive and behavioral frameworks of the decision-maker.

Business analytics is composed of (1) integration of data analyses, (2) pattern identification, and (3) cognitive positioning. This leaves us with the uncharted territory or space of the behavioral aspects of the decision-making process. This is the area where we embark beyond the mere listing of the information and classifying it for the records of the organization. This is the point beyond which the information becomes an integral part of the behavioral practice of transforming the raw data into useful and meaningful cognitive constants (Bannister and Griffith 1986; Borgman 1999; Chen and Chun-Yang 2014; Drucker 1988; Zwolenski and Weatherill 2014).

A Summary Review of the Foundational Literature on Models of Data Analytics

In the past five decades there have been several attempts to formulate systems that are designed to analyze the architecture and the performance of business enterprises. These systems or models have had some success in their empirical implementation within businesses. The need for good business analytics has also spurred the creation of business software and enterprise platforms to mine an organization's data in order to automate some of these measures and pick out meaningful insights. Although the term has become a bit of a buzzword, business analytics is a vital part of any business, making up a large portion of decision support systems, continuous improvement programs, and many other techniques used to keep a business competitive. Consequently, accurate business analytics, like efficiency measures and capacity utilization rates, is the first step to properly implementing these techniques (Kiron et al. 2013; L'Huillier and Maldonado 2011; Madtiavan and Grover 1998; Polydrack 2018). Following is a condensed description of the more popular or used systems.

Decision Analytics refers to decisions made by members of the organization whereby the decision-maker utilizes mental and other models that describe the decision-maker's reasoning in making such decisions (Kraemer and King 1986; Hult and Lennung 1980; Kahneman and Tversky 1973).

Descriptive Analytics examines organizational historical data in order to gain insights and knowledge about the organization and its progress. These data include reports, memos, scorecards, and similar correspondence and reporting produced by members (Fox and Tversky 1998; Geisler 1979; Etner et al. 2012).

Predictive Analytics refers to the use of predictive models that employ statistical data, tools, and platforms (Geisler and Kostoff 1999; Geisler 2002).

Prescriptive Analytics refers to the use of methods and models such as simulations and optimization. These models yield alternative decisions that can be employed by the decision-maker who can select those alternatives deemed to be appropriate for the situation when a decision is required or recommended (Gao et al. 2011; Hammer 1996; Hubbard 2014; Jenkins and Johnson 1997).

Over time, business analytics has become an organizational instrument routinely used for data analyses. It is a remarkable tool that gives actual, relevant, and current information about events that are of interest to the organization (Burrows and Savage 2014; Court 2015; Ghosh and Scott 2011; Kiron et al. 2010).

Business analytics is also an instrument that can be used *en masse* or sparingly. That is, managers may wish to collect a considerable amount of data so they can analyze events for the entire organization or they may wish to limit their endeavor to selected aspects or events in the organization (Kristoffersen et al. 2021).

Examples of the Types of Business Analytics

Decision Analytics

In many ways, decision analytics replaces the hitherto prevalent decision analysis. The key difference between the two modes is the ability of analytics to sort through massive amounts of data and to identify patterns. However, this ability does not replace human intuition and human judgment. Rather, these human capabilities become "must have" components of sound decision-making. Decision analytics should reinforce and complement human intuition, an innovative mind set, and human judgment.

Ulvila and Brown (1982) describe the 1970s as a time when "... decision analysis was still an experimental management technique, a fairly straightforward application of statistical decision theory" (p. 130). They also list the experiences of various companies. For example, larger petroleum companies (Union Texas Petroleum, Champlin Oil and Gas, and Gulf Oil) routinely employed decision analysis models and techniques in their selection of sites for digging wells in their search for oil and gas (Bannister and Griffith 1986; Davenport 2014a; Geisler 2013; Ghosh and Scott 2011; Horner 2018).

Decision analytics is used routinely and comprehensively throughout the business world, as well as in public organizations such as municipal, state, regional, and federal entities. However, successful implementation of this method or technique is not automatically guaranteed. In my 1997 book (*Managing the Aftermath of Radical Corporate Change*), I offer a critique of the quasi-ubiquitous use of Business Process Engineering (BPE). I argue that the failure of many such programs "... is but another attempt in the long tradition of corporate-wide programs which overpromised but did not deliver" (p. 52).

This is, in my view, the key strength of decision analytics. The ubiquitous usage and widespread applications make this mode of decision-making a very useful tool for managers. Some organizational scholars have argued that decision analytics, in its formats of description prediction and prescription, is the most powerful instrument for managerial action because this decision mode not only focuses on results but also uses human judgment (Borgman 1999; Davenport et al. 2013; Elgendy and Elragal 2016; Etner et al. 2012).

As this form of decision analytics permeates both the public and private sectors, its importance as the principal instrument for analysis grows, to the point of becoming the indispensable component of any analysis in which decisions are involved. In this manner, Decision Analytics is embedded in most scenarios of decision-making. Moreover, due to the fact that this tool exists, decision-makers are encouraged to use it, to the point where they may find themselves almost obliged to incorporate this instrument into their routine processes where decisions are required (Agor 1986; Braunstein 1974; Cosentino 2015; Dahl 1963; Davenport et al. 2010; Davenport 2014b; Drucker 1988).

Descriptive Analytics

The most precise and ubiquitous definition of descriptive analytics suggests that descriptive analytics offers us a glimpse into past events. In this mode, data are collected describing past occurrences so that statistical evidence exists that tells the story of the past. Such data include historical accounts in documents and human-recorded testimonies that are preserved in many forms, for instance, paper documents, inscriptions on monuments such as stone and on utensils, war instruments, and similar historical and archaeological relics (Conboy et al. 2020).

As I explained in my book, *The Metrics of Science and Technology* (Quorum Books, 2000), even such non-obtrusive, seemingly objective sources of information are also subject to careful scrutiny. Written or inscribed documents do not necessarily mean that they recount or represent the true events. As a general rule, all data memorialized in historical documents have political, social, religious, military, and ego-enhancement motives. The rulers or other influential persons who design and construct such monuments do so largely in order to enhance their legacy. They do so by telling the story from their subjective perspective to fit their own interests, ambitions, and outlook (Geisler 2000).

Thus, descriptive analytics owes its veracity and its accurate representation of events to the frailty of humans and to their desire to leave a personal mark on history by telling a story that reflects their biases, predilections, subjectivity, friendship, or animus against other humans. In fact, they do so also by the conniving use of the language in describing past events. A slim advantage on the battlefield becomes a "monumental victory" and a "decisive defeat" of the enemy. The victors indeed write the history of their struggles. All over the world, historical and even prehistorical monuments, inscriptions, and drawings are found in caves and on magnificent structures such as buildings, portals, obelisks, and murals. There is hardly any limit to the human desire of looking into infinity and reminding those who come after of the greatness left behind by this individual (Aydiner et al. 2019; Kraus et al. 2020).

Such ulterior motives of humans who describe events for posterity must be taken into account when we quantify past events. When stories are transmitted across generations, there is a natural tendency of the story tellers to embellish the facts and to aggrandize the original protagonists in the story. We tend to attribute to them superhuman qualities, characteristics, and abilities. Many Biblical stories and those of the Mesothelium and Greco-Roman traditions are excellent illustrations of these magnified historical tales. Geisler (2000) argues that all instruments we deploy to describe and measure past events are biased to some or to a large degree. This includes unobtrusive as well as obtrusive instruments.

Unobtrusive instruments measure events after the facts. These instruments are unobtrusive because they do not or did not intervene or influence the course of events these instruments purport to measure. For example, a simple thermometer or a pressure gauge provides measures of temperature and pressure without impacting the phenomenon they measure. Historical accounts of events are after-the-fact narratives, which offer a look or a glimpse into past events. When we thus collect a volume of information about past events, we are essentially generating descriptive analytics, providing that an analysis can be done of such information so as to extract various attributes of the inputs, structure, processes, or outputs of the original events thus measured (Kristoffersen et al. 2021).

The advantages of unobtrusive measurements that we employ to develop descriptive analytics are its relative objectivity (not associated with the event) and the ease of application. However, the disadvantages are the over-reliance on archival information that may be biased due to the negative aspects of keeping records (Geisler 2000).

Conversely, obtrusive instruments are those where the intrusive human participant is also the story teller. This is the case whereby the person narrates the events "in real time"—as the events are actually happening. War correspondents are an example of the reporting of events as they are occurring by those who are in the midst of such events. In this case, the glimpse offered is not into past events, but in real time. In many cases, such correspondents then write a book as they distance themselves in time and place from the original events. *The Rise and Fall of the Third Reich* (William Shirer) is a good example of the description of two decades of crucial historical events from the viewpoint of a correspondent who was actually on the scene while the events unfolded and was able to interact with some of the key protagonists in the story.

Both obtrusive and unobtrusive instruments describe events, albeit from two different, yet sometimes also complementary, perspectives. Because of this difference in approaches, these instruments sometimes narrate events that may not be identical in their different interpretations of the same set of facts. As Daniel Patrick Moynihan (1927–2003) famously said: "Everyone is entitled to his own opinion, but not to his own facts."

Interpretations vary according to the interpreter's level of education, his or her view of the world, and his or her inherent biases and predilections. In this manner, the interpreter may choose to utilize a given set of indicators that will describe, for the interpreter's use, the events under study and consideration. This action is carried out by selecting a set of indicators of events, preferably macro-indicators, which allow the interpreter to conjure events and to assemble them into a narrative that allows for analysis and interpretation.

Over-Reliance on Records or Unobtrusive Instruments

This over-reliance on instruments that utilize the information obtained from records that are kept by humans—across civilizations—manifests itself in the following attributes or characteristics of the instruments that collect and describe such archival information. Records are valued in many cases because they are the remaining outcomes produced by people and civilizations long gone. However, they tend to suffer from (1) lack of accuracy, (2) lack of precision, (3) repeatability, (4) inherent or built-in errors, (5) validity, and (6) reliability.

Validity refers to the degree to which the instrument used to collect information is itself designed to collect and analyze the information it purports to analyze. Validity is thus the strength of the instrument to indeed furnish the information we desire and for which it was enacted. For example, does the IQ (Intelligence Quotient) indeed measure intelligence? Similarly, are the measures of Gross Domestic Product (GDP) levels, or the rate of inflation, or the rate of current unemployment, or the level of national debt indeed good measures of growth of a national economy (Geisler 2000)?

Reliability refers to the degree to which the measures provided by the instrument are consistent over time or under varying environmental conditions or with different sets of subjects. For example, does the IQ test, when applied across different groups of people (varying degrees of ages, gender, socio-economic background, or national origin) indeed provide outcomes that are consistent so that there is little and acceptable variance in the readings or outputs of the instruments? Thus, will the IQ test provide consistent readings with subjects from the United States, Latin America, Central America, Western Europe, or Southern Asia? Similarly, will this test provide consistent readings when applied in the very wealthy and the poorest suburbs of a large metropolitan area? Another way of approaching this issue is to ask whether the test will generate consistent readings when applied over time, that is, in time intervals of ten, perhaps twenty, or even fifty years.

Developing Macro-Indicators

Another issue in the development of higher-order indicators is the use of macro-indicators. Macro-indicators are a given set of measures that are assembled under a single construct. They are normally employed to describe complex constructs or phenomena. The use of multiple indicators for a single construct may present several issues or inherent difficulties. First, the indicators selected may not measure or adequately represent the entire phenomenon. More likely, these sets of multiple indicators may capture some aspects of the phenomenon yet miss other, perhaps crucial, aspects or variables. For example, measures of technology in corporations tend to cover some facets of the phenomenon but ignore others. Organizational technology is often measured by the type of the technology itself (simple or complex) and by the value such technology provides to organizational members. Most of the measures of technology that are routinely used, such as count of patents or the count of new products, tell a very limited story of corporate innovation and the commercialization process of its innovative activity and contributions to the members.

Secondly, the indicators selected for assembly into macro-indicators may not be amenable to easy manipulation and convergence to form higher-order constructs. The indicators may be measuring different aspects of the phenomenon, such as both its positive and its negative attributes. For example, the positive indicators may measure the positive impacts and contributions of the technology to the organization and to society, whereas negative indicators may be measuring the negative impacts of the technology, such as pollution, workplace-related accidents, and the like.

In all of these instances, there is a reliance or even over-reliance on records that members of the organization keep for their routine operations and for the purposes of managerial and executive control. Since records are easily assembled and maintained over time, they tend to be the preferred mode of data collection for indicators. But, in the case of macro-indicators, the biases that are encased in these sets of indicators may multiply and thus have a more powerful negative impact upon the organization (Liedtka and Ogilvie 2011).

These biases inherent in records include the well-known fact that records do not necessarily describe the real facts as they happened. The following instances show these biases.

1. Records are generated by human beings who have a well-defined agenda. They use records to embellish their accomplishments. Sir Winston Churchill once famously remarked that history is written by the victors in wars, hence the records we have of these wars reflect the victor's agenda, viewpoint, biases, and preferences. For example, from antiquity to modern times, victorious leaders have erected monuments into which they inscribed their victories while happily pointing to the defeat of their enemies. From Atalae in Babylon to the Arc de Triumph in Paris, the victors left us magnificent records of their martial victories.
2. Historians are purported to be the objective narrators of our past. Yet, individual historians sometimes succumb to their nationalistic allegiances and describe historical occurrences in light of their nativist biases. For example, the British historian Arnold Toynbee (1889–1975) wrote the 12-volume work *A Study of History*. In this work, Toynbee argues that world history can and should be described in terms of the rise and the fall of civilizations. He studied twenty-eight such civilizations in human history. His conclusions were based on the fortunes of such civilizations. Since Toynbee defined the notion of a "civilization," he was able to skillfully manipulate historical data so as to fit his pre-established ideas of, for instance, good and evil. According to Toynbee, when a civilization begins its downfall, it may disappear from the world's stage, even though its influence may survive in the language, culture, religion, and other attributes of people and societies. Toynbee was criticized by Jewish historians because his framework of history considered the Jews to be an extinct civilization.
3. The interpretation of historical records by contemporary scholars, politicians, and religious leaders may be biased to fit the person's own religious agenda, political, or economic outlook, as well as biases due to the person's upbringing and the influence of family, friends, teachers, and mentors. I repeat the quote of Daniel Patrick Moynihan: "Everyone is entitled to his own opinion, but not to his own facts." Nonetheless, many people in positions of note and

> power tend to willfully ignore this sound advice. They create their own reality and they strongly believe in it. This aspect of human tendency may lead, and has led, to both positive and negative outcomes.
>
> On the positive side, this leads to dreams and aspirations. President Kennedy's call to the nation to reach the moon in less than a decade had considered the enormous difficulties in achieving such a goal not as impediments, but as challenges, which the human adventurous spirit can master and vanquish. Arthur Schlesinger Jr. captured this spirit and the enormous influence that Kennedy's challenge had on an entire generation of young Americans in his book *A Thousand Days: John F. Kennedy in the White House*. (In 1966, this book won both the Pulitzer Prize and the National Book Award.)
>
> Conversely, politicians may interpret historical facts in a manner that leads them to create mental images of threats and unabashed inimical characterization of an opposite party or leader as a menacing power, intent upon inflicting on the unsuspecting prey the utmost in destruction of the prey's cherished way of life. This dangerously sardonic interpretation eventually leads to policies of separation, distancing from the other party, as well as severing established ties of commerce, educational exchanges, even tourism and membership in international bodies.

Although unobtrusive instruments such as organizational and personal records describe past events with a degree of realism and accuracy, the subjective nature of their creation imbues a modicum of suspicion that the narrative is less than objective, hence should be considered with caution. But, as in many other human situations, the actors in a given situation are confronted with the dilemma of having only one weapon in their arsenal. Thus, if they wish to record a given event for their own use or the use of their family and other members of their tribe or community, they must resort to the least objectionable mode of historical recording, namely, unobtrusive instruments such as records and, preferably, contemporaneous records (Davenport 2014a; Fox and Tversky 1995; Geisler 2013).

The discussion above referred to narratives that exist in records, mostly in some form of writing. The invention of the ability to write and therefore to keep a record beyond the life span of the recorder has immensely contributed to the progress of the civilized world. It is widely assumed that such record keeping emerged as a solution to the basic human need to record their accumulated wealth. Two main reasons or needs accounted for such actions. First, the need to pay taxes to any form of political, civilian, religious, or military authority under which these humans functioned, transacted, and prospered. Simple rules were adopted to compute and assess the taxes they owed, such as one-tenth of their assets, which could be measured. For example, numbers of sheep, cattle, goats, and a portion of their harvest would be allocated to pay their taxes.

With the appearance of precious metals and other forms of monies, these were assessed in equivalence to the portion of assets owed to the tax collector. The authorities would send tax assessors who made their own computations of the assets and wealth of the taxpayer, and they would have the last word as to the level of taxes owed. More sophisticated nations, such as the ancient Romans, conducted periodical census to verify each citizen's manner of subsistence, his assets, and level of wealth; hence, what and how much he owed the empire. With such taxes, the citizens received a modicum of security and peace (*Pax Romana*), which allowed them to function and to have a normal life without fear from lawless bandits.

The accurate and objective mode of record keeping allowed the ancient Romans to maintain an enormous empire, spreading throughout the ancient world. Emissaries on horseback moved throughout the empire, carrying with them a diverse form of communications, such as written reports to Rome from the civil servants all over the empire, as well as letters exchanged among the Roman aristocrats who maintained a high level of literacy. The remainder of the population lacked the minimum form of literacy. They depended on scribes, who would compose letters and formal documents or requests that the citizen was required to have when transacting with the authorities. Some of the earliest written documents, discovered in Mesopotamia, contain a letter from a wealthy merchant to his son in which the merchant lists forms and mechanisms to avoid paying taxes.

Another need and reason for the Roman's effort of keeping objective records had to do with the need to recruit soldiers from the citizenry and to maintain a standing army. Records had to be kept of the recruitment of mostly peasants and the need to allow them to return to their farms as soon as the military crisis was over. The ancient Romans even engineered a system by which soldiers who served for twenty years could thereafter retire, with a certain remuneration and a piece of land that they could farm and where they could raise and feed a family. Some historians argue that this custom forced the Romans to expand their empire and to conquer more lands, because they simply ran out of land available to them to distribute to their veterans.

A Historical Perspective: The Middle Ages

In his book *The Decline and Fall of the Roman Empire*, Edward Gibbon (1737–1794) offers an outstanding description of Roman practices. With incisive logic, he demonstrates how the Roman empire found itself in an unstoppable state of decline. Further, the decline of the Roman power and influence in the ancient world inevitably led Western Europe into political, cultural, and scientific decline, even chaos. At this stage, the Catholic Church, as the only viable institution within the feudal system of political and economic power, intervened and filled the void left by Rome. As feudal lords used their time to fight among themselves, thus adding confusion to the chaos, the Catholic popes redirected their martial energies toward the crusades, whereby the lords traveled to the Holy Land to fight the infidels, Muslim rulers of the Levant.

While all this activity was taking place over several centuries in the Middle Ages, the Catholic monks in the various orders and in their secluded and peaceful monasteries took over the arts and sciences, recording the history of their church and the countries in which they practiced their religion. They recorded the stories of the apostles, the saints of the church, and the glories of the papal experience. Thus, the history and culture of the Roman empire were kept alive by the religiously copious effort of priests and monks of the Catholic church.

In the feudal society, where illiteracy was rampant, the officers of the church served in various capacities as assistants to the federal rulers and even to the kings on top of the feudal hierarchies. They served as scribes, clerks, and even managers in the emerging bureaucracies of the feudal lords. Moreover, when these western European lords went to fight in the crusades, they worked with such orders as the Hospitallers to gain rights to stop at their monasteries on the way to Jerusalem—where they could be fed, have beds for the night, and where their horses and servants could be cared for by the monks, all at a price. The religious orders would issue a letter so that the lord could travel and stop at monasteries along his route. This was the early use of letters of credit. Many such lords perished in the Levant and their lands and assets were appropriated by the church. Many lords who died without heirs would bequest their land and assets to the Catholic church.

There was a need to maintain accurate and current records for all these transactions. This was a particularly urgent need when, for example, Italian merchants in the port cities of Genoa and Venice assigned their fleets of ships to the service of the lords in order to ferry their troops across the Mediterranean Sea to the ports of the Holy Land. All over Western Europe, the lords had to barter with the newly created merchants in the emerging cities, including those in the northern part of Europe, where afterwards these cities created leagues with economic and financial power—such as the Hanseatic League. This league of German cities, headquartered in Lübeck, was a dominating power in Northern European commerce from the fourteenth to the sixteenth centuries. Since these transactions focused on international shipping across diverse jurisdictional entities, such as feudal lords, municipalities, and royal highways (each of which demanded certain payments and imposed certain taxes and fees), all parties involved in such transactions found it to be in their best interests to maintain accurate and current records.

The Modern Era

As the middle ages gave way to the modern era, the invention of the printing press and a more comprehensive public educational system across Europe and the Americas facilitated an almost universal proliferation of literacy. This led to the emergence of writers—historians and poets—who proceeded to document their environment with an honest and precise recording of past and current events and the daily life of common folks, including the unadulterated description of their successes, failures, painful experiences, exasperations, and the ecstasy of some successful achievements. The literary outputs of these writers became a monumental and timeless exposition of the human experience. We continue to be delighted, and also shocked, to read the narratives of Charles Dickens (1812–1870), Victor Hugo (1802–1885), and Fyodor Dostoyevsky (1821–1881), who frankly describe the drama of their fellow citizens and the lives of the less fortunate of citizens. Similarly, across the ocean, Mark Twain delights us with his description of the people, including children, who lived along the mighty Mississippi. These authors did not write to indulge some wealthy or noble benefactor. They recorded their world as they saw it: raw, unadulterated, and replete with more questions than answers, and offering a platform for a crude yet honest analysis of the past and the present. They offered more of the individual's viewpoint of the world and much less dogma.

The modern era also engendered a novel and powerful approach of the quantification of the human experience. Societies began to collect as much information as they could and desired about their citizens and the affairs of their citizens—including commercial, political, civic, and religious activities. With the ubiquitous use of electronic systems and devices, corporations, countries, states, cities, and not-for-profit organizations are now able to collect an enormous amount of information on each person in their society. There is ample recording of patterns of behavior, consumption, predilections, and political and economic thought processes of the citizenry. Never before in human affairs was there such a concentration of information on so many by so few organizations.

Much has been said and written in our times about the continuous loss of our privacy in exchange for a flow of goods, services, and information by entities in the private sector and by organizations in the public sector. Moreover, at least in the United States, Canada, and Western Europe, the governments of these nations collect, analyze, and share the vast amounts of information they routinely collect, with the full acquiescence and cooperation of their citizenry. Thus, in order to learn and to know more about ourselves (how we consume, how we work, how we play, and how we live our lives), we abrogated our rights to privacy and we happily provide these private and public entities with massive amounts of information about ourselves. Many governments conduct a census of their population once a decade, whereby much is learned about who we are and what we do. This practice goes back to ancient Rome and to ancient Greek city states, where authorities routinely surveyed their populations for the purposes of taxation and for obtaining information about human assets and resources needed in times of war.

Philosophers, sociologists, and political scientists have long questioned whether we are happier and more satisfied with added knowledge about ourselves. The human quest for knowledge is a powerful incentive, which propels us to explore, to investigate, and to incessantly continue to learn about ourselves and our environment. No other species is concerned with matters beyond its immediate surroundings. No other species is constantly questioning not only its surroundings but also its own existence. We continually ask: Who are we? Where did we come from? Where are we going?, and, of course Why?

The modern era also gave us dramatically improved technology, as well as the outcomes from scientific explorations. In all human endeavors and experiences, science and technology have given us fantastic contributions to vast improvements in our lives. We are now able to vanquish many horrendous diseases that in the past (even a century ago) left a devastating trail of death, morbidity, and suffering. Consider the much-dreaded disease leprosy. Once a scourge on human lives, it is now merely a bacterial infection, treatable with antibiotics. Also known as Hansen's disease, leprosy is caused by *Mycobacterium leprae*, yet it can now be cured with a multi-drug therapy within 6–12 months.

Predictive Analytics

In many ways, predictive analytics is similar to the technique of long-range planning Predictive analytics is concerned with forecasting future events. This is done by the employment of models such as machine learning algorithms. These models, in turn, are based on data or information collected by the organization and its members. For example, forecasting sales figures, when properly configured and used, allows the manager to prepare the organization by matching production levels to the levels predicted by the model. This type of analytics is essentially a reasoned prediction of future events with probabilities that may be somewhat better than mere chance and that allows for data-base decisions.

Prescriptive Analytics

This is a technique designed to provide the manager with the ability to propose selected courses of action in order to arrive at the desired outcomes. In this method, proposed actions and their outcomes are constantly evaluated. Feedback is given to the decision-maker, so that he/she is able to adjust, recalibrate, and improve the decision-making process.

Actual data are generated and evaluated as one goes along. Some models offer various potential courses of action, such as (1) optimistic, (2) pessimistic, and (3) realistic. The optimistic approach assumes that the conditions encountered by the decision-maker will be favorable and will facilitate a smooth decision process. The pessimistic approach refers to conditions that will be unfavorable to the decision-maker, who will encounter several types of barriers, such as organizational impediments.

The realistic course of action is based on the assumption that conditions will be neither highly favorable nor highly unfavorable. Thus, the decision-maker will be able to navigate the system without unforeseen negative conditions in the immediate future.

The prescribed course of action will be the course of action that will be proposed or will be forthcoming in response to the configuration of the conditions in the organization. I am reminded of a scene in the movie *Clear and Present Danger* (1994). In this movie, the president of the United States says: "The course of action you are suggesting is the course of action I cannot suggest." This is with regards to the American "war on drugs" when the president is forced with the extreme course of action of invading the South American country where drugs are cultivated.

Administrative/Organizational Analytics

This category of analytics is not often used in the relevant literature. These are variables, mostly quantitative, which describe administrative processes in the organization. They include measures that are inherent in the organizational system as well as those that are generated by specific surveys and studies conducted by managers. Some managers generate these variables or indicators for their own use, often for particular analysis and assessment of their organizational division, department, or other similar units within the organization. They also use such measures to describe and assess their interdepartmental relations, as well as their interaction with organizations and people outside the boundaries of their own organization.

A good example of this category of analytics is the specialized organizations in the area of health care. These organizations would include (a) those that provide health care (hospitals) and (b) those that insure the health care industry (e.g., HIPPA [Health Insurance Portability and the Accountability Act of 1996]). These, and similar organizations, have a dual purpose: they regulate the industry and, in order to carry out their mission, they collect massive amounts of data. Similarly, the healthcare providers also collect information in order to fulfill the requirements of these regulatory agencies, as well as to provide information to the health insurance companies that ultimately pay the bills of caring for the patients of these providers.

Some notable examples that represent these national healthcare organizations are (1) the American Hospital Association (AHA), (2) the National Academy of Medicine (NAM), and (3) the Joint Commission on Accreditation of Hospitals (JCAH). They perform a crucial regulatory mission, which includes a tight grip on the quality of care, the continuity of care, and the obeyance by these organizations to the rules, standards, and regulations of high-quality care given to all patients.

In all, the healthcare sector has a number of constituents, each with its mission, priorities, and procedural and organizational exigencies. This creates a situation whereby the sector has to navigate through a plethora of different organizations. This evidently leads to a "give and take" situation.

My experience on the Board of Directors of a large urban healthcare system may shed some light. The Board of Directors found itself between the need to comply with state and city standards in the decaying state of its buildings, while it was also tested with delays in payments from the state and other insurers of its patients. This situation required the hospitals to procure commercial loans in order to stay solvent and to pay its bills, such as salaries, materials, and equipment. The regulatory agencies, concerned with and focused on quality of care, were constantly threatening the hospitals with the removal of their accreditation—which led to very nervous directors of the organizations. In addition to all this, the hospital network needed to continually collect data on (1) its services, (2) the quality of its services, (3) demographics, and (4) the professional proficiencies and currency of its medical staff. I remember being handed a suitcase-sized bunch of voluminous documents describing the workings of the hospital system and the various demands of its constituents.

In summary, the health care example shows the criticality of the data collected by its organizations. These data are not only administrative, but are also descriptors of life-preserving and disease-combating activities of these organizations. Moreover, as a cloud hanging above these organizations was the permanent threat of legal actions, which invariably followed negative patient outcomes and the medical decisions undertaken by the medical staff of these organizations. Thus, the data/information continually collected by these organizations had to be relevant, current, compliant with regulations, complete, and accurate. These various types of healthcare data constituted the analytics of these healthcare delivery entities. These data were a combination of *clinical* data and *administrative* data, both of which were required by the healthcare sector.

The Three Dimensions of Business Analytics

Business analytics may be defined by three dimensions: (a) integration of data analysis; (b) pattern identification or recognition; and (c) use of cognitive skills and cognitive positioning.

1. Integration of Data Analysis

This dimension is historically one of the early applications of what would later be described as business analytics. This dimension describes the integration or assembly of the various modes of data analysis into one comprehensive and coherent description of the data. A more correct title for this mode of data analysis might be the *macro* dimension of data analysis. In fact, the correct spelling would be data *analyses*, whereby the dimension refers to multiple analyses that are assembled under one roof.

This dimension of business analytics depends on the availability of data from multiple sources so that they can be integrated into one overall dimension. This array of different analyses brought under one roof gives this reconstituted dimension a powerful value as a tool in the analysis of organizations. The various sources provide the breadth across dimensions of the organization, so that this dimension is a good representation of data analysis across the multidimensional organization.

The integration of the data analysis into a comprehensive, coherent, and representative dimension gives us a picture of the organization—across its units, departments, and divisions. This is a very useful input for decision-makers, who need to have a grasp on information across the organizations and on the overall assessment of what constitutes the focal organization.

Moreover, this comprehensive view is a crucial aspect of what business analytics is. The notion involves the entire organization. A good example is the practice of management and accounting/financial consulting companies. A suitable illustration is Ventana Research Corporation founded in 2002. This company conducts surveys and research on the intersection of business and technology. The key constituencies of the company are buyers of business technology and the suppliers of such technologies. When this company analyzes technology in the business context, it is compelled to focus on the overall corporate processes *and* product and services generation, since such technologies are pervasive throughout the organization. Another example is a company called Workiva. Workiva provides its customers with a platform in which data from disparate business units from multiple companies that are networked or collaborating with Workiva are assembled and managed under a common base.

2. Pattern Identification or Recognition

Statistical methods greatly improved in the past two decades, allowing researchers and managers to identify patterns in larger volumes of data. Such patterns can then be seamlessly translated into workable components of the decision-making process. The patterns in the data produce several diverse interpretations of large volumes of data and allow for meaningful descriptions of organizational realities.

Following the identification of patterns in the large data base, the need to "make sense" of such data occurs. Questions that arise include what do the patterns mean and how do they translate into conceptual constructs. Such questions enable us to subjugate the data to workable propositions. The more viable and valid that these propositions are, the more they reliably describe reality.

The recognition or identification patterns in the data validate the data base and its applications and contributions to our construction of reality. Thus, the data vindicates the proposed existence of a usable and highly relevant batch of information.

3. Cognitive Skills or Cognitive Positioning Systems

Often used as a mode of achieving accurate adaptation of cognitive radios, the Cognitive Positioning System (CPS) allows for location awareness for indoor as well as outdoor environments. The analysis of this mode employs such methods as simulations and the implementation of cognitive models.

This mode influences the extent and the accuracy of mental processes. The CPS is essentially the framework within which interpretations of data and the decisions that they inspire are conjured by the human brain, so that rational thinking and intuition are controlled within the limitations and the expertise of our mental abilities and life experience.

The CPS is an extremely useful mechanism that allows us to sort through and organize the vast array of data floating in our brain. The result is our enhanced ability to form complex phenomenon as a mental picture. This, in turn, simplifies the process of translating events into concepts. This also allows us to coordinate our presence in the world with our perception of the elements of the external environment in which we exist and operate.

In their insightful and provocative book, *The Way We Think* (2002), Gilles Fauconnier and Mark Turner advance the notion of "blending and selective projection." They elaborate upon the notion of "conceptual integration" as the process of "… setting up mental spaces, matching across spaces, predicting selectively to a blend, locating shared structures, projecting backwards to inputs, recruiting new structure to the inputs or the blend, and running various operations in the blend itself" (p. 44). These authors even go as far as to define blending as a "science." Building upon Karl Popper's definition of science as the making of falsifiable propositions and predictions, they depart from Popper by stating: "Actually, sciences like evolutionary biology are not about making falsifiable predictions regarding future events. Given the nature of the mental operation of blending, it would be nonsense to predict that from two inputs a certain blend must result or that a specific blend must arise at such-and-such a place and time. Human beings do not think that way." (p. 55).

I beg to differ. In no way—by reason or by mental agility—do these authors undo, defy, or challenge Popper's understanding of scientific exploration. The standard of falsifiable propositions can indeed be fully applied and it partially explains the way human beings think. My research is also increasingly showing that humans are very adept at compiling disparate information pieces and then weaving them into a tapestry of reasoned thinking and conceptual structuring. Higher-order concepts, such as progress, war, danger, peace, and prosperity are supposedly formed by bringing together, or by systematically collating, disparate information elements. At a given point, this sorting of the elements produces a purposeful mental picture of the event or the phenomenon that we are exploring and does so in much more detail.

Forming or Assembling Indicators

How do we form these higher-order concepts by collating disparate information elements? By employing *indicators* of the information elements.

Indicators are usually defined as fact-based quantities that measure or gauge the state or the level of an entity. There are three characteristics of indicators.

Firstly, there is a need for multiple indicators to measure the entity or the phenomenon because one predictor is insufficient to provide a complete and trustworthy description. Each indicator measures a fraction of the entity, or a limited factor and only a limited number of the attributes of the entity. The *Business Dictionary* defines an indicator as the "measurable variable used as a representation of an associated (but non-measured or non-measurable) factor or quantity. For example, the consumer price index (CPI) serves as an indicator of the general cost of living that consists of many factors, some of which are not included in computing CPI. Indicators are common statistical devices employed in economics."

Secondly, indicators are crucial elements in the formation of conceptual constructs. They are the building blocks and define the space or the structure of the construct that the indicators occupy. Thus, indicators are combined or assembled to form the higher-order construct. The sum total of the indicators therefore measures as much of the construct as the indicators singularly, then *en masse*, are designed to measure.

Several key methodological questions seem to arise. Firstly, how many information elements are initially ***sufficient*** to form a conceptual fabric or construct? Secondly, how many individual concepts are initially ***needed*** to be aggregated and thus to form a coherent and systematic description of a phenomenon? Thirdly, once a phenomenon has been identified and described, how will this description help us to justify the existence of such a phenomenon, so that we can integrate the phenomenon into our conversation of our reality?

- *Answering the First Question: How many information elements are initially sufficient to form a conceptual fabric or construct?*

The answer to the first question is complex and also, at best, it is a cautious estimation. The nature of the conceptual construct is such that there seems to be a need for multiple information elements in order to achieve a reliable measurement of the conceptual fabric. Such multiple variables tend to create the following two methodological questions.

How many information elements are initially required and are also sufficient to form a concept? The number of such elements should vary with the nature of the construct. For example, a construct that is similar, in frequent usage, and also known to the person or entity would require fewer information elements than the case where the construct is unfamiliar to the person or entity. In work organizations, for instance, the construct of "work effectiveness" would be more amenable to measurement by the set of information elements than, for example, a construct used subjectively by individuals, such as "self-accomplishment" or "dissatisfaction with the workings of the organization."

The employment of multiple information elements is normally done in the form of additive usage of the elements until such an instance where the set of elements is sufficient enough to offer a reliable and useful description of the notion or of the phenomenon. Thus, the measurement is conducted by the operational mode described as "continuous addition or assembly" or "continuous collating" of data elements in the incessant effort to form cohesive conceptual constructs. In some instances, three such elements are sufficient to form a reliable description of the notion. For example, physical phenomena such as tornadoes may be described by attributes of the winds that cause them: (1) velocity, (2) direction, and (3) level of expected damage.

- *Answering the Second Question: How many individual concepts are initially needed to be aggregated and to form a coherent and systematic description of a phenomenon?*

The answer to the second question is one step higher in the conceptual hierarchy. That is, we employ as many individual concepts as the data allows for a sufficiently robust and useful aggregation to the point by which a good description of the notion or the phenomenon can be accomplished.

For example, a phenomenon such as a country's economic strength may be measured by the Gross Domestic Product (GDP) and also by the measure of trade: the import and export ratio or the balance of trade. These two measures are indicators of what the national economy produces over a given time period (e.g., a year) and the level of exports compared to how much the national economy has imported during the year. These indicators offer a measure of the national economic output versus inputs, thus providing us with a "net" quantity of imports versus exports.

Although the two aforementioned measures are related, they nevertheless describe two distinct phenomena. The GDP indicates the level of economic outputs, whereas the balance of trade (the ratio) describes the level of imports versus exports. That is, the GDP is a single quantity, and the balance of trade is a ratio of two quantities. It is also widely accepted that a more complex notion (such as the balance of trade) would be more vulnerable to errors in measurement and in the collating of the notion of the balance of trade than a simpler notion such as the measure of the expansion of the economy versus the contraction or diminution of the economy. This means that the latter notion would consist of a single quantity of how much (e.g., in US dollars) has the economy grown or has it slowed down or contracted.

The number of notions necessary for the formation of the phenomenon would depend on the nature of the phenomenon. In the example above, we looked at the economic health of the national economy. The answer to the second question thus takes us to the point where we now aggregate individual concepts and apply these aggregations to describe the higher-order notion or the phenomenon.

As described above, we employ measurement-by-indicators, therefore we are *de rigueur* obtaining a measure that is incomplete and inevitably measuring only a portion or part of the phenomenon. It should be emphasized that the act of measuring-by-indicators is not necessarily misleading, *ignis fatuus*. We are unavoidably constrained by the effectiveness of the tools available to us for measuring a given phenomenon. Hence, whichever tool we employ, there will be some measure of bias and internal error, which will be embedded in our measurement technique. In this respect, the important aspect of measuring the phenomenon is that we obtain a sufficient measure of the attributes of the phenomenon, so that we can then confidentially define it as an acceptable representation of the phenomenon.

A philosophical issue that arises within this mode of measurement is that of the validity of the synthesis of disparate indicators into a viable conceptual construct. Does the construct indeed represent the assembly or the indicators? In most cases the resulting construct is valid, so when we advance a conceptual construct or notion, we are indeed advancing a construct that is composed of these indicators. The flow from individual indicators to the conceptual construct is thus maintained seamlessly.

- *Answering the Third Question: Once a phenomenon has been identified and cogently described, how does this description help us to intelligibly justify the existence of such a phenomenon?*

Answering the third question is even more complicated. How do the indicators, which helped us to cogently describe the phenomenon, also assist us to justify the existence of the phenomenon? In the previous example, we asked how changes in the GDP or levels of employment explain the variability in the nation's economic strength. This is the crucial issue of how variability in one indicator (however critical) describes or explains the variability in another indicator as in the phenomenon itself.

The use of a small set of indicators to describe a complex phenomenon is commonplace in the literature of economics and social sciences. The idea is to have a small set of indicators that describe selected dimensions of the phenomenon. There is no agreement among scholars in this area of inquiry as to how many indicators are sufficient to adequately describe the phenomenon. In a way, it is similar to a "wild west" where each author deals with a small set of her/his choosing. Subsequent authors rely on these earlier scholars in selecting and utilizing their own set of indicators.

This idea can also be found in the description of the market for stocks and bonds. The Dow Jones Index, for example, is based on the representativeness of a sample or a small set of companies whose stocks are traded on the New York Stock Exchange. Presumably, variations in this small set of stocks is an indicator of the performance of the individual companies and of the state of the entire market—and, by extension, of the national economy. This also means that the existence of these indicators acts as a proof of the existence, the performance, and the vitality of the companies that are part of this sample.

It is therefore hardly surprising that economists debate this issue in a consistent manner without achieving an acceptable degree of consensus or accommodation. They agree for or against not only the use of the specific indicators—as to their validity—but also as to the degree to which the indicators selected for the analysis represent and even explain the phenomenon. Nevertheless, in order to achieve a useable manner of analysis, economists and others who use the selected indicators do so regardless of the conceptual and methodological issues and constraints embedded in these indicators. At some point, one must acquiesce to the difficulties and accept a feasible set of indicators as a sufficient and adequate set with adequate validity.

The use of these indicators, albeit in an "imperfect" or less than "ideal" manner, can be explained by examining the conclusions reached by Herbert Simon, 1978 Nobel laureate in economics. Simon suggested that humans make decisions that are not designed to maximize outputs or to minimize costs. Rather, they make decisions that are *good enough* or *sufficient* to be acceptable to the decision-maker.

There is a large measure of compromising by the decision-maker. The constraints of time and cost make it very difficult, perhaps unfeasible, for the decision-maker to pursue the "perfect" route to make the "best" decisions that the data will allow. The compromise allows the decision-maker to arrive at an acceptable outcome, which then permits the decision-maker to continue seamlessly the pursuit of solutions.

The answer to the third question also takes us to the examination of the issue of how we assemble or bring together disparate items of knowledge (e.g., variables) to form a higher-order notion or concept. The following methodological queries seem to emerge.

1. How many variables are *sufficient* to form the notion or phenomenon?
2. What is the *nature* of these variables? That is, what aspects of the phenomenon do these variables measure? For example, do they measure quality? quantity? or a given relationship (e.g., correlation) among the said variables?
3. How do these variables coalesce to form higher-order constructs? That is, what are the individual aspects of their correlation? For example, are they correlated due to their measures of the construct that are designed to cover diverse attributes of the construct? Put another way, what makes these variables correlate to form higher-order concepts?

Imagine the notion of speed of vehicles on the ground. The variables would include (1) type of race car, (2) maximum speed that the race car can reach, and (3) the nature of the terrain. A similar illustration is the speed of an exceptional race horse. The speed would depend, among other variables, on the type of terrain, the weather, the jockey, and the attributes of the horse (training, pedigree, age, prior experience of the horse with the terrain and the jockey).

In the case of the race horse, the attributes refer to the overall ability of the horse to manage the course and the terrain. The attributes of the horse coalesce to describe an animal that has been designed to race with other horses and has also been bred, selected, and trained for competition and speed. The problem of how disparate indicators combine, coalesce, and assemble to form a higher-order notion has been of interest to me for several decades, since the research I conducted for my dissertation in 1979. I certainly pondered: How *do* these indicators form higher-order notions? In practice, we tend to overlook this issue and to accept, without question, the formation of higher-order notions as a direct result of the assembly of indicators.

However, in theory this problem vehemently persists, disobeying all the futile attempts by researchers to overlook its relevancy to our understanding of organizational behavior. The questions that continue to haunt researchers are (1) how do these indicators combine and coalesce to form higher-order notions? That is, what is the *process* by which these indicators are brought together to create higher-order notions? The next question is an inquiry; (2) what are the *drivers* (individuals, groups, or organizations) that make this happen? That is, how do these drivers compel the process to take place and thus to direct or force the indicators to coalesce into higher-order notions or constructs?

And then, there is a third question that is inherent in this problem: (3) *who* are the organizational members who undertake the process as the drivers of this process? That is, who are the individuals/members of the focal organization who take upon themselves to carry out this process of bringing together disparate indicators and combining them into conceptual frameworks?

Organizational Perspective Theory

The traditional definition of perspective theory in psychology and sociology is a theory that proposes self-reports of outlooks on scales that are based on the position and the content of the individual. This is different from the perspective theory in architecture whereby perspective refers to the converging of lines onto a point in a background, thus allowing for a modicum of a three-dimensional interpretation of reality.

The Differences Between Perspective Theory and Prospect Theory

To avoid confusion, *perspective* theory differs from another theory, namely *prospect* theory. The latter is a "behavioral model that shows how people decide between alternatives that involve risk and uncertainty (e.g., percent likelihood of gains and losses). It demonstrates that people think in terms of expected utility relative to a reference point (e.g., current wealth) rather than absolute incomes. Prospect theory was developed by framing risky choices and indicates that people are loss averse; since individuals dislike losses more than equivalent gains; they are more willing to take risks to avoid a loss."

"The model is descriptive: it tries to model real life choices, rather than optimal decisions, as normative models do." In this manner, the model is therefore similar to the decision model proposed by Herbert Simon, whereby individuals make decisions that are not the best possible decisions. Rather, they make decisions that are "good enough" or "satisficing" to fulfill the needs of the decision-makers or the organization.

Organizational perspective theory is defined here as the convergence of indicators to a point where a concept is thus congealed. Therefore, disparate or distinct elements of an event or of an organizational phenomenon are assembled, combined, or coalesced to form a cohesive notion or concept. For example, distinct indicators of human resources management in an organization, such as attributes of the workforce (age, education, and tenure in the organization) are combined and analyzed in this format to describe the level of obsolescence, if any, in this workforce. From here, the next step in organizational analysis suggests that obsolete organizations are less likely to be innovative, hence less likely to compete, to succeed, and to survive in their competitive environment.

This description of organizational perspective theory allows us to compare organizations and to do so by comparing for each organization the way in which the distinct elements are combined by the organization to form a concept. The degree of effectiveness of this process of coalescing is thus the variable being compared. The underlying assumption here is that the more effective the process, the more resilient is the organization to external pressures and challenges.

Organizational perspective may—and perhaps should—be viewed as a platform in which decisions are made, risks are taken, and a causal link to organizational performance and survival is established.

This means that perspective theory is adapted to the dimensions and the variables of organizational reality. The data collected under the umbrella of business analytics is made a part and parcel of the organization. In essence, organizational perspective theory describes how information items—which are developed by members of the organization—flow toward a unique collection point in the perspective field, where they coalesce into higher-order notions. Thus, this process is not occurring in a vacuum. Rather, it is driven and controlled by the members of the organization. The members receive and absorb disparate ideas of information (data) and then proceed to coalesce them into higher-order notions.

References

Agor, W. 1986. The Logic of Intuition: How Top Executives Make Important Decisions. *Organizational Dynamics* 14 (3): 5–18.

Aydiner, A., S. Tatoglu, E. Bayraktar, S. Zaim, and D. Delen. 2019. Business Analytics and Firm Performance: The Mediating Role of Business Process Performance. *Journal of Business Research* 96: 228–237.

Bannister, B., and R. Griffith. 1986. Applying a Causal Analytic Framework to the Mobley, Horner and Hollingsworth (1978) Turnover Model: A Useful Reexamination. *Journal of Management* 12 (3): 433–443.

Beller, M., and A. Barnett. 2009. Applying a Causal Analytical Framework to the Mobley, Horner, and Hollingworth (1978) Turnover Model: A Useful Reexamination. *Journal of Management* 12 (3): 433–443.

Borgman, C. 1999. The User's Mental Model for an Information Retrieval System: An Experiment on a Prototype Online Catalog. *International Journal of Human-Computer Studies* 51 (2): 435–452.

Braunstein, D. 1974. Beyond Leavitt's 'Narrow' Analytic Manager. *Interfaces* 4 (4): 28–31.

Burrows, L., and M. Savage. 2014. *After the Crisis? Big Data and the Methodological Challenges of Empirical Sociology*, 1–6. April–June: Big Data & Society.

Chen, C.L., and Chun-Yang. Zhang. 2014. Data-Intensive Applications, Challenges, Techniques and Technologies: A Survey on Big Data. *Information Sciences* 275: 314–347.

Chen, H., R. Chiang, and V. Storey. 2012. Business Intelligence and Analytics: From Big Date to Big Impact. *MIS Quarterly* 36 (4): 1165–1188.

Conboy, K., P. Mikalef, D. Dennehy, and J. Krogstie. 2020. Using Business Analytics to Enhance Dynamic Capabilities in Operations Research: A Case Analysis and Research Agenda. *European Journal of Operational Research* 281 (3): 656–672.

Cosentino, T. 2015. Data Preparation Is Essential for Predictive Analytics. Perspectives, Ventana Research.

Court, D. 2015. Getting Big Impact from Big Data. *McKinsey Quarterly*, January. http://www.mckinsey.com/insights/business_technology/getting_big_impact_from_big_data. Accessed 13 July 2015.

Dahl, R. 1963. *Modern Political Analysis*. Englewood Cliffs: Prentice-Hall.

Davenport, T. 2014a. *Advanced Analytics and Big Data Adoption Report*. Portland, OR: International Institute for Analytics.

Davenport, T. 2014b. *Big Data at Work: Dispelling the Myths, Uncovering the Opportunities*. Cambridge, MA: Harvard Business Review Press.

Davenport, T., M. Iansiti, and A. Sereis. 2013. *Managing with Analytics at Procter and Gamble*. Boston, MA: Harvard Business School Publishing.

Davenport, T., and J. Harris. 2007. *Competing on Analytics: The New Science of Winning*. Boston: Harvard Business School Press.

Davenport, T., J. Harris, and R. Morrison. 2010. *Analytics at Work, Smarter Decisions, Better Results*. Cambridge, MA: Harvard Business Review Press.

Drucker, P. 1988. The Coming of the New Organization. *Harvard Business Review*, January–February, pp. 45–53.

Elgendy, N., and A. Elragal. 2016. Big Data Analytics in Support of the Decision Making Process. *Procedia Computer Science* 100: 1071–1084.

Etner, J., M. Jeleva, and J. Tallon. 2012. Decision Theory Under Ambiguity. *Journal of Economic Surveys* 26 (2): 234–270.

Fox, C., and A. Tversky. 1995. Ambiguity Aversion and Comparative Ignorance. *Quarterly Journal of Economics* 110 (3): 585–604.

Fox, C., and A. Tversky. 1998. A Belief-Based Account of Decision Under Uncertainty. *Management Science* 44 (7): 879–895.

Gao, S., R. Alhaij, R. Rokne, and J. Guan. 2011. Mining Sequential Patterns with Extensible Knowledge Representation. *Intelligent Data Analysis* 15 (6): 889–911.

Geisler, E. 1979. An Empirical Study of a Proposed System for Monitoring Organizational Change in a Federal R&D Laboratory. Unpublished dissertation, Evanston, Illinois, Northwestern University.

Geisler, E. 2000. *The Metrics of Science and Technology*. Westport: Quorum Books.

Geisler, E. 2002. On the Ubiquitous Inadequacy of Co-Variation Design in Strategy Research. *International Journal of Technology Management* 23 (6): 558–577.

Geisler, E. 2013. Beyond Analytics: The Special Case How Technology Managers Translate Big Data into Actionable Decisions. In *Proceedings of the PICMET (Portland International Conference on the Management of Engineering and Technology) Conference*, Aug 3–5, San Jose, CA.

Geisler, E., and R. Kostoff. 1999. Strategic Management and Implementation of Textual Data Mining in Government Organizations. *Technology Analysis & Strategic Management* 11 (4): 493–525.

Ghosh, B., and J. Scott. 2011. Antecedents and Catalysts for Developing a Healthcare Analytic Capability. *Communications of the Association for Information Systems*. 29 (22): 395–410.

Hammer, M. 1996. *Beyond Engineering*. New York: Harper Business Publishers.

Horner, P. 2018. Analytics Extravaganza. *Informs/Analytics Magazine*, November–December, p. 2.

Hubbard, D. 2014. *How to Measure Anything: Finding the Value of "Intangibles" in Business*, 3rd ed. Hoboken: Wiley.

Hult, M., and Sven-Ake. Lennung. 1980. Towards a Definition of Action Research: A Note and Bibliography. *Journal of Management Studies* 17 (2): 241–250.

Janssen, M., H. van der Voort, and A. Wahyudi. 2017. Factors Influencing Big Data Decision-Making Quality. *Journal of Business Research* 70 (C): 338–345.

Jenkins, M., and G. Johnson. 1997. Linking Management Cognition and Organizational Performance: A Preliminary Investigation Using Causal Maps. *British Journal of Management* 8 (2): 77–90.

Kahneman, D., and A. Tversky. 1973. On the Psychology of Prediction. *Psychological Review* 80 (4): 237–251.

Kaufman, M., and D. Kirsch. 2014. *Advanced Analytics: The Hurwitz Victory Index Report*. Needham, MA: Hurwitz & Associates.

Kiron, D., R.B. Ferguson, and P.K. Prentice. 2013. *From Value to Vision: Reimaging the Possible with Data Analytics*. MIT Sloan Management Review, Research Report. Government Organizations. *Technology Analysis & Strategic Management* 11 (4): 493–525.

Kiron, D., R. Shockley, N. Kruschwitz, G. Finch, and M. Haydock. 2010. *Analytics: The Widening Divide: How Companies are Achieving Competitive Advantage Through Analytics*. IBM Institute for Business Value.

Kraemer, K., and J. King. 1986. Computing and Public Organizations. *Public Administration Review* 46 (November): 488–496.

Kraus, M., S. Feuerrigel, and A. Oztekin. 2020. Deep Learning in Business Analytics and Operations Research: Models, Applications, an Managerial Implications. *European Journal of Operational Research* 281 (3): 628–641.

Kristoffersen, E., P. Mikalef, F. Blomsma, and J. Li. 2021. Towards a Business Analytics Capability for the Circular Economy. Technological Forecasting & Social Change 171.

L'Huillier, G., and S. Maldonado. 2011. "Future Trends in Business Analytics and Optimization. *Intelligent Data Analysis* 15 (6): 1001–1017.

Laurson, G.H.N., and J. Thorlund. 2010. *Business Analytics for Managers: Taking Business Intelligence Beyond Reporting*. New York: Wiley.

Leavitt, H. 1975. Beyond the Analytic Manager. *California Management Review* 17 (3): 5–12.

Liedtka, J., and T. Ogilvie. 2011. *Designing for Growth: A Design Thinking Tool Kit for Managers*. New York: Columbia Business School Publishing.

Madtiavan, R., and P. Grover. 1998. From Embedded Knowledge to Embodied Knowledge: New Product Development as Knowledge Management. *Journal of Marketing* 62 (4): 1–12.

Nutt, P. 1990. Strategic Decision-Making by Top Executives and Middle Managers with Data and Process Dominant Stages. *Journal of Management Studies* 27 (2): 173–194.

Polydrack, R. 2018. *The New Mind Readers: What Neuroimaging Can and Cannot Reveal About Our Thoughts*. Princeton, NJ: Princeton University Press.

Rockart, J., and D. DeLong. 1988. *Executive Support Systems: The Emergence of Top Management Computer User*. Homewood: Irwin Publishers.

Schroeck, M., R. Scockley, J. Smart, D. Romero-Morales, and P. Tufano. 2012. Analytics: The Real-World Use of Big Data: How Innovative Enterprises Extract Value from Uncertain Data. Business Report, IBM Institute for Business Value.

Siegel, E. 2013. Predictive Analytics. *Analytics Magazine*, July/August, pp. 38–43.

Taylor, L., R. Schroeder, and E. Meyer. 2014. Emerging Practices and Perspectives on Big Data Analysis in Economics: Bigger and Better or More of the Same? *Big Data & Society* July–December 2014: 1–10.

Ulvila, J.W., and R.V. Brown. 1982. Decision Analysis Comes of Age. *Harvard Business Review* 60 (5): 130–141.

Wang, G., A. Gunasekaran, E.W. Ngai, and T. Papadopoulos. 2016. Big Data Analytics in Logistics and Supply Chain Management: Certain Investigations for Research and Applications. *International Journal of Production Economics* 176: 98–110.

Zwolenski, M., and L. Weatherill. 2014. The Digital Universe: Rich Data and the Increasing Value of the Internet of Things. *Journal of Telecommunications and the Digital Economy* 2 (3): 47.1–47.9.

CHAPTER 2

The Notion of Beyond Business Analytic: Examples of Business Applications

From Raw Data to Notions: The Framing of Conceptual Constructs

Several important questions emerge in our effort to advance from data elements to the framing of conceptual constructs. First, what is the *minimum* number of data elements necessary to formulate or to create a complex cognitive notion? (Adrian and Westerfield 2009; Fagin and Nash 2010). The question is not only how many elements are the minimum number sufficient to form these concepts, but also: how many are too many, or superfluous? This search is for a special number, which is both sufficient and not overbearing.

The number of new elements necessary to form a conceptual construct depends on the complexity of the construct. For example, a construct such as "the attributes of an organizational structure" would be a simple quantity. This means that we can describe an organizational structure by the number of layers of bureaucracy or managements. Therefore, a small number of layers would describe a "flat" structure, whereas a large number of layers describe a complex organization.

As discussed above, the exact number of layers required to make the transition from "flat" to "complex" is not defined with precision in the organizational literature. Rather, the attributes "flat" and "hierarchical"

E. Geisler, *Beyond Business Analytics*,
https://doi.org/10.1007/978-3-030-43718-3_2

(or complex) seem to be sufficient to describe this attribute of the organization without delving into specific quantities (Elgendy and Elragal 2016; Geisler 2013; Hubbard 2014).

There is also a phenomenon in human behavior in organizations by which members of the organization are routinely creating complex notions in their minds (Davenport 2014; Gao et al. 2011; Geisler 1979; Janssen et al. 2017). They do so by assembling raw data in the form of indicators and measures of organizational variables, which describe (quantitatively and qualitatively) selected attributes of the structure and the processes of the organization (Johnson et al. 1993; Kahneman and Tversky 1979; Ghosh and Scott 2011).

The Power of the Few

Human beings in general and the members of human organizations are endowed with the capability of working with a small set of variables to formulate complex notions. In this manner, people need a limited number of data elements (also expressed in human speech) in order to generate complex notions and to communicate them to other human beings.

In Western philosophy there have been several attempts to define simplicity and the principle of parsimony, that is, that the simpler or more straightforward definitions or explanations of a phenomenon are preferable to the more complex explanations. One of the more cited principles is *Occam's Razor*. This principle proposes that if there are two theories that equally explain the empirical evidence, then the "best" theory would be the one that is simpler, less complex, and with fewer components, arguments, data, or in Aristotelian terms: fewer postulates (Bollier 2010; Burrows and Savage 2014; Fortuna 2018).

This theory is also known as the *Theory of Parsimony*, as proposed by William of Occam, in medieval England, about 1280–1350 CE. It is an excellent example of the empirical application of the notion of "the power of the few." This application exemplifies the productive use of few indicators, or items of information. Thus, the notion of the "power of the few" proposes that very few items of information are sufficient to make critical decisions and that people are endowed with the innate ability to make such decisions, even with a very limited set of information (Taleb 2010; Tuchman 2009; Sankararaman et al. 2014).

Some Illustrations of the Power of the Few

Here are some examples of the use of the notion of the "power of the few."

Malcolm Gladwell

Malcolm Gladwell (2002) suggested that there is a "tipping point," which means how many ideas are introduced and are propagated in a society's culture. Some ideas succeed and others fail. According to Gladwell, there are three factors that determine the success or failure of ideas or trends. The first factor is the *law of the few*. He defines this factor as the role of a few key types of people who champion an idea and work to make the spreading or diffusion of the idea a reality.

The second factor, according to Gladwell, is the "stickiness factor." In general terms, this is the attribute of the idea or trend that will attract people to the idea (or product). In many instances this factor appears unplanned, whereby people, or consumers, for example, will support the idea or buy the product because of a given quality that they perceive in the idea or product, and which was not so designed or intended by the generator of the idea.

The third factor is what Gladwell calls the "power of context." This factor examines the degree to which an idea or a product will propagate. This factor is broadly defined as small changes in the external environment that can precipitate the tipping point. Examples include small changes in public tastes, predilections, or affinities toward an idea or a product. These minor changes are sufficient to engender a tipping point, so that the idea or the product will succeed or fail. In many instances, such environmental changes—however minute—are unpredictable. Only after they occur, and their influence is noted, can people link them to the changes they are experiencing in their environment or in the level of proliferation of their ideas or products.

The Notion of the "Black Swan," Suggested by Taleb (2010)

This is the occurrence of a *minor* incident or action by an individual or organization that can lead to or trigger a massive and unequal response or reaction. For example, the assassination of the Grand Duke of the Austro-Hungarian Empire. On June 28, 1914, Franz Ferdinand, Archduke of

Austria-Este and a nephew of the emperor Fran Joseph, was traveling with his wife in an open car in a motorcade through the city of Sarajevo. A young man, 19-year-old Gavrilo Princip, shot the archduke and his wife Sophie with a Browning pistol. Because of his young age, Princip received a sentence of twenty years in prison.

This incident triggered several unstoppable events. On July 28, 1914, the Austrian empire declared war on Serbia, which is considered to be the country behind the assassinations. Thus, the alliance of Austria, Germany, and Italy declared war on Serbia. Due to its political engagement, Serbia was allied with Russia, France, and Great Britain. These countries came to the aid of Serbia and declared war on Austria, Germany, and Italy. World War I had therefore begun. The assassination of a European royal couple had thus triggered a worldwide conflict that engulfed most of Europe, Russia, and, later, the United States.

The Consequence of World War I

The human toll of this war amounted to nine million soldiers killed. In France alone, over 20 percent of men in the age group of 20–40 years in 1914 were killed in this war. A similar number of civilians also perished due to famine and diseases, leading to the Spanish epidemic of influenza in 1918–1919, which caused the death of 20 million worldwide. Europe was economically, politically, and socially devastated. The war also precipitated the collapse of the Russian house of the Romanov czar and the takeover by the socialists and then Lenin's communists. Two decades later, these consequences of the First World War had facilitated the rise of Hitler and Mussolini, thus laying the ground for the Second World War.

A few shots in Sarajevo in 1914 ultimately triggered a world war, then a second world war, and political and military arrangements that Europe had known until the collapse of the Soviet empire in 1991. The "black swan" incident in June of 1914 had massive consequences, unimagined at the time, when Gavrilo Princip assassinated the Archduke and his wife. One small incident resulted in gigantic changes in the political, economic, demographic, and social landscape of Europe and the world.

As Europe and the world were reeling from the horrors of the First World War, many people opted to name the conflict "the war to end all wars" and "the great war." There was a prayer and the hope among people throughout the globe that this was "the last war," and that people who experienced its tragic outcomes would never be willing to repeat them.

Alas, the next generation, which grew up in "the roaring twenties," a time of living the good life, was imbued with the belief that the "good times" will last for many decades to come. The crash of 1929 was a rude awakening, not only because it exploded the "bubble of prosperity" but also because it shattered the optimism and the confidence of an entire generation in both Europe and in the United States. This deplorable situation gave rise to political manipulators who decried the "failures" of Western democracies, while at the same time unwilling to reinstitute the monarchies with its absolute powers. The solution seemed to be non-monarchic autocracies, such as national-socialism and communism. In Germany, it was the emergence of Hitlerism; in the Soviet Union, it was Stalinism, and in other countries such as Poland, it was the time for army officers to capture control of the government.

The Thirteen Days of the Cuban Missile Crisis

On the morning of October 16, 1962, the American intelligence services showed President John F. Kennedy concrete proof that the Soviet Union led by Premier Nikita Khrushchev, had deployed ballistic missiles on the island of Cuba, some 90 miles from the coast of Florida. This was the apex of the "cold war" between the Soviet Union and the United States. This state of potential conflict emerged after the Second World War, when the Soviet Union (then under Stalin's dictatorship) seized control of Eastern Europe and assiduously worked to propagate the Soviet communist system around the world, in particular among the recently emerging countries in Asia, Africa, and Latin America. Under the rule of Fidel Castro, Cuba became a prime target for such Soviet expansion.

Faced with solid proof of the Soviet missiles in Cuba, the Kennedy administration decided to act forcefully and without delay. The administration had identified several potential courses of action: (1) do nothing; (2) diplomacy; (3) secret approach such as confronting Fidel Castro with an ultimatum: abandon the Soviet influence or face invasion; (4) actual invasion; (5) air strikes, pinpointed at the known missile bases; and (6) a naval blockade of the island of Cuba.

In order to minimize the risk of a full-scale nuclear confrontation with the Soviet Union, the Kennedy administration chose to deploy the naval blockade option. All vessels headed toward Cuba and, suspected of carrying military cargo, were ordered to turn back. This situation continued for almost two weeks. It was defused by a secret agreement between the United States and the Soviet Union. Premier Khrushchev agreed to dismantle the missiles, return them to the Soviet Union, and to not deploy them again. The United States agreed not to invade Cuba or to aid those who wished to do so.

Essentially, the agreement led to a resolution that was the *status quo ante*, as it was before the Soviets introduced the missiles. Fidel Castro remained in power, while enduring no commercial or other ties with the United States. The flow of American tourists to Cuba had dried out, due to the total embargo imposed by the United States. Fidel Castro had to totally rely on the Soviet Union and its satellite countries for its exports and imports.

Thus, a unique act of deploying missile bases on a small, almost insignificant island in the Caribbean Sea, located at the confluence of the Caribbean Sea, the Gulf of Mexico, and the Atlantic Ocean, had almost catapulted the world into a possible nuclear catastrophe. The fact that the two global superpowers became entangled in this situation, with ominous ramifications for world peace, was undoubtedly a most perilous and deplorable state of affairs, and a direct consequence of the tensions of the "cold war." Any action by one of the world powers or their allies would have been considered a direct provocation and a menace to the status quo, requiring an immediate and proportional reaction. However minute or innocent would be the deviation from the *status quo ante*, the response from the opposing power could have been catastrophic (Taleb 2010; Tuchman 2009).

The American Civil War

Another example of the mushrooming impacts of a seemingly unique action into an enormous conflagration is the American Civil War. Also known as the "war between the states," this war began on April 12, 1861, when Confederate forces attacked Fort Sumter in South Carolina. President Abraham Lincoln called upon the free states to send volunteers in order to recapture the fort, which he considered federal territory. What ensued was that other Southern states, which allowed slavery, joined the rebellion. The total number of rebel states increased to eleven. It is estimated that the total cost of this internecine conflict was over 77 billion dollars in today's (2019) currency.

Clearly, there were various factors which were embedded in the fractured relationship between the Northern and the Southern states. These factors may have contributed to the armed confrontation. However, the triggering factor that initiated and really launched the war had been the unique act of the attack on the fort. Perhaps, under different circumstances, the reasons for the attack could have been negotiated to a peaceful solution. But, the sentiments on both sides were ablaze. There was no room nor hope for any compromise. The climate was ripe for an armed conflict. This set of circumstances led directly to the willingness of the opposing parties to go to war. All they needed was a "spark," namely an incident which, however minute or innocent, would ignite the odious relationship and catapult it into open hostilities. These went on for four years (1861–1865) at a horrendous cost and lasting consequences for the nation and its inhabitants.

The Defeat of the Spanish Armada

Another example of the "power of the few" is the defeat of the Spanish Armada by Sir Francis Drake and his English naval forces. The Spanish King Phillip II decided to conquer Protestant England and its Tudor Queen Elizabeth and impose Catholicism on the renegade island. To this end, Phillip assembled a mighty armada of 130 large ships with 2500 guns and over 30 thousand men. The English fleet consisted of 200 smaller ships and 16 thousand men. Thus, England could muster only half the manpower of the Spanish armada. On August 8, 1588, the English navy resolutely defeated the Spanish armada. Only 67 ships returned to Spain.

The power of the smaller English naval force resulted in the ascendance of England as a global naval power. This fact imbued the English with the determination to explore the seas, thus emboldening their leaders to expand their global power and ultimately engineer the British Empire that ruled the world for two centuries—protected and serviced by the British Navy. Thus, one day in the summer of 1588 resulted in the emergence of the largest empire that the world has ever seen since the heydays of the Roman Empire. The one summer day in 1588 had catapulted the small island off the European continent into a global empire. Even today, the British Commonwealth of Nations is composed of 53 sovereign nation-members from all five continents. This group of nations had also exported its language, customs, and culture to all of its member nations. English is today the *lingua franca* of the civilized world, as well as of the world's diplomacy and the world's scientific community (Laurson and Thorlund 2010; Ryan 2016; Siegel 2013).

Planning and Evaluation Techniques

In the period 1950s–2000 there emerged a considerable literature containing various techniques for planning and evaluation of organizational projects and programs. The following are examples of these techniques.

Gantt Chart

This technique was invented by Henry Gantt (1861–1919), an American project manager. The chart identifies tasks that may be executed in parallel and those that are dependent on other tasks. The technique also helps to detect and to anticipate bottlenecks. This graphic depiction of the schedule of a project provides start and finish dates; the resources needed for the project; the milestones to be achieved; the tasks to be accomplished; and the dependency of the elements of the structure and processes of the organization.

The Gantt chart also provides a visual depiction of events on a long timeframe of days, weeks, months, even years. These attributes of the chart make it easily understood and interpreted by supervisors and managers without specialized training on how to read and interpret the charts.

Nevertheless, the simplicity of the Gantt chart is also a disadvantage in the wide usage of the technique. It does not allow for a more complex evaluation of a project because it lacks the display and the analysis of the relationship among the components of the tasks under evaluation.

Zero-Based Budgeting (ZBB)

This technique for planning and evaluation considers all the expenses necessary for a project and the justification for needing such resources. This justification is repeated for every time period, so that the evaluator begins from a "zero base." For each time period, the building of the budget for the period starts from a zero-initial point, regardless of how high or low the budget was in the previous period.

ZBB strives for a quantitative evaluation, and by doing so it also tends to under-evaluate the activities that are not easily quantifiable, such as research and development, services to the customers of the organization and interdepartmental services, and the transfer and absorption of new technologies and knowledge. In addition, ZBB is also dependent upon the subjective assessments by managers, so that managers with less experience may be less capable to provide an adequate evaluation.

PERT (Program Evaluation and Review Technique)

Under the command of Admiral Hyman Rickover (1900–1986), the US Navy developed naval nuclear propulsion and the first nuclear submarine, The U.S.S. Nautilus, which was launched in 1954. Jointly with the US Navy, the consulting firm of Booz Allen Hamilton and Lockheed Corporation developed PERT (Program Evaluation and Review Technique) for a Polaris missile submarine project. The PERT system allowed these companies to undertake the massive naval project and to meet the demands of the US Navy for accurate and timely reporting of their progress and the resources and time expended in this project.

1. The PERT system provides the following:
2. The logical sequence of the project's activities.
3. A diagrammatic view of the network.
4. The list of critical activities.
5. The critical path of activities in the network.
6. The activity slack.
7. The overall project duration.
8. The probability of achieving the planned completion data of the project.

The advantages or benefits of PERT are:

1. Allows managers to evaluate time and resources and to track required assets.
2. Allows for three-point estimation of expected duration of activities:
    (a) Optimistic time for completion (if all goes well, without any glitches),

(b) Pessimistic time for completion (if unexpected glitches or delays occur), and
(c) Most-likely time (if normal and expected events occur).

3. Allows for identification of locus of responsibility.
4. Help to improve communication among members and departments.
5. Allows for "what if analysis."

The disadvantages or shortcomings of PERT are:

1. The system is subjective: based on the manager's experience.
2. The system needs continual review and revisions as assets change with time.

Finally, although PERT has lost some of its luster since the heydays of the 1960s–1980s, often replaced by more recent techniques such as Agile, it is nevertheless still considered an important and reliable instrument to evaluate projects and programs.

PPBS: Planning-Programming-Budgeting System

This system was developed by the Rand Corporation of Santa Monica, California, in the late 1960s. It provides an analytical basis for decision-making and for moving these decisions into operations. The system consists of:

1. A program structure: a classification of the courses of action available to the decision-maker.
2. An approved program document with precise quantitative data on needs, resources, and program outputs—extending into the foreseeable future.
3. A decision-making process, which establishes functions, rules, and time lines for PPBS.
4. An analytical process to measure effectiveness and for weighing alternative decisions.
5. An information system, which supplies data required to implement the system.

The advantages of the PPBS are:

1. The system covers a wide range of activities, from the initial planning stage to the budgeting of the specific operations.
2. The system is superior to the previous systems (GANTT, ZBB, and PERT), primarily because it supplies managerial data from several areas or departments.
3. The system provides analytical data, which is needed for the implementation of the system.

These advantages provide the decision-maker with an evaluation instrument that covers much of the organization and that collects data from across divisions, areas, and departments.

The disadvantages of the PPBS are:

1. The system does not provide an analysis of the outputs.
2. The system does not provide a link to the evaluation effort by managers.
3. The system does not provide a link to the objectives of the evaluation.

These shortcomings of the PPBS restrict the system to the initial stages of planning. Although it may be defined as "a good start," the system nevertheless fails to extend its reach to the downstream stages of the evaluation effort.

If we compare the advantages and the disadvantages side-by-side, it becomes evident that this evaluation system is not a strong instrument in the service of management. It is also evident that the techniques described above are utilized by evaluators mainly because each evaluation technique offers some benefits, since it provides one or more dimensions of the evaluation space required by managers.

Critical Path Analysis (CPA) or Method (CPM)

This technique employs the following principles:

1. Mapping every key task needed to complete the project or program,

2. Mapping the amount of time needed to complete each task or activity, and
3. How the tasks or activities are dependent on each other (inter-dependency of tasks).

This technique of CPA is also defined as the critical path method (CPM). It entails the activities needed for completion; the time it takes to complete each activity; and the degree to which each task/activity may or may not depend on another task/activity.

The early version of the CPM technique was initially developed in the 1940s, and is credited by some historians with its contribution to the management of the "Manhattan Project," which led to the development and the construction of the first nuclear weapons, later used at Hiroshima and Nagasaki in Japan.

The CPA technique provides a process of identifying the longest path in a schedule-network diagram. It indicates the steps and the completeness of project schedule, ***and*** ascertains the degree of schedule flexibility. In addition, the CPA reveals the minimum time duration required to successfully complete a project, as well as the link between project activities and the permissible delays that are not identified on the critical path.

This means that some delays are tolerable and do not raise alarm—if they occur in activities that are not part of the Critical Path to completion—that is, are not essential to the completion of activities that make up the critical path to completion. Moreover, the CPA also focuses on the inter-dependency of activities, so that selected activities cannot start unless and until other activities are completed. This characteristic of the CPA is essential for reliable planning. It also gives the manager the ability to identify "busy" time frames as well as slack times between activities. Thus, managers have much more flexibility in their planning and the implementation stages of their plans.

Summary: The Evaluation Techniques

The sections above described the five evaluation techniques most in use by managers/evaluators: (1) GANTT Charts; (2) Zero-Base Budgeting (ZBB); (3) PERT; (4) PPBS; and (5) Critical Path Analysis (CPA) or Method (CPM). These techniques vary with the degree to which they are useful to the manager. For example, the PERT technique is better than the GANTT Chart because it is more complete. That is, PERT allows the use of data from the diverse areas and departments of the organization, and it also identifies lines of responsibility, channels of communication, and a "what if analysis" scenario. These characteristics of PERT were attractive enough so that the US Navy, under Admiral Rickover, used the technique to manage and to evaluate the highly complex Polaris program: the design and construction of the first nuclear submarine.

The famous implementation of these techniques occurred during the American War in Vietnam. Then Defense Secretary Robert McNamara (1916–2009) insisted on the application of many such techniques in the conduct of the war. One outcome from these techniques was the ability of McNamara and his team to have periodic quantitative analyses of the war effort—including budgets and the human toll of the war in terms of casualties and other variables in the utilization, effectiveness, and losses of the troops in Vietnam.

Another famous application was the planning and execution of the landing on the Moon during the decade of the 1960s. The National Aeronautics and Space Agency (NASA) was under a time constraint, because President John F. Kennedy had declared in 1962 that the United States would send an astronaut to land on the moon and return him safely to earth.

It is abundantly clear that all the techniques described above are, in many ways, the essential components of the notion of *Analytics*. These techniques offer the portfolio of techniques or methods that can be used to analyze project, program, and organizational activities and their outputs. These techniques are the tools, at the disposal of the manager, allowing for a workable and valid analysis. Clearly, this is where the "buck stops." This is merely the analysis of where we stand, and what quantities we have available to classify in our evaluation of projects, programs, and organization.

These techniques fall short of providing us with the tools necessary to link these projects and programs to their objectives, their logical formulations, and their meaning to the manager. It is necessary, at this juncture, to resort to a more comprehensive, more responsive, and more elaborate technique that will have a strong appeal to the practicing manager. This is the time for the notion of "Beyond Analytics."

References

Adrian, T. and M. M. Westerfield. 2009. Disagreement and Learning in a Dynamic Contracting Model. *Review of Financial Studies* 22 (10): 3873–3906.

Bollier, D. 2010. *The Promise and Peril of Big Data*. Aspen CO: The Aspen Institute.

Burrows, R., and M. Savage. 2014. After the Crisis? Big Data and the Methodological Challenges of Empirical Sociology. *Big Data & Society*, April-June, 1–6.

Davenport, T. 2014. *Advanced Analytics and Big Data Adoption Report*. Portland, OR: International Institute for Analytics.

Elgendy, N. and A. Elragal. 2016. Big Data Analytics in Support of the Decision Making Process. *Procedia Computer Science* 100: 1071–1084.

Fagin, R., and A. Nash. 2010. The Structure of Inverses in Schema Mappings. *Journal of the ACM* 57 (6): 1–57.

Fortuna, N. 2018. Beyond Analytics. *MHI Solutions* March 23, 2018.

Gao, S., R. Alhaij, R. Rokne, and J. Guan. 2011. Mining Sequential Patterns with Extensible Knowledge Representation. *Intelligent Data Analysis* 15 (6): 889–911.

Geisler, E. 1979. *An Empirical Study of a Proposed System for Monitoring Organizational Change in a Federal R&D Laboratory*. Unpublished dissertation, Evanston, IL, Northwestern University.

Geisler, E. 2013. Beyond Analytics: The Special Case. How Technology Managers Translate Big Data into Actionable Decisions. In *Proceedings of the PICMET (Portland International Conference on the Management of Engineering and Technology) Conference*. Aug 3–5 2013, San Jose, CA.

Ghosh, B., and J. Scott. 2011. Antecedents and Catalysts for Developing a Healthcare Analytic Capability. *Communications of the Association for Information Systems* 29 (22): 395–410.

Gladwell, M. 2002. *The Tipping Point: How Little Things Can Make a Big Difference*. New York: Back Bay Books.

Hubbard, D. 2014. *How to Measure Anything: Finding the Value of "Intangibles" in Business, 3rd Ed*. Hoboken, NJ: John Wiley and Sons.

Janssen, A., C. Klein, and M. Slors. 2017. Cognitive Ontologies in Philosophy of Mind and Philosophy of Psychiatry. *Philosophical Explorations* 20 (2): 123–128.

Johnson, E., J. Hershey, J. Meszaros, and H. Kunreuther. 1993. Framing Probability Distortions and Insurance Decisions. *Journal of Risk and Uncertainty* 7 (1): 35–51.

Kahneman, D., and A. Tversky. 1979. Prospect Theory: An Analysis of Decisions Under Risk. *Econometrica* 47 (2): 263–292.

Laurson, G. H. N., and J. Thorlund. 2010. *Business Analytics for Managers: Taking Business Intelligence Beyond Reporting*. New York, NY: Wiley & Sons.
Ryan, V. 2016. Special Report: The Promise of Predictive Analytics. *CFO*, October 16, 2016.
Sankararaman, S. et al. 2014. The Genomic Landscape of Neanderthal Ancestry in Present-Day Humans. *Nature* 507: 354–357.
Siegel, E. 2013. Predictive Analytics. *Analytics Magazine*, July/August, 38–43.
Taleb, N. 2010. *The Black Swan: The Impact of the Highly Improbable*. New York: Random House.
Tuchman, B. 2009 Reprint. *The Guns of August*. New York: Random House.

CHAPTER 3

The Concept of Beyond Business Analytics

In their 1963 seminal book, Donald Campbell and Julian Stanley introduced what they called quasi-experimental designs for research. They argued that in the managerial and organizational sciences—unlike in the exact sciences—true experiments like those conducted in a laboratory, are not feasible. Human subjects are too fickle, too individualistic, and too unpredictable to participate in such true experiments. Thus, one must understand the advantages as well as the disadvantages of dealing with human subjects in a field research project.

A similar notion is in place regarding "beyond analytics." Analytics provide data and its initial analysis. However, the next step introduces such questions as: (1) what does it all mean, (2) how do I translate the data into adequate managerial decisions, and (3) how can I manipulate the "big data" thus assembled in my data base so that I am able to translate such data into a workable description of my organizational reality (McCarthy et al. 2018; Polyrack 2018).

The notion of "Beyond Analytics" is designed to fill the space between the analysis of the data and the meaning of the data (or information) and its input into the decision-making process (Davenport 2014; Hand 2018; Kiron et al. 2010). Moreover, the notion of Business Analytics is the set of the skills, technologies, and practices that occurred in the past time frame. This set is then used to assess past performance and, from this set of variables, to deduce the understanding of business processes and

E. Geisler, *Beyond Business Analytics*,
https://doi.org/10.1007/978-3-030-43718-3_3

outcomes, and from them to gain new insights into the present situation and the planning of future events (Dane and Pratt 2007; Davenport 2014; Geisler 2013; Kachelmeier and Shehata 1992).

It is precisely because the insights gained from analytics have a limited capability of describing events and predicting them that we resort to the employment of "Beyond Analytics." This concept not only refers to the analytical space between the analysis and the managerial decision process, but also provides the decision-maker with the explanation of how the information/data that results from the analysis effort can be used as credible inputs to the decision process.

What Is Beyond Business Analytics?

The notion of Beyond Business Analytics (BBA) is a complex concept that is composed of two complementary parts, one quantitative and the other cognitive. The first part is the quantity in the space we call analytics. the *description* of the phenomenon or the notion. The second is the *meaning* of this quantity to the decision-maker. In essence, ***analytics is the data, whereas beyond analytics is the meaning of the data*** to the decision-maker.

Moreover, analytics is also an instrument that reveals the truthful situations or variables within the organization. It may also be described with the ancient Roman principle of *res ipso loquitor* (the thing speaks for itself) or, put another way, the thing, variable, or situation is self-evident or self-explanatory. In German the term is *selbstverstandlich* and, in French, *évident ensoi* (Kaplan and Norton 1996).

When fed complete and truthful information, the instrument of analytics offers the manager a powerful tool for decision-making. However, to arrive at a point where the manager is capable of utilizing analytics to make sound decisions, the notion of analytics must be constructed in a format that will give the manager a sufficient and seamless assessment of the information, so that the manager can easily feed the information into the decision process.

This is where the notion of *Beyond Business Analytics* comes into being. It contains a sufficient amount of relevant information necessary for a sound decision, as well as the description of a business situation or a business phenomenon (Simon 1982). As described above, the term "beyond" signifies the venturing into the cognitive space between the data or the information and the meaning of such data—which then can be interpreted by the decision-maker and can provide input for a business decision.

Therefore, the notion of "beyond" is the link between the quantitative data and the sound decisions by the manager. In this manner, the notion of "beyond" enriches the data, as it connects the data to the cognitive manipulation of the data by the manager. This also means that until the advent of the notion of "beyond," the manager is almost solely engaged in "working" with the data at his disposal so that the manager is inevitably confronted with data and information and, in many instances, the manager is challenged by large amounts of such data or "big data".

"Big Data" generally refers to a very large amount of data that is composed of various and sundry types of data—all mixed together. Such a mixture may contain qualitative ***and*** quantitative data assembled into the set, without a prior categorization or classification of the data. The notion of "Big Data" does not necessarily mean or even imply a certain mix of, say, half qualitative and half quantitative data. In fact, the mix of raw data in the notion of "Big Data" may be of any type and classification—as long as it contains large amounts of data brought together within the same system (Bannister and Griffith 1986; Blok and Pedersen 2014, Braunstein 1974; Chen et al. 2012; Dahl 1963; Levine et al. 1993; Liberatore and Luo 2010; Reiter and List 2013).

Some Evidence from the Literature

The large volume of organizational data are thus assembled and processed in the mind of the manager. There is an already fertile and constantly growing literature on the topic. Greene et al. (2019) describes the European Union's General Data Protection Regulation (GDPR) of May 2018. They suggested that data and behavioral scientists should strive to fully understand this legislation and to familiarize themselves with its key concepts, definitions, and principles.

Similarly, Minelli et al. (2013) also linked the accumulation of big data to what they call Big Analytics, and the impact of these on business intelligence. Other writers such as Franks (2012) and Davenport (2014) have focused on the implementation or the utilization of big data in developing the strategic plan of the firm, as well as in its operational decision-making processes. For example, Bernard Marr (2012) argued that business leaders should not be skeptical about big data that crosses their desk. Rather, they should consider such data as a strategic asset. Marr also suggested that managers should find ways to identify their strategic data needs, the means and methods by which they would collect the relevant data, and to make such data relevant inputs to their decision process.

These scholars, in effect, advanced the notion that managers should ensure that their data is indeed considered and treated as an essential asset to their organization. The road from raw data to strategic insights must be clearly understood and scrupulously followed by these managers. Therefore, vast amounts of data collected by the organization are to be treated constructively and consistently as critical components of the firm's strategic planning.

The concern about the utilization of data analytics is a global phenomenon. For instance, West et al. (2018) described the learning analytics experience among academics in Australia 3 and Malaysia. They conducted a survey of 355 Australian and 224 Malaysian academics. The study focused on (1) involvement in learning analytics activities, (2) responses of these academics to their institutional capacity in supporting learning analytics, and (3) their concerns about ethical issues regarding the learning of analytics. This study concluded that academics in both countries are very interested in the use of learning analytics and very concerned with issues of such usage and implementation.

The relevant literature thus supports the notion that managers and academics are acutely concerned with large volumes of data and considerably involved in the practices of utilizing such data in their organizational decision processes (Connor 2012; Davenport and Harris 2007; Drucker 1988; Franks 2012).

Summary: What is Beyond Business Analytics

Beyond Business Analytics (BBA) is therefore the theoretical *and* the empirical space between the collection of data and the application of such data in conjuring concepts for managerial usage. This also means that this is the concept that emerges in the "Valley of Nothingness" between concept and implementation. As mentioned above, the notion of "beyond" is the link between the raw or quantitative data and the decisions made by the manager. In other words, "beyond" refers to how the manager transforms the raw data about a variable, a situation, or a phenomenon into the conceptual description of the data—as it is used for sound decisions (Kaplan and Norton 1996).

Beyond Analytics in Different Contexts

The notion of Beyond Analytics has several ramifications into other areas besides business. One such area is policy-making and politics in all forms of government: municipal, county, state, and country.

In these policy-making cases in the public sector, beyond analytics encompasses the space between the data or information supplied to the office holder in a public sector organization and the decisions made by the office holder with all its ramifications and impacts on the budget, the human resources function, operations, and the strategic planning of the organization (House and Shull 1988; Evans et al. 2019).

Evans et al. (2019) address applications of analytics in over a dozen areas in the public sector such as education, military, public health, and criminal justice. For example, in Chapter 2 they discuss the use of operational data in the public bus services in South Korea, whereas in Chapter 10 they focus on the use of analytics in the US criminal justice system. In this case they argue that the expenditures in the United States associated with crime averaged 1.5 trillion dollars, or 20.9 percent of the gross domestic product (GDP). Thus, the expenditure related to crime averaged almost 1/3 of the federal budget and about 6.8 percent of the GP.

These are indeed very big numbers! For example, the total expen ditures of the government of the United Kingdom in 2016 were 1.03 trillion US dollars. This is about 66 percent or 2/3 of what the United States spent that same year on crime-related activities Conversely, the United Kingdom expended only 4.4 percent of its 2016 budget on public order and safety. This figure is only about 1/5 of what the United States was spending as a portion of its budget.

It is therefore abundantly clear that these enormous sets of data must be carefully managed, hence the need for analytics as a tool to measure and manage these big data (Schroeck et al. 2012).

This book addresses these issues on the measurement and the management of big data, as well as the space beyond such management and measurement quantities. This book focuses on the question: how do we connect the quantities we gather with the instrument of analytics to the cognitive content of the manager's use of such data. This is accomplished with the use of the linking mechanism we connote as "Beyond Business Analytics" (Wouters and Noyons 2014).

The Case of the University of California System Admissions Requirements

The University of California System's administration has announced on April 1, 2020 that it will extend its policy for the 2022 and 2023 incoming freshman classes whereby it will no longer require SAT or ACT scores for admission decision. The university system, however, also gave the individual campuses of the system a choice to make the test an option for the incoming classes of 2021 and 2022.

This change in policy means that the admissions director does not need any longer to abide by a quantitative measure of qualification for admission. Rather, it can rely solely on such evaluation instruments as the high-school grades of the applicant and, if so needed, a thesis or written paper on "why I wish to enroll at the University of California campus?" Thus, the admission decision is now primarily a subjective evaluation by the admissions staff of the applicant's record of high-school scholarship, and where necessary, the applicant's analytical ability for expression via a paper or a thesis. The idea is that the applicant's written output will be an additional and sufficient measure of the applicant's probability of a successful graduation from the academic studies at the University of California, and a successful career at the conclusion of these studies.

This case of the University of California admissions process is a good illustration of the notion of Beyond Business Analytics. The university may henceforth disregard the quantitative aspects of the admission procedure, which until now was used as an indicator of future success of the applicant. Rather, it may now solely rely on the subjective analyses and subsequent conclusions by the admissions office.

References

Bannister, B., and R. Griffith. 1986. Applying a Causal Analytic Framework to the Mobley, Horner and Hollingsworth (1978) Turnover Model: A Useful Reexamination. *Journal of Management* 12 (3): 433–443.

Blok, A., and M. A. Pederson. 2014. Complementary Social Science Quali-Quantitative Experiments in a Big Data World. *Big Data & Society* 5: 1–6.

Braunstein, D. 1974. Beyond Leavitt's 'Narrow' Analytic Manager. *Interfaces* 4 (4): 28–31.

Chen, H., R. Chiang, and V. Storey. 2012. Business Intelligence and Analytics: From Big Date to Big Impact. *MIS Quarterly* 36 (4): 1165–1188.

Connor, K. 2012. Taming the Data Tidal Wave. *Analytics Magazine*, 21–24.

Cook, T., and D. Stanley. 1979. *Quasi-Experimentation: Design and Analysis Issues for Field Settings*. Boston, MA: Houghton Mifflin Company.

Dahl, R. 1963. *Modern Political Analysis*. Prentice-Hall: Englewood Cliffs.

Dane, E., and M. Pratt. 2007. Exploring Intuition and its Role in Managerial Decision-Making. *Academy of Management Review* 32 (1): 33–54.

Davenport, T. 2014. *Advanced Analytics and Big Data Adoption Report*. Portland: International Institute for Analytics.

Davenport, T., and J. Harris. 2007. *Competing on Analytics: The New Science of Winning*. Boston: Harvard Business School Press.

Drucker, P. 1988. The Coming of the New Organization. *Harvard Business Review* 1: 45–53.

Evans, G., W. Biles, and Ki-Hwan Bae. 2019. *Analytics, Operations, and Strategic Decision Making in the Public Sector*. Hershey, PA: IGI Global.

Franks, B. 2012. *Taming the Big Data Tidal Wave*. New York: Wiley.

Geisler, E. 2013. Beyond Analytics: The Special Case How Technology Managers Translate Big Data into Actionable Decisions. In *Proceedings of the PICMET (Portland International Conference on the Management of Engineering and Technology) Conference*, August 3–5, 2013, San Jose, CA.

Hand, D. 2018. Who Told You That? Data Provenance, False Facts, and Separating the Liars from the Truth-Tellers. *Significance* 15: 8–9.

House, P., and R. Shull. 1988. *Rush to Policy: Using Analytics Techniques in Public Sector Decision-Making*. London, UK: Routledge.

Kachelmeier, S., and M. Shehata. 1992. Examining Risk Preferences Under High Monetary Incentives: Experimental Evidence from the People's Republic of China. *American Economic Review* 82 (5): 1120–1141.

Kaplan, R., and D. Norton. 1996. *The Balanced Scorecard*. Boston, MA: Harvard Business School Press.

Kiron, D., R. Shockley, N. Kruschwitz, G. Finch, and M. Haydock. 2010. *Analytics: The Widening Divide: How Companies are Achieving Competitive Advantage Through Analytics*. New York: IBM Institute for Business Value.

Levine, J., L. Resnick, and E. Higgins. 1993. Social Foundations of Cognition. *Annual Review of Psychology* 44 (4): 484 612.

Liberatore, M., and W. Luo. 2010. The Analytics Movement: Implications for Operations Research. *Interfaces* 40 (4): 313–324.

McCarthy, B., C. McShea, and M. Roth. 2018. Rebooting Analytics Leadership: Time to Move Beyond the Math. McKinsey & Company, NewYork, November 2018.

Minelli, M., M. Chambers, and A. Dhiraj. 2013. *Big Data Big Analytics: Emerging Business Intelligence and Analytic Trends for Today's Businesses*. New York: Wiley.

Polyrack, R. 2018. *The New Mind Readers: What Neuroimaging Can and Cannot Reveal About Our Thoughts*. Princeton, NJ: Princeton University Press.

Reiter, N., and B. List. 2013. An Analytics Maturity Model: How Analytically Mature is your Organization and How Can it Do Better. *Analytics*, Nov-Dec. Accessed July 8, 2015. http://www.analytics-magazine.org/november-december-2013/904-informs-analytics-maturity-model?format=pdf.

Schroeck, M., R. Scockley, J. Smart, D. Romero-Morales, and P. Tufano. 2012. Analytics: The Real-World Use of Big Data: How Innovative Enterprises Extract Value from Uncertain Data. Business Report, IBM Institute for Business Value.

Simon, H. 1982. *Models of Bounded Rationality*. Cambridge, MA: MIT Press.

West, D., T. Zaidatun, et al., 2018. Learning Analytics Experience Among Academics in Australia and Malaysia: A Comparison. *Australasian Journal of Educational Technology* 34 (3): 122–139.

Wouters, P., and E. Noyons. 2014. Context Counts: Pathways to Master Big and Little Data. In *Proceedings of the Science and Technology Indicators Conference*, Leiden, The Netherlands, University of Leiden Press.

CHAPTER 4

Representations of Organizational Events

This chapter addresses the ways in which we represent organizational events. This is the description of the various formats with which we collate or assemble organizational events under a single coherent description. There are several ways to describe organizational events—each of these with its own attributes, strengths, and weaknesses (Bannister and Griffith 1986; Boudreau 2015; Braunstein 1974; Chen et al. 2012; Geisler 2001).

This chapter contains six sections. The first discusses the knowledge matrix and the periodic table of knowledge. The second section deals with the individual preferences in their view of such organizational events. The third section explores tacit knowledge. The fourth section deals with representation, which is how the human mind creates representation of events as its cognitive components. The fifth section is on decision making, and the so-called threshold effect. Finally, the sixth section deals with the power that a few elements may have over the overall phenomenon (Burrows and Savage 2014; Charan 2015; D'Eredita and Barreto 2006; Fox and Tversky 1995).

Models of Knowledge

The cogent literature on knowledge and knowledge management offers several models that describe and classify personal and organizational knowledge. Some models are presented below.

E. Geisler, *Beyond Business Analytics*,
https://doi.org/10.1007/978-3-030-43718-3_4

The Wiig Model

In 1993, Karl Wiig proposed a four-stage model or process of what constitutes knowledge in organizations:

1. Building Knowledge
2. Holding Knowledge
3. Pooling Knowledge, and
4. Applying Knowledge

The idea is to build and hold or maintain the amount of knowledge that organizational members are able to procure (Geisler 2006).

The Periodic Table of the Elements

In 1869, the Russian scientist, Dimitri Mendeleev (1834–1907), conceived a classification scheme for the elements by their atomic number. To date, the elements from number 1 (hydrogen) through number 118 (oganesson) inhabit seven full rows of the table. The first 97 elements exist in nature, whereas elements 95 through 118 are the product of syntheses in laboratories and in nuclear reactors—that is, humans have engendered the conditions in which such elements may be detected (Agor 1986; Charan 2015; Geisler and Kostoff 1999).

In describing his discovery, Mendeleev wrote: "I saw in a dream a table where all elements fell into place as required. Awakening, I immediately wrote it down on a piece of paper, only in one place did a correction later seem necessary." This was indeed one of the rare instances in history when people are endowed or blessed with an idea—or a thought, or a theory, or explanation—that is fortuitous, the result of serendipity, and, perhaps, simply pure luck. Sometimes these ideas or discoveries are obviously revolutionary whereas in other cases they emerge without fanfare, only to be rediscovered years later as great contributors to our state of knowledge (Geisler 2002; Halper and Krishnan 2013; Hand 2018; Isabella 1990; Kaplan 2011; Lavalle et al. 2010).

Bloom's Taxonomy

In 1956 the American psychologist Benjamin Bloom (1913–1999) proposed a framework for the classification of learning based on levels of the vigor and complexity of cognition. In 2001, Lorin Anderson and David Krathwohl published a revision to Bloom's taxonomy. Their revision was designed to make the taxonomy more effectively useful. Anderson was a student of Bloom's, and Krathwohl was Bloom's research partner during the time when Bloom conceived his taxonomy.

Bloom's model includes the following descriptions of knowledge: (1) Remembering; (2) Comprehension; (3) Application; (4) Analysis; (5) Synthesis; and (6) Evaluation. Anderson and Krathwohl also had six levels: (1) Remembering; (2) Understanding; (3) Applying; (4) Analysis; (5) Evaluating; and (6) Creating (getting the elements together in order to form a functional whole). It is assumed that the "creating" process is the most difficult mental task in the taxonomy, (d) ***Anderson and Krathwohl*** also identified four levels of knowledge:

1. Factual Knowledge: basic elements necessary to solve a problem.
2. Conceptual Knowledge: Inter-relationships among the basic elements.
3. Procedural Knowledge: Methods, techniques, and criteria of how to do or proceed with a given task.
4. Metacognitive Knowledge: Defined as the awareness of one's cognition. This type of knowledge is more strategic in nature.

In summary, the above four classifications or models of what constitutes knowledge are essentially designed to facilitate human workings and the applications of such knowledge.

Models of Knowledge and Beyond Business Analytics

As described above, Beyond Business Analytics is both an *instrument* for analysis and the *link* to the content of a business situation or phenomenon. It is the link between the quantitative content and the behavioral aspects of the situation.

The four models of knowledge listed above offer a description of the types of knowledge that humans possess. These models provide the *context* or the structures where knowledge resides. For instance, the Periodic Table of the elements gives us the structure of the positioning of the elements of nature—akin to art objects positioned on a wall unit.

The relationships among these categories of data describe how what transpires within the organization can be used to take us beyond the analyses and into the space of the behavior of the managers of the organization.

The five dimensions (5 Ps) of the relationship between business analytics and the firm are:

- Why? (**P**urpose: To what end?)
- How? (**P**rocess: In what way?)
- By whom? (**P**eople involved: Who are they?)
- How well? (**P**erformance of the people involved.)
- With what consequences? (**P**ayback: What is the fallout, reaction, upshot, aftermath, or effects of such performance?

This relationship can also be elucidated, explicated, or expounded by how beyond analytics is a notion that explains the need for the information collected by the analytics effort and the usefulness of such information as critical inputs to sound managerial decision-making activities (Jenkins and Johnson 1997; Kachelmeier and Shehata 1992; Kahneman et al. 1982; Kramer et al. 2014; Leavitt 1975a, b; McCarthy et al. 2018; Plomp 1990; Poldrack 2018; Rubenstein et al. 1992).

Beyond Analytics: Illustrative Special Cases in Human History

This section portrays three cases of historical illustrations of the applications of the notion of "beyond analytics" to real-life situations. In this context it should be clarified that the notion of analytics is not the decision process itself. It is rather the *inputs* to the decision process. Thus, the cases below are examples of misjudgments and misinterpretations of analytics (data and events).

The Case of Napoleon's Campaign in Russia

In 1812 the French Emperor Napoleon Buonaparte invaded Russia. This army was known as "Le Grande Armee" (the great army). In late June 1812, the total strength of Napoleon's army is estimated at about 685,000 men (of which about 400,000 were French soldiers) and over 50,000 horses. The remaining 285,000 soldiers were conscripts from all over Europe, particularly from Poland, Austria, Italy, Bavaria, Saxony, and Prussia.

Throughout his previous campaigns in Italy and Spain, Napoleon was a master of accumulating intelligence on his adversaries. His battle plans had been tailored to the information which he gained on the size of his enemies and their disposition in and around the battlefield.

When Napoleon invaded Russia, he rapidly advanced his armies toward the Imperial Russian capital, Moscow. The Russians, led by their emperor, Alexander I, and under the command of Mikhail Kutuzov (1745–1813) abandoned Moscow to Napoleon, but executed a "scorched earth" strategy, thus depriving Napoleon the bounty of the Russian countryside. The harsh winter of 1812 and the lack of adequate supplies forced the "Grande Armee" to retreat to Prussia, thus abandoning any hope of defeating the Russians.

Although Napoleon had information on the Russian forces opposing him, he could not transform this information into actionable knowledge. Napoleon had information (analytics), yet he failed to think beyond the information and to integrate it into his overall strategy and its operational tactics. Napoleon was thus faced with the famous dilemma of the "go" versus "chess."

"Go" versus "chess" is a choice between two different strategies. The "Go" strategy calls for conquering as much territory as possible, regardless of the size of the remaining enemy forces. The *chess* strategy is based on the systematic destruction of enemy forces. In the game of chess, the object of the game is to eliminate the opponent's pieces in the tactic of attacking and eliminating the king, which is the ultimate object of the game. In the game of chess, conquering territory is not the object of the game—as it is rather a secondary goal since the remaining pieces, by their range of movement on the board, thus control the territory around them.

The case of Napoleon Buonaparte in Russia is perhaps one of the best examples of a "go" strategy, whereas his enemy, the Russians, employed the "chess" strategy. The Russians gave up territory but kept their forces relatively intact for future battles. The large tracts of land that Napoleon conquered (including Moscow) were of no good use to him. He now faced an almost intact Russian army, fighting in its homeland and enjoying the benefits of relatively short supply lines, contrary to Napoleon's inability to adequately exploit the lands he now possessed in the Russian steppes.

In addition, an extremely powerful Russian winter has descended upon the French and their allies. Most of these armies had originally come from temperate climates where winters are difficult but not extreme. The French troops thus painfully lacked the appropriate clothing and accommodations that could protect them from the harsh winter weather. These conditions vastly contributed to the disastrous fortune of the "Great Army." Only about 110,000 French soldiers survived this disastrous ordeal, out of 685,000 who first crossed the Russian frontier. This means that only about 16 percent of the grand army survived. The remainder perished in the freezing weather, as well as victims of the constant attacks by the Russian elite units of the Cossack cavalry.

Another aspect of this case that displays a critical lack of information or intelligence about Russia was the disastrous realization by Napoleon that Russia had an extremely underdeveloped network of roads. This fact had forced Napoleon to move his army on a very narrow front, hence opening himself to constant attacks on his flanks by Russian troops who did not necessarily need to maneuver on their poor system of roads. Perhaps Napoleon and his Marshalls knew that the roads were in poor state of repair, yet had decided to use them anyway because they were the only navigable system of movement and transport of troops and supplies that were available to them.

The Case of the First Crusade

The first crusade was a popular movement in Western Europe, whose objective was to recapture the Holy Land and the city of Jerusalem, which had been conquered by the surging power of the Islamic military forces. The first crusade was also known as the "People's Crusade." In 1096 A.D., at the instigation of Peter the Hermit, who evoked a religious fervor in mobs of peasants and others in Western Europe. This was a disorganized eruption of energy, driven by deep religious belief endowed with the sacred mission to "liberate" the Holy Land and restore the church's control of the holy shrines in the Holy Land. These early crusaders attacked Jewish communities in Germany on their way to the Holy Land via the Ottoman Empire in Turkey. In October 1096 the Turks attacked the Crusaders at Civetot. By some accounts, over 60 thousand crusaders were killed by Turkish arrows. This was the end of the "People's Crusade."

The first Crusaders had no information or intelligence of the enemy's forces that awaited them. The People's Crusaders simply marched ahead, led by nonmilitary men such as Peter the Hermit. They had no plan. They had a very limited knowledge of the terrain, and of the strategic and tactical disposition of their adversaries. They lacked the basic information about their mission and what they were about to encounter. This is a classic example of an amateurish enterprise, involving many thousands of untrained and undisciplined peasants and city dwellers.

In our terminology, we can safely attest to the fact that the first crusaders were simply a mob of hooligans, who instead of constant quarreling among themselves had turned their combative and destructive energy first against their Jewish neighbors, and then against the Islamic inhabitants of the Levant.

Following the disastrous "People's Crusade," several European nobles, particularly from France, heeded the call for help from Pope Urban II and from the Byzantine Emperor Alexios Komnenos. They attacked and conquered Jerusalem in July 1099, thus establishing the kingdom of Jerusalem.

The Case of Navarre at Dien Bien Phu

The French general Henri Navarre (1898–1983) was the commanding general of the First Indochina War, and in this capacity was also the military commander during the battle of Dien Bien Phu, when the French Army was resolutely defeated by the Viet Minh in May 1954.

General Navarre commanded a garrison of about 13 thousand soldiers, whereas the Viet Minh had over 50 thousand fighters. Following a siege which lasted 54 days, the city was lost to the enemy. General Navarre had failed to consider the psychological effects of this defeat on the French people. His defeat contributed to the loss of support for the war by the people. On May 8, 1954, peace negotiations began in Geneva. The first war in Indochina had ended.

General Navarre was relieved of his command on June 3, 1954. He retired from the French Army in 1956. He was disillusioned and upon his retirement, General Navarre published a book *Agonie de L'Indochine*. This book was highly critical of the French military and political bureaucracies.

This is a case whereby General Navarre was in possession of good intelligence (Analytics) of the numbers and dispositions of the Vietnamese forces. He chose to disregard and to discount this information. By so doing, he also misjudged the military capacity of his enemy. He could not accept the fact that a native force of rebels could amount to a serious military threat to his forces of regular army formations.

A similar misjudgment was repeated a decade later in the same geographical region by an American commander, General Westmoreland. His forces were bogged down in the harsh Vietnamese terrain of tropical forests, rivers, and lagoons. The topography was largely unpassable—even to a modern army.

Summary: What These Cases Tell Us

These cases illustrate situations in which the leaders lacked adequate and actionable analytics, or were in possession of some or much information—sufficiently assembled as inputs to good decision-making. Clearly, the question, how much analytics is necessary and sufficient to make a good decision? is still very relevant to this discussion.

These cases also tell us that the existence of Analytics in any form, in a given situation, determines to a large extent the resolution of the situation or the problem depicted in the given scenario. There seems to be no urgent need for a surfeit of evidence; rather, an amount of analytics that would provide acceptable input for a good managerial decision.

In some instances, the analytics provided to the decision-maker is not sufficient for a good decision.

Case A

Case A shows that although the analytics may have been good and sufficient, the decision-maker made the wrong decision by selecting the wrong alternative from the set of possible alternative solutions that were available to the decision-maker. The wrong choice may have been the result of a gross misinterpretation of the information or the decision-maker's affinity or existing predilection, thus biasing the choice toward a given alternative.

An example of Case A is the unmitigated defeat of the American General George Custer by the Sioux Indians at the Battle of the Little Big Horn. He was in possession of adequate information about his opponents, yet he decided to engage them with the inadequate forces at his disposal rather than disengage the enemy and postpone the attack until reinforcements arrived.

Case B

Another situation is Case B. This is the case where the analytics are wrong, incomplete, or misleading to such a degree that the problem or situation could not be resolved. Such a case may be the implementation of a wrong policy or the choice of a poor strategy. The decision-maker is in possession of inadequate amounts of information (analytics), thus unable to make a reasonable decision.

Examples of Case B include the first Iraq War of 2003. This conflict was predicated upon analytics of Iraq's possession of an arsenal of weapons of mass destruction (WMDs), such as nuclear, chemical, and biological weapons. The analytics proved to be erroneous as upon occupying Iraq, such weapons could not be found. The analytics was wrong.

According to the US Center for Disease Control and Prevention, 8 out of 10 deaths from the coronavirus have been 65 years old and older. 4–11 percent of adults 65–85 years old and 10–27 percent of adults 85 years old and older have died as a result of this disease. Also, 11–31 percent of adults 65–84 years old required admission to intensive care. This means that about one in four or one in three older adults required admission to intensive care. Finally, 31–59 percent of adults 65–84 years old required hospitalization. That is, from one-third to one-half of such adults required hospitalization. These data show with abundant clarity that the burden on American hospitals may become insupportable.

Case C

This is the case where the decision-maker works on the wrong problem, or where the decision-maker solves the wrong problem. There is an abundance of historical cases that illustrate this specific case of analytics.

Cases of Leaders Who Lacked Adequate Analytics, yet Decided to Act

The cases below illustrate situations whereby leaders lacked adequate analytics, and were fully aware of this fact yet decided to act regardless of this limiting constraint that they were facing.

The Case of the Battle of the Bulge

The Battle of the Bulge occurred as a result of the German counteroffensive through the mountainous terrain of the Belgian Ardennes. This battle between German and American units was fought during the period December 16, 1944 until January 16, 1945. The term "bulge" described the wedge or the area in which the Germans penetrated the Allied lines.

The German offensive is said to have caught the Allied commanders totally by surprise. However, the facts on the ground and at the Allied Headquarters present a different scenario. Due to the Allied mastery of the German cyphers, General Dwight D. Eisenhower, the Allied supreme commander, was able to anticipate the enemy's intentions and plans. Although the Allies received good intelligence that the Germans were massing troops in the wooded area of the Ardennes, their commanders chose to ignore such specific intelligence. The Allied commanders mistakenly believed that the Germans lacked the necessary armored forces for such a massive winter campaign and, secondly, that the rugged wooded terrain of the Ardennes prohibited the use of armored formations. Some Allied commanders strongly believed that tanks could not maneuver among the trees of a dense forest, such as the Ardennes. Based on such erroneous assumptions, the Allied forces, mostly American, consisted of 80 thousand mainly exhausted and inexperienced divisions. It is thus believed that these 80 thousand men faced in the Ardennes a German force of 250 thousand men, consisting of 14 German infantry and 5 Panzer divisions.

The Americans bravely resisted the continuous attacks by the Germans, particularly in the strategically located city of Bastogne. The Germans lacked adequate fuel supplies for their tank formations and, when confronted with the heroic stand of the American forces, their counterattack collapsed. The "bulge" was recaptured by the Allies, and the German forces retreated to their original lines.

Although the Germans were cognizant of the Allied forces opposing them, and of the continuous influx of Allied reserves coming through the ports of Normandy and from the Belgian port of Antwerp, they stood their ground. Their leader issued an order to fight on, regardless of the human losses and the clearly untenable situation of their units.

The German commanders lacked the means to obtain intelligence on their opponents. They could barely supply and maintain their lines. These commanders simply believed that the Allies had an almost inexhaustible supply of manpower and materials. The Allies controlled the skies and also controlled the ports and the sea lanes.

The order that the German commanders received to stand their position and to not retreat or reposition or regroup their troops was based solely on the will of their leaders—not on solid intelligence of the state of their enemies The order was purely subjective, without the input from military intelligence and an adequate picture of the situation in the field of battle. At the end, the Germans had over 120 thousand casualties, while the Allies lost 75 thousand. But, in addition to the horrific loss of lives, the Germans also lost enormous tonnage of supplies and material, which their war economy could not resupply in time for further military actions.

The escalation of the German “counterattack” in the Ardennes effectively meant a defeat of the German forces in the Second World War. This misjudgment of the German command had accelerated the defeat of Germany and the end of the war.

Since the Germans had a good idea of the forces opposing them, the “Battle of the Bulge” could be considered a “fool’s errand,” perhaps an almost suicidal enterprise. That is, the Germans were in possession of intelligence about their enemies so that the deadly outcome of their counterattack was quite predictable. The German Field Marshal Walther Model, for example, commented on the planned attack:

> “Hitler’s plan has not got a damned leg to stand on.”

The German generals knew, in advance, that the counterattack was doomed from the start. They went along with it because of their military code of obedience to higher authority.

The Case of General Ritchie

In my book *Managing the Aftermath of Radical Corporate Change* (1997), I describe the case in which General Sir Neil Ritchie commanded a British army in the North African desert. In late May 1942, General Ritchie received credible information about the German Field Marshal Erwin Rommel. The British intelligence services had decoded Rommel's battle plan. Ritchie did not know the source of the information, but he knew that his superiors were satisfied that the information was reliable.

General Ritchie decided to ignore the detailed intelligence he possessed and proceeded to commit his army to battle. Rommel sprang his trap on June 13, 1942. Ritchie endured a humiliating defeat. He lost 300 tanks and had to retreat to Egypt.

As I concluded in my account of this incident, the mere possession of critical information is not a guarantee that the commander who possesses such information will indeed incorporate it into his decision-making process. General Ritchie had ignored the intelligence he had received. This behavior is not uncommon. Commanders tend to ignore and reject intelligence that, *prima facie*, appears to be trustworthy. Several reasons animate such behavior. Commanders might not trust the source of the intelligence or the people who bring such intelligence to them. Also, the specific intelligence may not fit their own view of the enemy, his disposition of forces, or his intentions—as they are reflected in his movement (Bliese and Hanges 2004).

The Case of Sir Francis Drake and the Spanish Armada

In the late 1580s, King Philip II of Spain was enraged by the raids of English marauders commanded by Sir Francis Drake, with the silent consent of Queen Elisabeth I. King Philip decided to forcefully act and destroy England's hold on the channel waters and the Atlantic Ocean.

The King ordered the construction of a giant fleet of 130 ships, manned by 8000 sailors, and equipped with 2500 guns and 20 thousand soldiers. On July 23, 1588, the English fleet attacked the Spanish armada, forcing it to turn back to Spain. On the journey back, the armada encountered strong storms and by October, when the surviving ships reached Spain, the armada had lost over half its vessels, and over 15,000 dead.

In these naval encounters, the English introduced a new form of attack. Instead of boarding the enemy's ships and conquering them with the use of their infantry, the English attacked the armada from a distance by using their superior long-range guns. In addition, Sir Francis Drake's ships were smaller, much faster, and could better manipulate the unpredictable waters of the English Channel.

This is a case where one combatant (the English) had analytics over the Spanish. They knew that the enemy ships were slow and cumbersome, and that their English ships could easily out-maneuver the slow-moving armada. The English also had better knowledge of the English Channel and its mortal perils (Bliese et al. 2020).

Sir Francis Drake was victorious because he had much better knowledge of the battleground (the sea) and the advantages of his agile fleet. Sir Francis gained some of this previous knowledge from his raid on the armada's port of Cadiz, in Spain, in early 1588.

The Spaniards knew very little about the English fleet, its characteristics, or its strengths and weaknesses. The Spanish commander, the Duke of Medina-Sidonia, did not bother with gaining intelligence on his enemy. His confidence in his fleet was unshakeable. He had the most fearsome armada the world had ever seen. Victory was just a matter of time and of engaging the enemy. He did not care to know what the enemy was like. Pure logic by looking at the numbers of vessels, led him to believe that a few English vessels could not pose a threat to his force. Perhaps, this was an early application of Analytics (Fiegenbaum and Thomas 1988; Kenny 1979; Thorndike 1939).

Cases in Antiquity

In ancient times, until later in the Roman Empire, kings and generals acted with very little intelligence about their enemies. It was, however, a common practice to send spies to the enemy's camp, who would return and report on what they had seen. In the Biblical account of Joshua (1355–1245 BCE), he sent two spies to the highly fortified city of Jericho. The spies befriended a prostitute, named Rahab. She hid them from the authorities and helped them leave the city undetected. The two spies returned unharmed and reported to Joshua that the population of Jericho was very afraid ("melting away") of the potential invaders (Joshua, 2:24). They also probably reported data on the city's walls, which helped Joshua destroy the walls.

Julius Caesar also employed spies, whom he sent to Gaul (today's France), so he could better understand the disposition of his troops, vis-à-vis the enemy. This was a common practice by the Roman legions. The reports were delivered to members of the Roman Senate but were considered to be state secrets (Kreft and de Leeuw 1998).

Legion commanders and the supreme commander of the Roman forces habitually sent spies to collect data on (1) geography and terrain, such as approaches, escape routes, weather, and food and water resources; (2) social and political data, such as quality of leadership, strengths and weaknesses of the population, and social and political institutions, including their religious practices and the nature of their holidays.

Other types of data include types and locations of fortifications, outposts, communication means (e.g., by foot or on horseback), and the topography of the enemy's terrain and its surroundings.

In 331 BCE, Alexander the Macedonian defeated the Persian army at Gaugamela, under the command of Darius III. The Macedonians had 35,000 men, against over 200,000 Persians. Alexander had studied the terrain and was thus able to lure the Persian cavalry to a very rough and rocky area, where their maneuverability would greatly collapse. Thus, Alexander was in possession of analytics about the battlefield and the enemy—and this helped him to achieve remarkable victory.

In all these cases, the victorious side had collected analytics about the terrain, the size of the enemy forces, and their disposition. Armed with such data, the victors could fight with the tremendous advantage of knowing much more than their opponent (Snijders and Bosker 1999; Bliese et al. 2020).

These four categories of cases illustrate the link between leaders and analytics. The cases show instances where leaders lacked sufficient and adequate analytics—yet decided to act. Their decision would sometimes lead to positive results and, in other cases to errors and disasters. In other instances, leaders had adequate analytics yet decided to ignore or disregard such assets of information.

Whenever leaders made use of their analytics, the resulting outcomes from their decisions were more positive. Prior to the D-day invasion in June 1944, American Supreme Commander, General Dwight D. Eisenhower, had his staff scrupulously study all the relevant variables, such as weather, terrain disposition of enemy units, whereabout of senior enemy generals, availability of landing crafts, the morale of the troops, etc. (Kitchin 2014).

Conversely, another example from the Second World War is the planning by the Germans of the invasion of Norway in 1940. The command of the operation was given to General Nikolaus van Falkenhorst. He later wrote that to learn about Norway, he went to a bookstore and purchased a Fodor's Travel Guide to Norway, so that he could familiarize himself with such key points of interest as major cities, parks, landing strips, highways, demographics, and cultural variables, such as language and money notes.

There is an obvious correlation between analytics and specific knowledge of a subject matter. The literature offers few clues of how to describe these similarities. Perhaps a good distinction would be that analytics is the result of some analysis of the subject matter, whereas knowledge is a very general descriptor of what is known about the subject matter—mostly without an analysis of any substantial type (Wenzel and Van Quaquebeke 2017).

Another fact that emerges from the use of analytics is that leaders (and managers) are not obligated to use this instrument of analysis. They would opt to use it mainly if they believed that such use would give them competitive advantage over both their colleagues and adversaries. As history clearly teaches us, there are numerous instances when leaders failed to use analytics, and thus had to pay for their mistake. Successful leaders and managers in their organizations excelled because they had recognized the value of analytics to their work and their accomplishments. Analytics is therefore a valuable asset, at the disposal of insightful leaders or managers.

The Example of the Rothschilds

Although this cliché has been criticized by several authors, there is some truth in the "knowledge is power" statement. The more leaders or managers know about their organizations, their human resources, and the conditions of the marketplace within which they operate, the more successful they will be. For instance, there is the famous example of the banking house of Rothschild. This financial empire was founded in the 1760s in Frankfurt, Germany. The patriarch of the family sent his five sons to the five main capitals of Europe, where they established and managed the bank's branches. The Rothschilds thus had a presence in Naples, Vienna, Paris, London, and Frankfurt. During the Napoleonic wars, the bank had established a network of messengers who communicated with each other across borders by "semaphore" (the use of two flags in certain positions to signify words). This network gave the bankers in London, Paris, and Frankfurt, immediate news of the outcomes of battles anywhere in Europe, so that the bank could purchase in a timely manner bonds of the victors and dispose/sell those of the losers. This was perhaps the first known case of "insider trading."

The Rothschild case clearly demonstrates that knowledge by itself has limited value unless it is obtained in a timely manner. Similarly, analytics is of value only when it is not just relevant, but also timely. Indisputably, the ownership of timely knowledge does indeed endow people and organizations with comparative advantage, which can therefore be translated into pecuniary gains.

In the following chapters I will discuss the cognitive aspects of analytics. That is, how the data collected by the instrument of analytics is entered into a system of synthesis, in which the data is assembled, then distinctly categorized and entered as inputs to how we link the data to the formation of conceptual framework.

A different approach to analytics and its relationship to the outcomes of a given problem—where analytics is used as the instrument of analysis—is shown in figure.

Figure shows three possible scenarios or cases. *Case (a)* is the case where the decision-maker selected the wrong alternative from a set of alternative solutions available to the decision-maker. For example, the decision-maker is considering some form of organizational redesign. The options-for-action which are available to the decision-maker may include: (a) redesign or restructure only one department or unit; (b) redesign or restructure several units; and (c) redesign or restructure the entire organization. The decision-maker selects one alternative. However, if the restructuring involves the entire organization (whereas only one unit had to be redesigned), this choice of alternative would be not only wrong, but also expensive to the organization, in that the cost of applying this wrong option would be added to the cost of implementing the "correct" option, thus making the restructuring economically onerous.

Case (b) is where the alternative was correctly selected, but the implementation of the tools of analytics was wrong. For example, as part of the analysis, the decision-maker employs various statistical methods or tests, such as multiple regression analysis, when the appropriate test should have been a Spearman nonparametric correlation. In this case, the application of the incorrect analytical test leads to the under-measurement or over-measurement of the phenomenon. Either way, the decision-maker is now in possession of an inadequate—perhaps even erroneous—measure.

Case (c) is where analytics is applied to the wrong problem. Thus, the problem could not be resolved, although analytics was used. This case illustrates the use of analytics in vain, whereby the analytics measuring tool had been flawlessly applied—but the original problem has not been solved at all. In some instances, the decision-maker may be able to draw a lesson from this wasted effort. The main lesson may entail the knowledge of where *not* to go, and the scenarios that should *not* be analyzed by the decision-maker.

Because analytics comprises more than one test instrument, the decision-maker has the ability to select an instrument that would best apply to the decision-maker's needs and capabilities to master and manipulate the instrument. This type of alternative action would also limit the decision-maker's range of potential implementation of the test-instrument. Hence, the outcomes or outputs from this problem would also be limited to those that can be applied by the decision-maker without much additional effort.

In summary, business analytics can be described as the manipulation of data within the organization, conducted with the application of selected measurement instruments. This is the quantitative aspect of measuring the selected organizational variables.

Beyond Business Analytics

The notion of "Beyond Business Analytics" (BBA) is a complex concept, which includes both *behavioral* and *business* elements. BBA occupies the space between the analysis of the business and the behavioral implications of the analysis. This is the space where the analysis stops and the *cognitive evaluation* begins. Thus, the analysis is the quantitative description and the following cognitive space is the "beyond analytics."

This cognitive space includes questions that the evaluator begins to ask. These questions include:

1. What have we gained from the analysis of the organization?
2. What are the organizational implications of these conclusions?
3. What are the individual implications of these conclusions?

4. How can we implement these conclusions as integral parts of the organization's evaluation systems?

The Inevitability of Numbers

There is an important scholarly view that measurement in the social sciences must rely on, or at least must include, some quantitative measures. I would call this "the inevitability of numbers." Clearly, however, this principle of inevitability does not, in any way, preclude or diminish the value of *qualitative* measures or indicators.

In my studies of the monitoring of changes in organizations (Geisler 1979), I concluded that both qualitative and quantitative indicators are essential for an effective measurement. The mix of these two types of indicators is a much more powerful evaluation tool than either qualitative or quantitative indicators alone.

Consider, for example, an evaluation system that assesses, measures, and evaluates the space that exists between the *quantitative* measures and the *cognitive* dimension. That is, how do people absorb, assess, evaluate, and integrate quantitative data or information into their cognition, thus making such data an integral part of their psyche?

Such an evaluation system will provide the evaluators a plethora of benefits and advantages. Not only will this system offer the quantitative indicators as a good measure of the system, but it also may include some qualitative measures. For example, the quantitative indicators may show upward or downward movement (depending on the indicators), but the qualitative evaluation seeks answers to such questions as: "How well are we doing?"

With this type of question, the evaluation will be moving toward the theoretical space, where the indicators describing the situation are supplemented with the *cognitive* indicators—in order to form a more compete evaluation framework. The closer the evaluation effort gets to the cognitive aspects, the more the evaluation then includes not only the quantities but also how they contribute to the evaluation. Without this link to the cognitive space, all we would have would be a bunch of numbers that lacked an anchor into the full appraisal of the phenomenon (Geisler 1979).

The Role of Semiotics

Semiotics is a study of sign processes, which includes any activities in which signs are used in lieu of or to supplement words. The signs thus produced have meaning, which can be transmitted to another party in the communication scheme. Consider signs produced by the hands or arms of a communicator. For example, before the advent of street traffic lights, a police officer would stand in the middle of the intersection of streets and continually move his arms to direct traffic. It worked, and traffic tended to flow smoothly. The introduction of traffic-lights technology was not a revolutionary technology but it did improve the effectiveness of traffic control.

Semiotics is largely defined as the analysis of the significance of any form of communication. In a way, this is a use of codes by which humans transmit meaning to each other. Signs made by people with their hands have a cultural significance and meaning. Signs made by facial expressions also transmit meaning. Such meaning is, of course, defined by cultural imperatives of the region or country. Similarly, the use of colors to express emotions and meaning also varies by region, country, and culture. For example, the wearing of black clothes is associated with mourning for a dead relative. The color white, as a sign of purity, is worn by brides at their wedding ceremony in various regions and religions around the world.

Semiotics is therefore a form of communication that emerges after the conclusion of analytics. Once the analysis of the data is completed, meaning emerges that can be attributed to the data and is the content of the space we have denoted as the "beyond analytics" space. Semiotics, therefore, is considered as one form of making sense of signs and other non-verbal communication. Clearly, when sensemaking is employed, the evaluator moves into the space of the cognitive evaluation and mental modeling of events, hence to the region of beyond analytics, i.e., away from the data and closer to a cognitive sense of the evaluation,

Examples from the Literature and Other Mass Media

The expression of the notion of "beyond analytics" in the literature and other forms of mass media (e.g., theater, radio, television, internet, and movies) has been a global phenomenon. The main formula in the application of this notion has been as a method or approach to solving crimes and to the identification of the perpetrators of these crimes.

The formula has been rather simple. A crime is committed. The law-enforcement authorities are baffled, overworked, and generally lack the insights and the thought processes necessary for an effective analysis of facts and for the building of a solid theory of the crime. The law-enforcement authorities then ask for the advice and assistance of private individuals who have a reputation and a track record of unraveling insolvable crimes. Here are some notable examples from the international literature.

Hercule Poirot
Hercule Poirot, the fictional Belgium detective created by Agatha Christie, is an eccentric individual who employs the "gray cells" of his mind in his analysis of a crime and the psychological makeup of the individuals involved in this crime. Poirot's gray cells go beyond the facts of the case. With their help, Poirot is able to synthesize events and, like a tapestry, weave them into a coherent picture of "who done it." Poirot's methods are notably unorthodox, yet he traveled among the British aristocracy of the 1920s and 1930s with ease and panache. He is flamboyant, has style and flair, and is able to consider even the minute fact or the human intent and behavior—as imperceptible as they may be to other humans. In his "grey cells," Poirot employs the mode of "beyond analytics." No criminal could outwit Poirot and his sidekick Captain Hastings.

Sherlock Holmes
Sherlock Holmes, the legendary private detective created by Sir Arthur Conan Doyle, an English physician and story teller who lived in the second half of the nineteenth century, like his counterpart Poirot, was an extraordinary fellow. He was addicted to cocaine, an avid reader, and an accomplished violinist. Like Poirot, Holmes had a companion, Watson, who shared his lodgings at 221 Baker Street, London. Dr. John Watson was a participant in many cases which Holmes solved and, in several occasions, also offered his medical advice and assistance. Through Dr. Watson, Sir Conan Doyle—trained as a physician—was able to insert medical situations and expert opinion in several of the cases in which Holmes was involved.

Holmes would routinely explain his methods of analysis of a crime scene to his trusted friend, Dr. Watson. Several such explanations became popular "pearls of wisdom." For example, (1) "when you have eliminated the impossible, whatever remains, however improbable, must be the truth," and (2) "elementary, my dear Watson." Holmes also related his methods of forensic science and acute observation to Inspector Lestrade of Scotland Yard. Invariably, Inspector Lestrade would follow a wrong approach to solving a crime. Only when Holmes offered his insight and his power of observation and analysis, would Lestrade then solve the crime—and take credit for doing so.

Lestrade and Holmes had observed the same crime scene and the same forensic data. Yet, Holmes was able to go "beyond analytics" and in his mind he would construe an accurate model of the reality of the crime. This helped him to arrive at the true perpetrator of the crime. Holmes incorporated into his analysis all the knowledge he had acquired in areas such as types of cigar, cigarette, and pipe ashes; indicators of the use of a piece of clothing, such as stains, smudges, and wrinkles; and the ways in which people decorated their apartments and houses. No detail was irrelevant. Every fact was of use to Holmes, as he conjured his mental image of the crime. Holmes considered his method as a natural way to analyze a crime scene. He would frequently admonish his roommate: "Elementary, my dear Watson."

Although Holmes was aware of his exceptional abilities and considered himself mentally vastly superior to his fellow men (including the detective inspectors of Scotland Yard), he, nonetheless, felt some compassion to those who sought his help—especially women. Dr. Conan Doyle had probably inserted some of his feelings as a physician toward his patients.

Conan Doyle's mental exceptionalism probably contributed to his standing in beyond analytics. His nimble mind—and by extension that of Holmes—had to constantly prove its superiority by transcending beyond analytics, namely beyond the facts and into the cognitive arena.

Perry Mason

The fictional character of Perry Mason was the creation of the prolific author Earle Stanley Gardner (1889–1970). He was the author of numerous nonfiction historical books as well as travel logs, describing his extensive travels in California and Mexico. Gardner translated his legal courtroom experience into his famous novels, which focused on cases handled by the fictional Los Angeles lawyer, Perry Mason, assisted by his private secretary, Miss Della Street, and the talented private detective, Paul Drake. In court, Mason always confronted the District Attorney for

Los Angeles County, Hamilton Burger, assisted by the indefatigable police Lieutenant Arthur Tragg.

Mason's outstanding court performances were excellent illustrations of "beyond analytics." He was always armed with all possible information about a case and about his clients, who were accused of a crime by Tragg and Burger. However, Mason went beyond the facts. He diligently explored the psychological makeup of both the accused and the victim. In addition to seeking answers to the question, What *happened*? Mason asked "*why*" it happened and looked for clues to "*how*" it happened in a mode that invariably challenged the conclusions drawn by the District Attorney and that offered a very different theory of the crime. One can clearly state that Mason routinely went "beyond analytics" to formulate a distinctly different theory of what happened, why it happened the way it did, and "who done it." To Mason, the facts of the crime were merely a springboard to a different theory.

With his mastery of suspense, Gardner wrote his novels in a format that invariably led to an explosive scene in the courtroom, where Mason would interrogate a witness with such psychological pressure, and exposition of the facts—that the witness inevitably would break down on the stand and either confess to the crime or point out the perpetrator, who was sitting in the courtroom.

The Perry Mason cases aired on television in the 1950s and 1960s. The title role was played by Raymond Burr from 1957 through 1966. The television series has popularized the story of the California lawyer. Gardner used the Mason character to explore and discuss several controversial legal situations and court rulings. He penned 146 books, with 85 of those being Perry Mason cases.

Why then do we include here the Perry Mason novels as an example of "beyond analytics?" Simply because Gardner weaves his mystery story as the professional effort by Mason and his associates to collect all available data and to search "for the truth." Except for what his client tells him, Mason mistrusts every character in the story until he identifies the "true" culprit. Nevertheless, in most instances, Mason places his complete trust in his clients. He starts his investigation with the absolute conviction that his client is telling the truth, even in those cases where the "truth" may be incomplete, shaky, and even implausible.

Examples from History

Radio Addresses During the Second World War

During the Second World War, the British Prime Minister Winston Spencer Churchill (1874–1965) was the leader of his country and of the British Commonweal of Nations. For over a year, in 1940, Britain stood alone against the might of the Nazi-occupied European continent. Only the 28 miles of the English Channel separated the British from the armored divisions of the Third Reich. Moreover, after the evacuation of the British Expeditionary Force from the French coast at Dunkirk between May 26 and June 4, 1940, over 300 thousand British soldiers were back in England. Although they had abandoned their armor and other heavy equipment in Dunkirk, they were seasoned soldiers, ready for a second chance at the Nazi menace.

After the "miracle of Dunkirk," Churchill gave one of his memorable speeches to the Parliament in London. His oration reverberated across the Atlantic and much impressed the American President Franklin Delano Roosevelt (1882–1945). Churchill did not list any numbers. His orations were composed of concepts and notions. He spoke of "blood, sweat, and tears." He spoke of the valor of the pilots of the Royal Air Force who defended their island from the might of the German Luftwaffe. He assured his countrymen and world leaders alike that Britain would continue to fight, with growing power and growing confidence. He said that "never in the history of human conflict was so much owed by so many to so few."

Churchill's prose was an excellent example of "Beyond Analytics." Without revealing numbers, Churchill was able to convince all who listened that Britain's military might was on the rise and that he and his people were determined to continue their fight to its ultimate conclusion.

Moreover, the cooperation between Churchill and Roosevelt led to the declaration of the "Atlantic Charter." This statement, published in August 1941, delineated the aims of Great Britain and the United States for the post-war era. The Charter was also signed by the European government in exile, including Belgium, Czechoslovakia, Greece, Luxemburg, the Netherlands, Norway, Poland, and Yugoslavia. This was a document that enumerated eight points, focusing on cooperation in the fight against Nazism and the economic and political collaboration among the parties. The document listed the free flow of people on the high seas and the assurance that "all men in all lands" may live without fear and want.

In his speech to the nation on January 6, 1941, President Roosevelt listed what he considered the "four freedoms" to which every citizen has the right. The four freedoms were:

1. Freedom of speech and expression,
2. Freedom of worship,
3. Freedom from want, and
4. Freedom from fear.

Although freedom of speech, for example, is guaranteed to every American by the American constitution, the First and Fourteenth Amendments to the Constitution give citizens the right to express ideas and opinions without the fear of government restrictions that are based on content. This definition is as close as one can get to "free speech" protected by the Constitution.

Upon reflection, I have conceived a more comprehensive list of 14 freedoms which are, in my view, inalienable rights with which we are endowed by our creator (to paraphrase Thomas Jefferson). The list of freedoms is:

1. Freedom of speech and expression,
2. Freedom to worship the religion of our choosing,
3. Freedom from want,
4. Freedom from fear,
5. Freedom from discrimination and persecution,
6. Freedom to choose the treatments for our illnesses and any invasive procedure, remedy, or cure recommended by medical or religious personnel, or any other professionals or people with any such power or authority given to them by the state,
7. Freedom to educate our children in our choosing,
8. Freedom to live in the location of our choosing,
9. Freedom of association for peaceful goals,
10. Freedom to move around and to travel everywhere in our universe,
11. Freedom to explore our world and to unravel its mysteries,
12. Freedom to choose our profession and to continually improve our skills and proficiencies,
13. Freedom to accomplish the utmost our potential will allow, and

14. Freedom to doubt conventions, and to devise and to offer to humanity new ideas, inventions, and innovations—however revolutionary and groundbreaking they may be—and any fruit of our talent and of our imagination.

The fourteen freedoms may be grouped into two categories (1) freedoms *from* a restriction imposed by a government power and (2) freedoms *to* act in a given manner without interference by a government entity. For example, freedom to educate our children in our choosing. The sixth freedom is a controversial statement, in that a choice of a medical treatment may include "end of life" decisions. These decisions are strenuously opposed by religious groups, thus curtailing the freedom to choose treatment. Many such cases end up in the courts, where they may languish for years while, for example, a patient continues to suffer, devoid of the freedom to choose the end to such suffering.

The main challenge to both Roosevelt and Churchill was their desire for a *lasting peace* in the aftermath of the Second World War. Roosevelt considered the maintenance of world peace via institutions whose mission would be to ensure global peace. The outcome of his view became the United Nations. Moreover, because Roosevelt did not trust the Europeans to maintain the peace and to abandon their nationalist acute mistrust of each other, he made it clear that the new world institution should be headquartered in New York. The Europeans agreed. Roosevelt also helped to create, within the United Nations, the Security Council, whose members are the five big powers. More recently, mainland China became a member.

This institutional instrument for global relations and world peace became an example of "Beyond Analytics." Soon after its birth, the Security Council of the United Nations was painfully challenged in 1950 with the Korean War. Despite this event and later the Berlin Wall, the institution survived. The Security Council had no armies or navy or air force. It depended on the goodwill of the big member nations. Although regional conflicts exist even today, there have been no major wars around the globe since the establishment of the United Nations and its Security Council.

Behavioral Perspective Theory

As mentioned above, the notion of "Beyond Business Analytics" (BBA) was introduced as a complex concept, which includes both *behavioral* and *business* components. The behavioral space in this concept includes the theoretical aspect of the *cognitive* evaluation of the phenomenon.

The best way to describe this phenomenon is by the use of Behavioral Perspective Theory (BPT). This means that the notion is now identified as a unique dimension that includes the various and disparate components or indicators that migrate or flow to it, and are thus integrated into it.

There are four key criteria for the coalescing of the indicators, or in their coming together in Behavioral Perspective Theory.

(1) *Familiarity*: Same or similar group or degree of correlation.
(2) *Relevance:* To the theory.
(3) *Measurability*: How well can we measure the indicator.
(4) *Comparability* (allows for comparison): How well can we compare the indicators to each other or to other non-related indicators?

My interest in this Behavioral Perspective Theory began during the period in which I was completing my doctoral dissertation at Northwestern University. My thesis explored the set of indicators needed to measure change phenomena in technology-driven organizations and, later, to all other types of organizations. (A detailed description of the underlying studies and the interview protocols are given in Chapter 5: The Quasi-Experiments.) I designed interview protocols with respondents in a random sample of fourteen organizations. The study yielded very interesting results. The first stage of the phase of data collection consisted of the accumulation of raw data from the various divisions, and the various functions of these organizations. The data categories included data on human resources, marketing, organizational behavior, financial analysis, and inter-organizational relations.

These data items, collected over the past several years, were then shown to respondents in two forms: (1) as tables and (2) as figures. This duality of presentation was created to facilitate the reading of the data by both types of people: (1) those who prefer tables and (2) those who prefer diagrams. In total, I prepared two groups or two sets of twelve measures or indicators to be used in the instrument.

The Field Research Instrument was administered to fourteen respondents during the field interview as a field protocol. The results from this field research can now be channeled as inputs to the key dimensions, which can be assembled or brought together to the major conceptual construct—in the way that individual lines converge on a central point in an *architectural perspective.*

The key purpose of these field studies was to test the proposition that people are able to create a mental image of individual variables converging to form complex conceptual frameworks. The results from these studies indeed supported the proposition. This was a considerable advancement in this theoretical space.

A complementary proposition suggested that decision-makers tend to utilize conceptual frameworks as variables in their decision-making processes. That is, decision-makers do not make decisions based on raw data. Rather, they use conceptual structures. For example, corporate decision-makers will rely on variables such as the additional market share, ascribed by a competitor, rather than the raw quantitative description of the increase in sales by the competitor. For the corporate decision-makers, just to know that a competitor sold an additional ten million dollars will mean very little. A much better variable would be that the competitor increased its market share by 20 percent.

In the public arena, for example, decision- and policy-makers are able to communicate and act only on the basis of concepts, such as "liberty," "equality," or "free market." Clearly, a concept such as "free market" is complex and is composed of several variables, which define its features, the economic transitions, and the aversion to government regulations and other economic, geographical, and similar constraints.

> By a process of "continuous clustering," decision-makers are able to assemble, condense, and translate data into higher-order concepts. This process, for example, may be applied by policy-makers, whereupon such continuous clustering leads to decisions made by policy-makers that determine the progress and the future of financial markets and economic conditions in general.

In this context, "Big Data" is simply a pool of data. It allows decision-makers to dip into it and thus collect, select, and form higher-order concepts. The one distinguishing characteristic of "Big Data" is that this is a pool of very large quantities of data—but a pool of data nonetheless.

> This feature of this concept means that decision-makers are able to form conceptual constructs with some flexibility as to the data that is available

to them. They are able to "tailor" the search for data to the conceptual constructs that they intend to formulate.

Behavioral Perspective Theory (BPT) is therefore similar to the architectural perspective theory. Instead of lines on a design or rays of light that converge on a singular point, it is the elements of data that converge toward a singular point and these elements coalesce to form a distinguishably unique conceptual construct.

Perspective in Italian Renaissance Art

In the period of Italian "Renaissance," there were four types of perspective that were employed by Italian artists (1) linear, (2) atmospheric, (3) color, and (4) planar.

Linear Perspective

This is a technique that allows the artist to create artificial depth by reducing the size of the elements of the painting in relation to their existence in the space of the painting. This is also known as the "vanishing point," toward which the lines of perspective converge. This generates, in the eyes of the observer, a sense of spatial depth.

Atmospheric Perspective

Here the artist creates the perspective by making the images in the artificial distance of the painting increasingly less defined, to the point where images in the distance appear hazy. This technique was often used by Dutch painters.

Color Perspective

This technique uses colors, such as blue and green, to create the effect of depth and space. The background of the painting contains color saturation that conveys the existence of foreground and background.

Planar Perspective

The artist paints the picture in layered planes, where the division of the planes is well executed and an observer can easily identify the plane of the foreground and the plane of the background of the composition.

Behavioral Perspective Theory and Prospect Theory

Behavioral Perspective Theory (BPT) is an extension of Prospect Theory, which was developed in the late 1970s by Amos Tversky and Daniel Kahneman. This theory is also known as "loss-aversion theory." Kahneman and Tversky developed this theory based on empirical studies of human choice behavior. This was the result of studies of choices in financial bets and gambles that people make.

Prospect Theory advances the notion that decisions made by humans depend on the choices that the decision-makers choose among options that are based on judgments that are already biased. This work is based on Kahneman and Tversky's studies of *judgmental heuristics* in the evaluation of frequencies and probabilities of these events. This means making choices among values; hence decision-making is a tradeoff among not only options, but values.

For example, when respondents were asked to make choices among policy plans by public institutions to respond to the outbreak of a contagious disease, the support for a plan rested on how the outcomes of the plan were presented to respondents as the number of people who would live versus the number of people who would die. Another example consists of actual patients with cancer who would make choices based on whether the data on outcomes was given to them as probabilities of survival versus mortality.

The above is considered by the Prospect Theory to be the first phase, in which the effects are prepared and framed for further analysis. The second phase is the *evaluation* phase. There are two components of the second phase. The first is the value function, where people make decisions based on where they find themselves and where they aspire to be and as they compare themselves to others. In this, they also consider the potential outcomes from the choices at their disposal. Thus, Tversky and Kahneman found that people are more risk averse when there are gains, and they are more risk takers where losses are prevalent. They do so with the hope that they can recover their losses.

Another important finding was that losses are more hurtful to people than the pleasure they derive from gains. People will have to be paid two and a half times more to risk a loss, than to risk a gain. Pain is more powerful than pleasure. People seem to be averse to pain.

Tversky and Kahneman also found that people assign more importance to events and outcomes of which they can count on with high probability. Examples of these phenomena are (1) insurance, where people take a current loss versus a small probability of a future event where larger loss is possible, and (2) lotteries, where people prefer to suffer a sure loss versus a very small probability of a gain. This is an example of a gamble, where people knowingly suffer a loss with a very slight chance of any gain.

Prospect Theory has been criticized for its failure to advance a theoretical framework, which will explain *how* and *why* people make their choices as rational decisions, selecting among similar alternatives. But, how do these choices or the framing of events take place? What are the dimensions that constitute these choices? Why do people prefer one alternative over another?

Behavioral Perspective Theory and the Coronavirus (COVID-19)

In 2019–2020, the world was exposed to a pandemic of the coronavirus (COVID-19). This was a new illness that affects the lungs and airways of the respiratory system. The symptoms of the disease appear 2–14 days after exposure and consist of a cough, high fever, and shortness of breath. This pandemic originated in China and quickly spread to other countries worldwide.

In the spring of 2020, for example, there were over 400,000 confirmed cases globally, with confirmed deaths of almost 20,000 (about 5 percent). At the same time, 107,000 patients recovered (26 percent). In the United States, in the same period, there were 50,138 confirmed cases with 622 deaths (about 1 percent). There were 107,073 patients who recovered (26 percent).

According to the US Center for Disease Control and Prevention, 8 out of 10 deaths from the coronavirus have been 65 years old and older. 4–11 percent of adults 65–85 years old and 10–27 percent of adults 85 years old and older have died as a result of this disease. Also, 11 to 31 percent of adults 6--84 years old required admission to intensive care. This means that about one in four or one in three older adults who contacted the coronavirus required admission to intensive care. Finally, 31–59 percent of adults with coronavirus who were 65–84 years old required hospitalization. That is, from one-third to one-half of such adults required hospitalization. These data show with abundant clarity that the burden on American hospitals could become insupportable.

The warning signs of the disease are (1) trouble breathing; (2) persistent chest pain or pressure; (3) confusion; and (4) bluish colored lips or face. The disease is highly contagious and is transmitted from person to person.

Older adults and people with respiratory illnesses such as asthma and HIV (human immunodeficiency virus) and pregnant women are at a higher risk of contracting COVID-19.

There are laboratory tests that can identify the virus with a high degree of confidence. These tests are real-time reverse transcriptase (RT-PCR) diagnostic panels. They can provide results within 4–6 hours .

Behavioral Perspective Theory can provide a platform on which the process of identification of COVID-19 and the triage of the severity of a case can be executed. The result of the triage determines the next steps in the process.

This means that there is a filtering of the various types or categorics of impacts and the outcome of such filtering in the form of a revised assessment of the threat of coronavirus to the given population. This revision would then be translated into revised policies and actions taken by the authorities (municipals, county, state, and federal) in the strategic fight against the virus.

How does this process actually work? First, the various categories of impacts flow toward the focal point of BPT, similar to the flow of lines toward a given point in the architecture of perspective. Second, these categories are then converted into a unique conceptual framework. The many converge to become one step higher in the continuous clustering process. Thirdly, what used to be individual and disparate categories of impacts is now a *notion* or a *concept*, and it can be related to other concepts such as "beauty," "usefulness," or "constructiveness." Thus, once a notion is created, decision-makers can confidently adopt their revised perception of threat into a cohesive and targeted policy and managerial action(s).

The behavioral perspective theory (BPT) contributes to an improved decision process by, in effect, condensing the various impacts into a workable and better manageable conceptual framework. The BPT absorbs disparate categories of impacts and creates a higher-level notion, which now allows managers to make credible and evidence-based decisions.

As these pages are being written, it is impossible to predict the final outcome of the coronavirus pandemic of 2019–2020. There is a concerted global effort to contain and mitigate the disease. But whatever the outcome may be, the BPT offers a good analytical instrument to assess the state of the global effort to combat coronavirus.

In addition to the contribution of BPT to a better decision process, the BPT also contributes to our ability to conjure or to conceptualize a set of variables and to combine them into a higher-order notion. This allows us to correlate and to compare this notion with other notions. This means that BPT is not a stand-alone notion. Rather, it is an important cog in a large machine of the notions and variables of human behavior in general and human behavior in organizations in particular.

Behavioral Perspective Theory and the Case of the Cuban Missile Crisis

In the month of October 1962, there occurred a confrontation between the United States and the Soviet Union. For thirteen days, from 15 to 28 October, the two superpowers were engaged in a most perilous game of "who will blink first."

The two key protagonists were the leaders of the two countries. John F. Kennedy was the American President and Nikita Khrushchev was the Premier of the Soviet Union and, for all practical purposes, the dictator of the Union of the Soviet Socialist Republics (USSR). This union was established in 1922 and ceased to exist in 1991. In all, this form of Russian Communist dictatorship existed for a period of 69 years.

The relationship between Washington and Moscow became very tense in the height of what was called "the Cold War." The two leaders lacked a dedicated line of communication. All of their interaction was conducted by cables flowing between their respective embassies, with all the diplomatic constraints that routinely created delays in what should have been seamless interchange between the two leaders.

On October 27, 1962, Major Rudolph Anderson, an American pilot of the U-2 spy airplane, was shot down over Cuba. The American navy had declared a blockade of Cuba, thereby stopping all Soviet ships that appeared to be carrying military cargo. The blockade was a response to evidence that the USSR was in the process of placing middle-range ballistic missiles in Cuba. The range of these missiles would then allow them to hit any city in the continental United States, except Seattle. Therefore, the United States was now confronted with a mortal threat just 90 miles from Florida.

From the days of the Monroe Doctrine to the American policy of the Cold War, such an action by the USSR was considered in Washington to be an unacceptable intrusion of Communist Russia in the most private American geographical territory.

In 2000, the movie *Thirteen Days* directed by Roger Donaldson portrayed the tension in the White House with regard to the Cuban crisis and President Kennedy's explicit order to avoid any shooting unless by his specific command. In 1999, the historian Arthur Schlesinger published his book *Thirteen Days: A Memoir of the Cuban Missile Crisis.* Many other books have since been written about this episode in the Cold War. All these narratives paint a dire picture of what I would call "the ladder of escalation" in the tense relations between the two superpowers leading to a situation whereby a compromise was necessary for the relations between the superpowers. The Soviet Union agreed to withdraw its military presence in Cuba and to never reinstall missiles or other military threats to the hemisphere. On its part, the United States agreed to dismantle its Jupiter missiles in Turkey, thus removing their threat to the Soviet Union. The world was spared a countdown of the "doomsday clock"—as established by the Bulletin of Atomic Scientists—to fewer than two minutes.

The Power of the Few

The blockade of Cuba by the United States in 1962 was a definite demonstration of the might of naval power and the ability of the American navy to exercise its unchallenged control of the world's waterways. Thus, naval power was shown able to control vast geographic areas with a minimum arsenal of vessels, accompanied by adequately equipped selected port facilities.

The Empire of Japan in the first half of the twentieth century Japan was a relatively poor country, devoid of many natural resources with a population of about 105 million souls. By comparison, the population of the United States in 1941 was 133 million—about 26 percent larger than

Japan. In addition, the United States possessed a multitude of minerals and other war materials, all ready to be used by a very large industrial complex, which was being converted to total war production.

During the period 1940–1945, the United States had manufactured a total of 296,000 aircraft, of which 200,443 were combat aircraft (65 percent). By contrast, Germany's aircraft production totaled about 92,000, Japan's production was about 71,000 aircraft, the USSR produced 149,000, and the United Kingdom manufactured about 123,000. The United States alone produced more aircraft than Germany and Japan *combined*. It is therefore no wonder that Winston Churchill called the United States "The Arsenal of Democracy."

The power of the few is also amply demonstrated in both naval power and air supremacy. Historically, England was a relatively small set of islands off the cost of the European continent. It owed its temperate climate to the flow of warm water known as the "Gulf Stream." This is an Atlantic current that brings tropical current from the Caribbean to the east coast of North America, and to northwestern Europe. Thus, the British Isles, which are at a latitude similar to that of Moscow (51° north versus 55° north) have a more temperate climate than Moscow. This climatic anomaly was a contributor to the productive agriculture in Britain and its ability to navigate the English Channel without the fear of ice and icebergs.

Thus, the population of this small island became seafaring people with enhanced skills in shipbuilding and navigation. These advantages allowed the British to explore the globe and to establish itself as a commercial hub, which led to their empire.

In essence, Japan and Britain are examples of relatively small countries with limited resources and populations who were able to build powerful navies and thus control their respective seaways. Similarly, small countries such as Spain and Portugal dominated—for several centuries—large portions of the globe. Brazil, for example, was discovered by the Portuguese in 1500 and only obtained its independence in 1822—over three centuries later. Analogously, Spain conquered vast territories from the Philippines to Mexico and to Central and South America.

Similarly, the Spanish Empire extended over large portions of the global areas of population. In 1790, this empire ruled over 60 million subjects. At its height, the Spanish Empire controlled some 7.5 million square miles in Europe, Africa, and Oceania. Originally a small country, the Spaniards built a powerful empire that controlled the importation of silver and other precious metals from the "New World." Spanish colonies extended in Central and South America and included Mexico, Peru, Central America, and Argentina, so named because of the Spanish desire to mine its silver.

After the defeat of its armada by the British in July 1588, Spain lost its position as a naval power and was replaced by the British, who dominated India and other territories in South Asia and vast territories in Africa including South Africa, Egypt, Uganda, and Nigeria.

The Power of the Few and the Battle of Britain

Another outstanding example of the impacts of the notion of "The Power of the Few" on historical events is the story of the Battle of Britain in 1940. The British Prime Minister Winston Churchill aptly described it in these immortal words: "Never in the field of human conflict was so much owed by so many to so few." He was referring to the heroic effort by the British Royal Air Force (RAF), which, although vastly outnumbered, stood alone against the might of the German Luftwaffe, thus preventing the Germans from having control over British skies. The Battle of Britain also prevented the Germans from invading the British Isles, because their military leaders made it abundantly clear that any invasion plan must include.

Behavioral Perspective Theory (BPT) and the Power of the Few

In Behavioral Perspective Theory (BPT), the key idea is that disparate dimensions of a notion or a phenomenon converge towards a unique point, like in the case of architectural perspective. This means that even a complex notion can be described by a small set of dimensions.

In the literature we find two complementary theories. The first is the framework of *perspective*, whereby the elements of the phenomenon flow *toward the concept*. The second framework can be defined as *amplitude*. This is a notion that I discussed in my book *Methodology, Theory, and Knowledge in the Managerial and Organizational Sciences* (1999). This is the case in which the dimensions are flowing *from the concept* toward the given set of elements that constitutes the concept.

However, there are some occasions where the concepts are in conflict with each other. For example, a metropolitan bus company finds itself with two conflicting strategies. One strategy is the objective of the company to run its buses on time. The other is to pick up as many passengers as it possibly can in any given route. All is well until traffic and weather intervene, so the buses may be delayed. In order to be on time, the buses must pick up speed, thus avoiding a few stops, and by doing so they don't take some passengers, who are therefore left at the bus stops waiting for the next bus.

These circumstances force the bus company to play a balancing act: on-time versus full capacity of passengers in each run of the bus. These are two conflicting concepts: be on time or pick up full loads of passengers. If buses focus on timeliness, not passengers, after a while the company will be bankrupt.

In such circumstances of conflicting strategies, a small number of elements can make a clear difference between profits and losses. Some buses are able to pick up a large number of passengers while also being on time. In the Behavioral Perspective Theory, this will be a case whereby buses will be *effective* (pick up as many passengers as possible) as well as *efficient* (doing so on time) simultaneously.

The elements of the behavior of the uses will converge toward the perspective of being on time.

Behavioral Perspective Theory (BPT) and Managerial Decision-Making: A Propositional Inventory

Proposition 1:

Managers decide with the use of notions, not with raw data.

The conclusion one can draw from the previous couple of pages is that managers make decisions based on notions or conceptual constructs that they form in their mind and that represent related dimensions or aspects of their reality. The raw data of this reality are not useful to the manager, in that such raw data does not, in and by itself, play a role in the mental picture that the decision-maker creates of his/her reality.

Thus, in order to make sound decisions, managers must first convert raw data of their perceived environment into notions or conceptual constructs of this environment. For example, the raw data of "There has been a change of 5 percent in human resources in the past five years" is essentially useless to the decision-maker. The data must be incorporated into a conceptual construct, which states that the use need and even the use of human resources has increased in the past five years because the mission of the organization has expanded, and consequently there emerged a need for an infusion of additional personnel and new skills.

Proposition 2:

> Managers use continuous or progressive clustering to go from raw data to conceptual notions, thus climbing up the hierarchical ladder—in a step-by-step manner.

The hierarchical ladder is the space between the raw data and the conceptual notion. In this space there are stages or steps, similar to a ladder. The road or way from raw data to conceptual notion goes sequentially through the stages or steps of this ladder. In other words, one cannot "jump" directly from the raw data to the conceptual notion One has to "climb up" the ladder, step-by-step.

"Continuous or progressive clustering" means that at each of the steps of the hierarchical ladder, the raw data thus accumulated, will continually be clustered into the higher-order categories or notions. The ultimate or final stage of this process will produce—as a final product—the clustered format we can then call a *conceptual notion.*

The practical implication of Proposition 2 is the ability that the decision-maker has to climb up the hierarchical ladder, and at each step to stop, to review the progress to that point, and to thus make a decision based on the data the decision-maker accumulated up to that point. In a way, this procedure is similar to the term "satisfying," which was introduced to the literature in 1947 by Herbert Simon, in his seminal book *Administrative Behavior*.

The term "satisfying" refers to a situation encountered by a decision-maker, in which an optimal or "best" decision cannot be attained, perhaps due to its nonexistence in the particular problem, or because the cost and effort to be spent on procuring such a solution are considered prohibitively high. Therefore, the decision-maker will need to accept a solution that is not optimal, but is acceptable as realistic and satisfactory—under the existing circumstances of the problem.

The "continuous clustering" approach is a very practical instrument at the disposal of the decision-maker. It gives the decision-maker the flexibility to make a coherent decision at every rung of the ladder—with enough data/information the decision-maker had accumulated up to that point. As explained above, this is not the "best" scenario and the decision-maker may have only some of the information needed for a good decision.

But to the decision-maker, this situation seems satisfactory and "good enough" for the decision-maker to make an acceptable decision. When, for example, the demands of time or cost in this decision regime would challenge the decision-maker, there emerges the need to make a decision without delay. Thus, the decision-maker has no slack time or slack resources to procure an "optimal" or "best" decision. The effort is therefore focused on a decision, which is "good enough" for the situation and for the problem.

An interesting paper was published by Dan Chenok and Michael Keegan (2020) as a paper of the *IBM Center for the Business of Government*. The paper was titled "Risk-Based Decision-Making: A Key Capacity for Government Today." The authors offered an introduction to the risk management research portfolio of the Center, and then continue to discuss the evolution of risk management in the US federal government. First, the authors define risk as: "Uncertainty that matters." They argue that "…defining risk as merely a threat that objectives will not be achieved leaves unanswered the question of how to actively balance risks that may pose opportunities as well as threats." Secondly, they listed such risks as: (1) strategic, (2) cyber, (3) legal, and (4) reputational. In addition, they included such risks as information security, human capital, financial control, and business continuity.

Chenok and Keegan had also identified three ways to how government agencies manage risk: (1) *use of internal controls*, (2) *use of silos* as mode of risk management, and (3) *use of Enterprise Risk Management (ERM)*. This third mode is defined by the International Risk Management Society as "strategic business discipline that supports the achievement of an organization's objectives." Thus, all risks are considered, in addition to the risks *within* the silos.

Thus, in order to manage with notions, managers must be able to discern between notions and nonclustered aggregations of raw data. To the trained manager such a distinction is relatively easy, since the manager's experience provides a useful tool that allows for such distinction to take place. The marginal experience also very clearly identifies for the manager the existence of a conceptual-hierarchical ladder, where "continuous clustering" phenomenon occurs.

Two examples will illuminate the managerial use of continuous clustering. These examples will highlight the stepwise cumulation of raw data on the rungs of the hierarchical ladder.

First Example: Traffic Data

The first example is the analysis of national data for such a variable as traffic jams in urban transportation. A 2018 report by the consulting firm of Price Waterhouse (PWC) on traffic congestion in urban areas had cited a 2016 US Census Bureau report that in 2017 the average person spent 41 hours in congestion, which was 8 percent higher than in 2010. This phenomenon is a worldwide urban problem. The public decision-makers have access to these data, both from their own jurisdiction to those of other countries, states, and municipalities. In other words, the data exist. Government agencies scrupulously collect and analyze these data, and are willing to offer it to third parties.

So, in addition to data on traffic flow, decision-makers also have access to data on conditions of the roads, as well as road construction projects—both current and planned, and the budgets allocated to construction and maintenance of public roads. Finally, decision-makers may have access to data on alternative means of transportation such as rail, fluvial, maritime, and air. Thus, decision-makers have access to almost all the data they need in order to make sound traffic decisions. These data are available, and in many instances are provided at minimal cost from government agencies.

The data thus available to decision-makers is multifaceted. It includes *municipal* data, as well as state data, *intrastate* transportation data, *interstate* data—and data on *international transportation*, such as passenger and cargo air-flights and maritime.

Second Example: Data Collection

Federal agencies routinely collect data on municipalities, counties, and states. They collect, for example, demographic data on the citizenry patterns of certain behavioral variables such as population movements, availability, quality, and utilization of education, health care, housing, and welfare.

In addition to the general census every ten years, these agencies track patterns in the dynamics of the nation's human resources. They collect data on levels of high-school graduations, college admissions and graduations, and economic variables such as levels and patterns of unemployment, and agrarian versus urban clustering of citizens.

> These patterns of continuous collection of data allow these agencies to map the behavior of these variables, in their current status, and also historically. Based on these data, the agencies may now make predictions: what will the future be like (5, 10, or 20 years hence)?

Since these data are open to the public and shared with business managers, these managers are now able to continually cluster the data and to thus derive higher-level conceptual notions.

Proposition 3:

Managers use internal and external organizational information in their formulation of the pro positions of the Behavioral Perspective Theory.

Figure shows the application of Behavioral Perspective Theory to the current state of the 2019–2020 coronavirus pandemic. The figure graphically displays the five categories of impacts on the Behavioral Perspective Theory (BPT) and how these impacts combine to influence the organization, so that it revises the assessment of the level of threat to humans from the coronavirus disease (covid-19). This disease is an infectious disease that is caused by the severe acute respiratory syndrome coronavirus 2 (SARS-CoV-2).

This disease was initially identified in late 2019 in the city of Wuhan, the capital of the Hubei province in China. The disease spread globally at a very fast pace. By late April 2020, 185 countries reported over 3 million cases and over 200 thousand deaths—about 7 (seven) percent reported fatalities. By comparison, the Ebola virus disease (EVD), also known as the Ebola Hemorrhagic Fever, had a fatality rate of about 50 (fifty) percent.

Another comparison is with the 1918–1919 Spanish flu epidemic. This disease infected over 500 million people—*one-third* of the entire world population at the time. This disease resulted in a death toll of about 50 million people. This lethal disease was caused by the H1N1 influenza

A virus, and is considered one of the deadliest pandemics in world history. The second pandemic caused by the virus was the 2009 swine flu pandemic, which raged between January 2009 and August 2010. It is estimated that between 11 and 21 percent of the world's population were infected.

Figure suggests that the threat of the coronavirus may be influenced by the conceptual threats, which define the notions of the dimensions that combine to threaten humanity. This threat may also be the subject of much attention and vigilance by the world's community. Our experience with the Spanish flu showed that the virus has a formidable ability to resurrect. In the case of the Spanish flu, the second wave of the 1918 flu pandemic was much deadlier than the first. A third wave occurred in 1919, affecting Spain, Mexico, Serbia, and Great Britain.

Behavioral Perspective Theory: Aspiring Toward the Apex of the Perspective Ladder

By and large, managers aspire toward the apex of the perspective ladder or hierarchical structure. This means that managers will continually aspire toward conceptual notions, and away from raw data. This behavior is designed to allow managers to think and reason in terms of higher-order categories or notions.

For example, when a manager is confronted with a set of corporate data—including data from marketing, manufacturing, R&D (Research and Development), finance, and legal (e.g., expiration dates for key patents held by the company)—the manager will opt to view such data not as a set of basic numbers, but as a set of questions and answers, such as (1) how well is our marketing effort doing?; (2) how well is our production program doing, that is, are we making our goods in a current and advanced manner, or are we losing precious ground to our competitors? And, how well is our human resources function doing? Are we hiring the right people? Are we able to keep them as our employees?

Some years ago I asked Bill Gates of Microsoft: what keeps you up at night? He replied: "A new Microsoft led by a fresh Bill Gates." This sentiment is shared by most, if not all, chief executives.

The perspective ladder is the stepwise movement upwards, by corporate managers. This is the point where all relevant information (and knowledge) of the enterprise converge to a single point, where the managers would have the definite answer to the fundamental question: "How well are we doing?" The term "we" means that the focus is on all relevant aspects of the enterprise—not one or two functions used as examples. The question is: How is the enterprise doing: both internally and in its relations with the external environment? This phenomenon may give managers the comparative advantage they need to compete in the marketplace.

But Behavioral Perspective Theory means that managerial behavior is purposely designed to cluster and to aspire toward the top of the perspective hierarchical structure (or ladder). This movement of the manager's behavior is geared toward a higher conceptual construct. This is possibly so because I propose here that this is the aspect of human behavior, when it deals with the convergence of disparate data elements. The human or managerial aptitude and desire is to impose some "order" or "structure" on these data, by congealing them into a higher-order construct—all the way toward the apex of the perspective ladder. This description of the phenomenon explains Proposition 2, which proposes that managers move, step-by-step, from raw data to higher-order conceptual notions.

The aspiration of managers toward the perspective ladder is similar to the concept of organizational effectiveness. Yuchtman and Seashore (1967) proposed a model of the concept of organizational effectiveness as the positive manner with which the organization is able to acquire the resources it needs for the survival (financial resources, human resources, technological resources, etc.). This model is deficient in that it neglected the "utilization" of said resources, as well as the ability of the organization to successfully market (sell) its products or services in the competitive marketplace.

It seems that organizational managers are limited by how far they can achieve an effective organizational structure and organizational processes that are necessary for an effective discharge of the organizational functions. This is also a much-needed comparative advantage. The more the manager is able to transact in the variables of the higher-order, or the behavioral perspective of the organization, the more the manager will be able to effectively compete.

In part, this phenomenon can be explained by the attributes of the nature of the competitive marketplace. Firms do not compete on the basis of fundamental variables. Rather, they fiercely compete on higher-order notions, such as Michael Porter's 5 forces model.

Porter proposed that the rivalry among firms in their industry is impacted by five forces: (1) the rivalry itself, (2) the bargaining power of suppliers, (3) the bargaining power of buyers, (4) the threat of substitutes, and (5) the threat of new entrants. These forces can be quantitatively measured by the metrics of, for example, the types of threats of new entrants; the types or factors of the threat of substitutes, and the factors that measure the bargaining power of customers and suppliers.

Thus, the measures of the variables that act as forces in shaping the firm's competitiveness, represent the "analysis" of competitiveness. Beyond analytics would therefore extend the notion to include what the notions mean to the decision-maker, and how they influence the decision itself.

Behavioral Perspective Theory therefore focuses on how the firm's decision-maker considers the impacts and the value of organizational notions on the decision process and on the decision itself. When the decision-maker conducts an organizational analysis of the relative situation of the firm in its relevant environment, such an analysis must contain the set of questions listed above, in addition to the raw data that the decision-maker assembles in the analysis.

Porter's Model and the Hertz Case

For example, in 2020 the icon of the world's car and truck rental company—Hertz—had filed for bankruptcy. This drastic action was forthcoming for at least several weeks. Customer behavior has changed: fewer trips for both business and leisure, combined with the reluctance to spend any slack funds that were still available to the consumer in an uncertain economy.

The Hertz bankruptcy case may be partially explained with Porter's five forces model. The autorental industry was concentrated among very few companies: Hertz, Avis, Enterprise, Budget, and Alamo. On May 23, 2020, Jack Pritcher and David Welch wrote an article in Bloomberg in which they blamed the bankruptcy on their assertion that the rental-car demand had basically vanished. They argued that the "…sweeping travel restrictions and the global economic collapse had destroyed demand for Hertz's vehicles." Paul Stone, the chief executive officer of Hertz said that "with the severity of the covid-19 impact on our business, and the uncertainty of when travel and the economy will rebound, we need to take further steps to weather a potentially prolonged recovery."

Hertz was founded in 1918 and a century later was operating 12,400 locations around the globe. The court petition for bankruptcy had the company with $25.8 billion of assets, and $24.4 billion in debt. The company also owns and operates other rent-a-car companies, including Dollar, Thrifty, Firefly, and Denzen. The combined Hertz and Dollar Thrifty group controlled about 24 percent of their industry.

The Porter model applies to Hertz in the following manner. The "buyer power" has diminished, with impact on the rivalry among competitors. This case was not a case of a single company in trouble. Rather, it is a case whereby an entire industry is experiencing a severe downturn. The threats to the focal company are a combination of threats that emanate from the collapse of key variables in the entire marketplace and across industries.

How, then, would the Porter Model apply to the notion of beyond analytics and Behavioral Perspective Theory? First, the Porter model examines competition rivalry in light of threats of new entrance. This notion goes beyond the quantitative listing of the forces. The Porter model focuses on threats, which are phenomena that senior management considers to be within its purview, thus dealing with it as an overall management notion.

In this manner, the manager would measure, for example, the notion of competitive rivalry by (1) number of competitors, (2) quality differences among competitors, (3) switching costs, (4) customer loyalty, and (5) the cost of leaving the market. Each of these variables is of value to the manager, as it indicates the trend and direction in which the variable changes. However, the most important occurrence is that the manager indeed considers all of these individual variables, but is ultimately concerned with how they form the phenomenon as competitive rivalry—which is now the object of the manager's attention.

By and large, scientists have focused on the processes of decision-making by humans, and by managers in particular—and on the risks they take and are willing to tolerate in these decisions.

> The Behavioral Perspective Theory departs from this focus. It explores the overall idea that decisions can only be effectively made with well-defined concepts. This formulation is delineated below in the basic equation of the theory.

Enter Fig. 6 About Here.

The congealing, coalescing, or assembly of the elements into higher-order notions is done according to the following criteria.

1. *Familiarity*: when the elements from disparate sets belong to the same or similar group, or are strongly correlated.
2. *Relevance*: when each element is relevant to the theory—per its own attributes.
3. *Measurability*: when each element can be measured, is to its effect or impact on the notion.
4. *Comparability: when the element can be easily compared with other elements.*

These criteria are applied to the assembly of the elements under the same conceptual roof, so that they come together to provide content to the Behavioral Perspective Theory. However, the congealing or assembly of the elements does not, by itself, endow them with the mantra of variables that compose the Behavioral Perspective Theory. The main criterion remains the integration of these elements with the cognitive dimension of the theory.

That is, when the elements, as they are affecting the framework, also have a meaning for the decision-maker. This occurs when these elements coalesce into a notion that "makes sense" to the decision-maker and that allow the decision-maker to comfortably incorporate them into the process of decision-making.

For example, consider a public enterprise that is engaged in managing a drastic change in its mission. In the mid to late 1970s, the National Aeronautics and Space Administration (NASA) was confronted with such a challenge. Its mission to land a man on the moon and bring him back alive had been accomplished. Apollo 11 had landed the lunar module "Eagle" on July 20, 1969 with Neil Armstrong and Edwin ("Buzz") Aldrin being the first humans to land on the surface of the moon. They spent two hours and fifteen minutes outside their lunar module.

The Apollo program started in 1961 and ended in 1975. Upon completion of the lunar program, the American public had lost its enthusiasm and much of its support for the space program. The goal had been accomplished. The United States won the race against the Soviet Union and it was the "Stars and Stripes" proudly erect in the Sea of Tranquility on the lunar surface.

Space: The Earthly Frontier

The national discussion about the future of the space program and NASA has begun. Republican presidential candidates have voiced their vision of what America should do and where to go net. Governor Mitt Romney's ideas are anchored in a solid view of the next steps. Instead of simply continuing to explore other planets and striving to inhabit the moon, the productive strategy should be to look down to earth for the commercial benefits from the space program.

This calls for three principles of the roadmap for America's future. The first is the transition from *exploration* to *exploitation* of NASA's contributions to science and technology. The benefits from the space program are numerous. They include the ubiquitous GPS, key innovations in telecommunications, much better weather prediction, and medical advances. As space above the earth is cluttered with satellites launched from several nations, NASA's mission should be to competitively race to commercialize thee innovations. There is so much to do and so much to create. In this century of a global economy and one based on knowledge, a new and promising industry is awaiting. Industrial companies and NASA must accelerate their cooperation, encouraged and supported by the federal government, with the aim of creating and producing commercial products and services based on space-generated know-how and innovations. Think about it: without the benefits from the space program, the iPad and iPhones, cellular technology, nanotechnology, maps by Google, and even the Internet itself would not have been possible. And these commercial applications are just the tip of the iceberg.

Another principle is the need to extract value from our investments in the space program. Since the mid-1950s this country has invested many billions of dollars into the various aspects of space exploration and space travel. Let's consider these expenditures as the research and development (&D) investments made by industrial companies. A company invests a good chunk of its revenues in R&D with the expectation of obtaining new products and processes, and introducing into the marketplace innovations that allow the company to compete and prosper. As a nation, we have expended many billions in the space program, and we can and should expect that these investments will bear fruits and provide us with innovations that may create new industries and new jobs for Americans, and give us the knowledge-base we need to compete globally. But, like a company, we need to commercialize the outputs from R&D and ensure that they are transformed into viable innovations of commercial value in the world's marketplace.

To let this huge reservoir of technology and knowledge go without a serious attempt to make it a commercial boon for the country is unacceptable and wasteful. We know of many companies who abandoned their R&D programs and thus ended up in decline. Xerox Corporation, for example, had shut down its Palo Alto Research Center (PARC) where many grand technological innovations had originated. Similarly, AT&T decided to downsize and transform its Bell Labs in a movie that accompanied its rapid loss of a formerly leadership position in the industry.

A third principle is our obligation to bring together the three main components of a massive commercialization effort for space benefits. First and foremost is the network of NASA laboratories. They are at the world's vanguard of science and technology. For decades these organizations served the mission of the space agency, while accumulating an incomparable reservoir of knowledge and technology. The other two partners in such an effort are industrial companies and our universities. We cannot go it alone with only one of these three institutions. Traditionally they had worked together, albeit not in as much of a cooperative mode as we would desire. Congress and the administration must push for a massive program of cooperation among universities, NASA laboratories, and industry, aimed at the commercialization and exploitation of the knowledge and technology that are stored in them. The mission is to create industries and jobs, to globally compete with what America has that no other nation currently has the cumulative potential of unexploited space technological outcomes waiting to be transformed into marketable products and services. Our economy has changed, moving away from manufacturing to service industries and then to high technology and knowledge-based businesses. The twenty-first century is the century of knowledge. We have what it takes to compete in this new world, and space technologies are at the leading edge of this trend.

To date, the federal administrations of both Democrats and Republicans have failed to seriously engaging in such space exploitation programs. In a way, they followed the popular mood that the era of space exploration is over, and that the scarce federal resources should be spent here on earth. The sole exception is the International Space Station, in which several countries have invested, together with the United States.

In view of the state of affairs described above, we must continue with targeted exploration, so as to ignite the public's imagination and to continue the R&D needed to feed the thirst for new knowledge and new technologies from our unrelenting space program. The quest for new knowledge and better understanding of our universe must go on, with the hope that even more benefits will be generated, later to be further exploited. The space program must ignite the imagination of a new generation of Americans. This program is an on-going national challenge that must be met, with enthusiasm and talent. It's much more important today than it was 50 years ago when President Kennedy called for putting a man on the moon. Today, the space program is not only a matter of national prestige, but one of the critical keys to our economic competitiveness in the global marketplace.

The American public had changed its mind. After the glory and the frustration with space had subsided, the public desired investments "down to earth," in such social areas as infrastructure and the public's welfare. This initial love affair between the public and the "star trek" television series gave birth to other TV space adventures series such as "Star Trek: The Next Generation" (1987–1994), "Star Trek: Deep Space Nine" (1993–2000), and "Star Trek Voyager" (1995–2001). In addition, several movies were produced with the star trek title. These included *Star Trek III: The Search for Spock* (1984); *Star Trek VI: The Undiscovered Country*, and *Star Trek Beyond* (2016).

In February 2012 I composed a short article, in which I listed the value to American society and its economy to be derived from the exploitation of the space program. The article proposed that the magnitude of the extraction of value from the space program could be equivalent to the effort expended in the space program itself, and that not employing such a national effort would dramatically diminish the nation's return on its enormous investments in space exploration.

Almost a decade ago the national discussion about the future of the space program and NASA has begun. At the time, the Republican presidential candidates have voiced their vision of what America should do and where to go next. Governor Mitt Romney's ideas were anchored in a solid view of the next steps. He argued that instead of simply continuing to explore other planets and striving to inhabit the moon, the productive strategy should be to look down to earth for the commercial benefits from the space program. Such a view was also supported by other politicians, such as Senator John Glenn (1921–2016).

The eventual termination of the space program had nevertheless salvaged funding for other earthly projects, because the government considered NASA to be national patrimony. The agency therefore continued to operate, with a modified mission, but with a subsistence budget, which had been inverted to such projects as the Space Station and unmanned missions to Mars and beyond. An impartial observer would invariably conclude that the American public simply "could not let go" of the idea of space in the next frontier for adventure and glory.

Thus, the perspective in this case is the adventure to "conquer" and to explore the interminable space, which lies beyond our home planet and expands to an infinity of heavenly bodies. Millennia ago, since humans looked up at the night sky and observed the tapestry of stars and planets that radiate their luminescence, humans have felt a sense of adoration of nature, the creation of their deities, and the humility they felt as tiny explorers in a small planet. All their efforts were geared and directed toward the heavens, as religious foci of adoration, and as scientific objectives that must be studied and analyzed.

This duality had produced conflicts between religious organizations and scientists, thus culminating in historic events, such as the conflict of Galileo Galilei and the Catholic Church in Italy in the seventeenth century. Galileo (1564–1642) advanced his proposition that the earth revolves around the sun. This was contrary to the religious belief of his time that the earth is at the center of the universe, and all planets revolve around it. Galileo published his findings in 1632. His book angered the Pope. Galileo was tried by the Inquisition in Rome. He was accused of suspicion of heresy, and was confined to his house, and all his movements and communications with other scientists were tightly monitored by the Inquisition.

Galileo introduced the scientific world in Europe to the conduct of science by observation and experimentation, in what is commonly known as "the scientific method." This method underlies the notion of perspective. All the empirical findings from experimentation are channeled toward the ultimate notion or concept. Although in the scientific method, as argued by Sir Karl Popper (1902–194), a scientific proposition can never be totally and finally accepted (because what is needed to reject the proposition is a single case in which the proposition is found to be false). The behavioral perspective theory may describe a phenomenon that is open to questioning and thus may be continually rejected by numerous attempts to disprove it. Until such time when an argument for rejection is advanced without challenge, the proposition (and its perspective) will continue to exist and will be accepted as a "temporarily true" description of reality.

References

Agor, W. 1986. The Logic of Intuition: How Top Executives Make Important Decisions. *Organizational Dynamics* 14 (3): 5–18.

Bannister, B., and R. Griffith. 1986. Applying a Causal Analytic Framework to the Mobley, Horner and Hollingsworth (1978) Turnover Model: A Useful Reexamination. *Journal of Management* 12 (3): 433–443.

Bliese, P., and P. Hanges. 2004. Being Both Too Liberal and Too Conservative: The Perils of Treating Grouped Data as Though They were Independent. *Organizational Research Methods* 7 (4): 400–417.

Bliese, P., et al. 2020. Bridging Methodological Divides Between Macro- and Microresearch: Endogeneity and Methods for Panel Data. *Journal of Management* 46 (1): 70–99.

Boudreau, J. 2015. Predictive Analytics for Human Capital: Think Outside the Line. *CFO*, April 27.

Burrows, R., and M. Savage. 2014. After the Crisis? Big Data and the Methodological Challenges of Empirical Sociology. *Big Data & Society*, April–June, 1–6.

Braunstein, D. 1974. Beyond Leavitt's 'Narrow' Analytic Manager. *Interfaces* 4 (4): 28–31.

Charan, R. 2015. *The Attacker's Advantage: Turning Uncertainty into Breakthrough Opportunities*. New York: Public Affairs.

Chen, H., R. Chiang, and V. Storey. 2012. Business Intelligence and Analytics: From Big Data to Big Impact. *MIS Quarterly* 36 (4): 1165–1188.

D'Eredita, M., and C. Barreto. 2006. How Does Tacit Knowledge Proliferate? An Episode-Based Perspective. *Organization Studies* 27 (12): 1821–1841.

Fiegenbaum, A., and H. Thomas. 1988. Attitudes Towards Risk and the Risk-Return Paradox: Prospect Theory Explanations. *Academy of Management Journal* 31 (2): 85–106.

Fox, C., and A. Tversky. 1995. Ambiguity Aversion and Comparative Ignorance. *Quarterly Journal of Economics* 110 (3): 585–604.

Geisler, E. 1979. *An Empirical Study of a Proposed System for Monitoring Organizational Change in a Federal R&D Laboratory*. Unpublished dissertation. Evanston, IL: Northwestern University.

Geisler, E. 2001. Organizational Change Phenomena, Managerial Cognition and Archival Measures: Reconceptualization and New Empirical Evidence. Working Paper, Illinois Institute of Technology.

Geisler, E. 2002. On the Ubiquitous Inadequacy of Co-Variation Design in Strategy Research. *International Journal of Technology Management* 23 (6): 558–577.

Geisler, E. 2006. A Taxonomy and Proposed Codification of Knowledge and Knowledge Systems in Organizations. *Knowledge and Process Management* 13 (4): 285–296.

Geisler, E., and R. Kostoff. 1999. Strategic Management and Implementation of Textual Data Mining in Government Organizations. *Technology Analysis & Strategic Management* 11 (4): 493–525.

Halper, F., and K. Krishnan (2013). *TDWI Big Data Maturity Model Guide*. Renton, WA: The Data Warehouse Institute.

Hand, D. 2018. Who Told You That? Data Provenance, False Facts, and Separating the Liars from the TruthTellers. *Significance* 15: 8–9.

Isabella, L. 1990. Evolving Interpretations as a Change Unfolds: How Managers Construe Key Organizational Events. *Academy of Management Journal* 33 (1): 7–41.

Jenkins, M., and G. Johnson. 1997. Linking Management Cognition and Organizational Performance: A Preliminary Investigation Using Causal Maps. *British Journal of Management* 8 (2): 77–90.

Kaplan, S. 2011. Research in Cognition and Strategy: Reflection on Two Decades of Program and a Look to the Future. *Journal of Management Studies* 48 (3): 665–695.

Kachelmeier, S., and M. Shehata. 1992. Examining Risk Preferences Under High Monetary Incentives: Experimental Evidence from the People's Republic of China. *American Economic Review* 82 (5): 1120–1141.

Kahneman, D., P. Slovic, and A. Tversky, eds. 1982. *Judgement Under Uncertainty: Heuristics and Biases*. London, UK: Cambridge University Press.

Kenny, D. 1979. *Correlation and Causality*. New York: Wiley.

Kitchin, R. 2014. Big Data, New Epistemologies and Paradigm Shifts. *Big Data & Society* 1 (1): 1–12.

Kramer, A., J. Guillory, and J. Hancock. 2014. Experimental Evidence of Massive-Scale Emotional Contagion Through Social Networks. *PNAS* 111: 8788–8790.

Kreft, L., and J. de Leeuw. 1998. *Introducing Multilevel Modeling*. London: Sage.

LaValle, S., M. Hopkins, E. Lessor, R. Schockley, and N. Kruschwitz. 2010. Analytics: The New Path to Value: How the Smartest Organizations are Embedding Analytics to Transform Insights into Action. *IBM Institute for Business Value*.

Leavitt, H. 1975a. Beyond the Analytic Manager. *California Management Review* 17 (3, Spring): 5–12.

Leavitt, H. 1975b. Beyond the Analytic Manager: Part II. *California Management Review* 17(4, Summer): 1121.

McCarthy, B., C. McShea, and M. Roth. 2018. Rebooting Analytics Leadership: Time to Move Beyond the Math. *McKinsey & Company*, November 2018.

Plomp, R. 1990. The Significance of the Number of Highly Cited Papers as an Indicator of Scientific Prolificacy. *Scientometrics* 19 (3–4): 185–197.

Poldrack, R. 2018. *The New Mind Readers: What Neuroimaging Can and Cannot Reveal About Our Thoughts*. Princeton, NJ: Princeton University Press.

Rubenstein, A., E. Geisler, M. Glaser, et al. 1992. Preliminary Design Features of a Series of Intelligent Support Machines for Professional Knowledge Workers. Paper prepared for IAMOT, 1992 and *Management of Technology III*, T. Khalil and B. Bayraktar, editors.

Snijders, I., and R. Bosker. 1999. *Multilevel Analysis: An Introduction to Basic and Applied Multilevel Analysis*. London: Sage Publications.

Thorndike, E.L. 1939. On the Fallacy of Imputing the Correlations Found for Groups to the Individuals or Smaller Groups Composing Them. *The American Journal of Psychology* 52 (2): 122–124.

Wenzel, R., and N. Van Quaquebeke. 2017. The Double-Edged Sword of Big Data in Organizational and Management Research: A Review of Opportunities and Risks. *Organizational Research Methods* 21 (3): 548–491.

Yuchtman, E., and S.E. Seashore. 1967. A System Resource Approach to Organizational Effectiveness. *American Sociological Review* 32 (December): 891–903.

CHAPTER 5

Beyond Business Analytics: Illustrative Cases in Human History

Beyond Analytics: Illustrative Special Cases in Human History

This chapter portrays three cases of historical illustrations of the applications of the notion of "beyond analytics" to real-life situations. In this context it should be clarified that the notion of analytics is not the decision process itself. It is rather the *inputs* to the decision process. Thus, the cases below are examples of misjudgments and misinterpretations of analytics (data and events).

The Case of Napoleon's Campaign in Russia

In 1812 the French Emperor Napoleon Buonaparte invaded Russia. This army was known as "Le Grande Armee" (the great army). In late June 1812, the total strength of Napoleon's army is estimated at about 685,000 men (of which about 400,000 were French soldiers) and over 50,000 horses. The remaining 285,000 soldiers were conscripts from all over Europe, particularly from Poland, Austria, Italy, Bavaria, Saxony, and Prussia.

Throughout his previous campaigns in Italy and Spain, Napoleon was a master of accumulating intelligence on his adversaries. His battle plans had been tailored to the information which he gained on the size of his enemies and their disposition in and around the battlefield.

E. Geisler, *Beyond Business Analytics*,
https://doi.org/10.1007/978-3-030-43718-3_5

When Napoleon invaded Russia, he rapidly advanced his armies toward the Imperial Russian capital, Moscow. The Russians, led by their emperor, Alexander I, and under the command of Mikhail Kutuzov (1745–1813) abandoned Moscow to Napoleon, but executed a "scorched earth" strategy, thus depriving Napoleon of the bounty of the Russian countryside. The harsh winter of 1812 and the lack of adequate supplies forced the "Grande Armee" to retreat to Prussia, thus abandoning any hope of defeating the Russians.

Although Napoleon had information on the Russian forces opposing him, he could not transform this information into actionable knowledge. Napoleon had information (analytics), yet he failed to think beyond the information and integrate it into his overall strategy and its operational tactics. Napoleon was thus faced with the famous dilemma of "go" versus "chess."

"Go" versus "chess" is a choice between two different strategies. The "Go" strategy calls for conquering as much territory as possible, regardless of the size of the remaining enemy forces. The *chess* strategy is based on the systematic destruction of enemy forces. In the game of chess, the object of the game is to eliminate the opponent's pieces in the tactic of attacking and eliminating the king, which is the ultimate object of the game. In the game of chess, conquering territory is not the object of the game—as it is rather a secondary goal since the remaining pieces, by their range of movement on the board, thus control the territory around them.

The case of Napoleon Buonaparte in Russia is perhaps one of the best examples of a "go" strategy, whereas his enemy, the Russians, employed the "chess" strategy. The Russians gave up territory but kept their forces relatively intact for future battles. The large tracts of land that Napoleon conquered (including Moscow) were of no good use to him. He now faced an almost intact Russian army, fighting in its homeland and enjoying the benefits of relatively short supply lines, contrary to Napoleon's inability to adequately exploit the lands he now possessed in the Russian steppes.

In addition, an extremely powerful Russian winter has descended upon the French and their allies. Most of these armies had originally come from temperate climates where winters are difficult but not extreme. The French troops thus painfully lacked the appropriate clothing and accommodations that could protect them from the harsh winter weather. These conditions vastly contributed to the disastrous fortune of the

"Great Army." Only about 110,000 French soldiers survived this disastrous ordeal, out of 685,000 who first crossed the Russian frontier. This means that only about 16% of the grand army survived. The remainder perished in the freezing weather, as well as victims of the constant attacks by the Russian elite units of the Cossack cavalry.

Another aspect of this case that displays a critical lack of information or intelligence about Russia was the disastrous realization by Napoleon that Russia had an extremely underdeveloped network of roads. This fact had forced Napoleon to move his army on a very narrow front, hence opening himself to constant attacks on his flanks by Russian troops who did not necessarily need to maneuver on their poor system of roads. Perhaps Napoleon and his Marshalls knew that the roads were in a poor state of repair, yet had decided to use them anyway because they were the only navigable system of movement and transport of troops and supplies that were available to them.

The Case of the First Crusade

The first crusade was a popular movement in Western Europe, whose objective was to recapture the Holy Land and the city of Jerusalem, which had been conquered by the surging power of the Islamic military forces. The first crusade was also known as the "People's Crusade." In 1096 A.D., at the instigation of Peter the Hermit, who evoked a religious fervor in mobs of peasants and others in Western Europe. This was a disorganized eruption of energy, driven by deep religious belief endowed with the sacred mission to "liberate" the Holy Land and restore the church's control of the holy shrines in the Holy Land. These early crusaders attacked Jewish communities in Germany on their way to the Holy Land via the Ottoman Empire in Turkey. In October 1096 the Turks attacked the Crusaders at Civetot. By some accounts, over 60 thousand crusaders were killed by Turkish arrows. This was the end of the "People's Crusade."

The first Crusaders had no information or intelligence of the enemy's forces that awaited them. The People's Crusaders simply marched ahead, led by nonmilitary men such as Peter the Hermit. They had no plan. They had a very limited knowledge of the terrain, and of the strategic and tactical disposition of their adversaries. They lacked the basic information about their mission and what they were about to encounter. This is a classic example of an amateurish enterprise, involving many thousands of untrained and undisciplined peasants and city dwellers.

In our terminology, we can safely attest to the fact that the first crusaders were simply a mob of hooligans, who instead of constant quarreling among themselves had turned their combative and destructive energy first against their Jewish neighbors, and then against the Islamic inhabitants of the Levant.

Following the disastrous "People's Crusade," several European nobles, particularly from France, heeded the call for help from Pope Urban II and from the Byzantine Emperor Alexios Komnenos. They attacked and conquered Jerusalem in July 1099, thus establishing the kingdom of Jerusalem.

The Case of Navarre at Dien Bien Phu

The French general Henri Navarre (1898–1983) was the commanding general of the First Indochina War, and in this capacity was also the military commander during the battle of Dien Bien Phu, when the French Army was resolutely defeated by the Viet Minh in May 1954.

General Navarre commanded a garrison of about 13 thousand soldiers, whereas the Viet Minh had over 50 thousand fighters. Following a siege which lasted 54 days, the city was lost to the enemy. General Navarre had failed to consider the psychological effects of this defeat on the French people. His defeat contributed to the loss of support for the war by the people. On May 8, 1954, peace negotiations began in Geneva. The first war in Indochina had ended.

General Navarre was relieved of his command on June 3, 1954. He retired from the French Army in 1956. He was disillusioned and upon his retirement, General Navarre published a book *Agonie de L'Indochine*. This book was highly critical of the French military and political bureaucracies.

This is a case whereby General Navarre was in possession of good intelligence (Analytics) of the numbers and dispositions of the Vietnamese forces. He chose to disregard and discount this information. By so doing, he also misjudged the military capacity of his enemy. He could not accept the fact that a native force of rebels could amount to a serious military threat to his forces of regular army formations.

A similar misjudgment was repeated a decade later in the same geographical region by an American commander, General Westmoreland.

His forces were bogged down in the harsh Vietnamese terrain of tropical forests, rivers, and lagoons. The topography was largely unpassable—even to a modern army.

Summary: What These Cases Tell Us

These three cases illustrate situations in which the leaders lacked adequate and actionable analytics, or were in possession of some or much information—sufficiently assembled as inputs to good decision-making. Clearly, the question, how much analytics is necessary and sufficient to make a good decision? is still very relevant to this discussion.

These cases also tell us that the existence of Analytics in any form, in a given situation, determines to a large extent the resolution of the situation or the problem depicted in the given scenario. There seems to be no urgent need for a surfeit of evidence; rather, an amount of analytics that would provide acceptable input for a good managerial decision.

In some instances, the analytics provided to the decision-maker is not sufficient for a good decision. For example, here are three cases that illustrate the situations when the analytics is not sufficient.

Case A

Case A shows that although the analytics may have been good and sufficient, the decision-maker made the wrong decision by selecting the wrong alternative from the set of possible alternative solutions that were available to the decision-maker. The wrong choice may have been the result of a gross misinterpretation of the information or the decision-maker's affinity or existing predilection, thus biasing the choice toward a given alternative.

An example of Case A is the unmitigated defeat of the American General George Custer by the Sioux Indians at the Battle of the Little Big Horn. He was in possession of adequate information about his opponents, yet he decided to engage them with the inadequate forces at his disposal rather than disengage the enemy and postpone the attack until reinforcements arrived.

Case B

Another situation is Case B. This is the case where the analytics are wrong, incomplete, or misleading to such a degree that the problem or situation could not be resolved. Such a case may be the implementation of a wrong policy or the choice of a poor strategy. The decision-maker is in possession of inadequate amounts of information (analytics), thus unable to make a reasonable decision.

Examples of Case B include the first Iraq War of 2003. This conflict was predicated upon analytics of Iraq's possession of an arsenal of weapons of mass destruction (WMDs), such as nuclear, chemical, and biological weapons. The analytics proved to be erroneous as upon occupying Iraq, such weapons could not be found. The analytics was wrong.

According to the US Center for Disease Control and Prevention, 8 out of 10 deaths from the coronavirus have been 65 years old and older. 4–11 percent of adults 65–85 years old and 10–27 percent of adults 85 years old and older have died as a result of this disease. Also, 11–31 percent of adults 65–84 years old required admission to intensive care. This means that about one in four or one in three older adults required admission to intensive care. Finally, 31–59 percent of adults 65–84 years old required hospitalization. That is, from one-third to one-half of such adults required hospitalization. These data show with abundant clarity that the burden on American hospitals may become insupportable.

Case C

This is the case where the decision-maker works on the wrong problem, or where the decision-maker solves the wrong problem. There is an abundance of historical cases that illustrate this specific case of analytics.

According to the US Center for Disease Control and Prevention, 8 out of 10 deaths from the coronavirus have been 65 years old and older. 4–11 percent of adults 65–85 years old and older have died as a result of this disease. Also, 11–31 percent of adults 65–84 years old required admission to intensive care. This means that about one in four or one in three older adults required of adults 65–84 years old required hospitalization. That is, from one-third to half of such adults required hospitalization. These data show with abundant clarity that the burden on American hospitals may become insupportable.

Cases of Leaders Who Lacked Adequate Analytics, Yet Decided to Act

The cases below illustrate situations whereby leaders lacked adequate analytics, and were fully aware of this fact yet decided to act regardless of this limiting constraint that they were facing.

The Case of the Battle of the Bulge

The Battle of the Bulge occurred as a result of the German counteroffensive through the mountainous terrain of the Belgian Ardennes. This battle between German and American units was fought during the period December 16, 1944 until January 16, 1945. The term "bulge" described the wedge or the area in which the Germans penetrated the Allied lines.

The German offensive is said to have caught the Allied commanders totally by surprise. However, the facts on the ground and at the Allied Headquarters present a different scenario. Due to the Allied mastery of the German cyphers, General Dwight D. Eisenhower, the Allied supreme commander, was able to anticipate the enemy's intentions and plans. Although the Allies received good intelligence that the Germans were massing troops in the wooded area of the Ardennes, their commanders chose to ignore such specific intelligence. The Allied commanders mistakenly believed that the Germans lacked the necessary armored forces for such a massive winter campaign and, secondly, that the rugged wooded terrain of the Ardennes prohibited the use of armored formations. Some Allied commanders strongly believed that tanks could not maneuver among the trees of a dense forest, such as the Ardennes. Based on such erroneous assumptions, the Allied forces, mostly American, consisted of 80 thousand mainly exhausted and inexperienced divisions. It is thus believed that these 80 thousand men faced in the Ardennes a German force of 250 thousand men, consisting of 14 German infantry and 5 Panzer divisions.

The Americans bravely resisted the continuous attacks by the Germans, particularly in the strategically located city of Bastogne. The Germans lacked adequate fuel supplies for their tank formations and, when confronted with the heroic stand of the American forces, their counterattack collapsed. The "bulge" was recaptured by the Allies, and the German forces retreated to their original lines.

Although the Germans were cognizant of the Allied forces opposing them, and of the continuous influx of Allied reserves coming through the ports of Normandy and from the Belgian port of Antwerp, they stood their ground. Their leader issued an order to fight on, regardless of the human losses and the clearly untenable situation of their units.

The German commanders lacked the means to obtain intelligence on their opponents. They could barely supply and maintain their lines. These commanders simply believed that the Allies had an almost inexhaustible supply of manpower and materials. The Allies controlled the skies and also controlled the ports and the sea lanes.

The order that the German commanders received to stand their position and to not retreat or reposition or regroup their troops was based solely on the will of their leaders—not on solid intelligence of the state of their enemies The order was purely subjective, without the input from military intelligence and an adequate picture of the situation in the field of battle. At the end, the Germans had over 120 thousand casualties, while the Allies lost 75 thousand. But, in addition to the horrific loss of lives, the Germans also lost enormous tonnage of supplies and material, which their war economy could not resupply in time for further military actions.

The escalation of the German "counterattack" in the Ardennes effectively meant a defeat of the German forces in the Second World War. This misjudgment of the German command had accelerated the defeat of Germany and the end of the war.

Since the Germans had a good idea of the forces opposing them, the "Battle of the Bulge" could be considered a "fool's errand," perhaps an almost suicidal enterprise. That is, the Germans were in possession of intelligence about their enemies so that the deadly outcome of their counterattack was quite predictable. The German Field Marshal Walther Model, for example, commented on the planned attack: "Hitler's plan has not got a damned leg to stand on."

The German generals knew, in advance, that the counterattack was doomed from the start. They went along with it because of their military code of obedience to higher authority.

The Case of General Ritchie

In my book *Managing the Aftermath of Radical Corporate Change* (1997), I describe the case in which General Sir Neil Ritchie commanded a British army in the North African desert. In late May 1942, General Ritchie received credible information about the German Field Marshal Erwin Rommel. The British intelligence services had decoded Rommel's battle plan. Ritchie did not know the source of the information, but he knew that his superiors were satisfied that the information was reliable.

General Ritchie decided to ignore the detailed intelligence he possessed and proceeded to commit his army to battle. Rommel sprang his trap on June 13, 1942. Ritchie endured a humiliating defeat. He lost 300 tanks and had to retreat to Egypt.

As I concluded in my account of this incident, the mere possession of critical information is not a guarantee that the commander who possesses such information will indeed incorporate it into his decision-making process. General Ritchie had ignored the intelligence he had received. This behavior is not uncommon. Commanders tend to ignore and reject intelligence that, *prima facie*, appears to be trustworthy. Several reasons animate such behavior. Commanders might not trust the source of the intelligence or the people who bring such intelligence to them. Also, the specific intelligence may not fit their own view of the enemy, his disposition of forces, or his intentions—as they are reflected in his movement.

The Case of Sir Francis Drake and the Spanish Armada

In the late 1580s, King Philip II of Spain was enraged by the raids of English marauders commanded by Sir Francis Drake, with the silent consent of Queen Elisabeth I. King Philip decided to forcefully act and destroy England's hold on the channel waters and the Atlantic Ocean.

The King ordered the construction of a giant fleet of 130 ships, manned by 8000 sailors, and equipped with 2500 guns and 20 thousand soldiers. On July 23, 1588, the English fleet attacked the Spanish armada, forcing it to turn back to Spain. On the journey back, the armada encountered strong storms and by October, when the surviving ships reached Spain, the armada had lost over half its vessels, and over 15,000 dead.

In these naval encounters, the English introduced a new form of attack. Instead of boarding the enemy's ships and conquering them with the use of their infantry, the English attacked the armada from a distance by using their superior long-range guns. In addition, Sir Francis Drake's ships were smaller, much faster, and could better manipulate the unpredictable waters of the English Channel.

This is a case where one combatant (the English) had analytics over the Spanish. They knew that the enemy ships were slow and cumbersome, and that their English ships could easily out-maneuver the slow-moving armada. The English also had better knowledge of the English Channel and its mortal perils.

Sir Francis Drake was victorious because he had much better knowledge of the battleground (the sea) and the advantages of his agile fleet. Sir Francis gained some of this previous knowledge from his raid on the armada's port of Cadiz, in Spain, in early 1588.

The Spaniards knew very little about the English fleet, its characteristics, or its strengths and weaknesses. The Spanish commander, the Duke of Medina-Sidonia, did not bother with gaining intelligence on his enemy. His confidence in his fleet was unshakeable. He had the most fearsome armada the world had ever seen. Victory was just a matter of time and of engaging the enemy. He did not care to know what the enemy was like. Pure logic by looking at the numbers of vessels, led him to believe that a few English vessels could not pose a threat to his force. Perhaps, this was an early application of Analytics.

Illustrative Cases in Antiquity

In ancient times, until later in the Roman Empire, kings and generals acted with very little intelligence about their enemies. It was, however, a common practice to send spies to the enemy's camp, who would return and report on what they had seen. In the Biblical account of Joshua (1355–1245 BCE), he sent two spies to the highly fortified city of Jericho. The spies befriended a prostitute, named Rahab. She hid them from the authorities and helped them leave the city undetected. The two spies returned unharmed and reported to Joshua that the population of Jericho was very afraid ("melting away") of the potential invaders (Joshua, 2: 24). They also probably reported data on the city's walls, which helped Joshua destroy the walls.

Julius Caesar also employed spies, whom he sent to Gaul (today's France), so he could better understand the disposition of his troops, vis-à-vis the enemy. This was a common practice by the Roman legions. The reports were delivered to members of the Roman Senate but were considered to be state secrets.

Legion commanders and the supreme commander of the Roman forces habitually sent spies to collect data on (1) geography and terrain, such as approaches, escape routes, weather, and food and water resources; (2) social and political data, such as quality of leadership, strengths and weaknesses of the population, and social and political institutions, including their religious practices and the nature of their holidays.

Other types of data include types and locations of fortifications, outposts, communication means (e.g., by foot or on horseback), and the topography of the enemy's terrain and its surroundings.

In 331 BCE, Alexander the Macedonian defeated the Persian army at Gaugamela, under the command of Darius III. The Macedonians had

35,000 men, against over 200,000 Persians. Alexander had studied the terrain and was thus able to lure the Persian cavalry to a very rough and rocky area, where their maneuverability would greatly collapse. Thus, Alexander was in possession of analytics about the battlefield and the enemy—and this helped him to achieve remarkable victory.

In all these cases, the victorious side had collected analytics about the terrain, the size of the enemy forces, and their disposition. Armed with such data, the victors could fight with the tremendous advantage of knowing much more than their opponent.

These four categories of cases illustrate the link between leaders and analytics. The cases show instances where leaders lacked sufficient and adequate analytics—yet decided to act. Their decision would sometimes lead to positive results and, in other cases to errors and disasters. In other instances, leaders had adequate analytics yet decided to ignore or disregard such assets of information.

Whenever leaders made use of their analytics, the resulting outcomes from their decisions were more positive. Prior to the D-day invasion in June 1944, American Supreme Commander, General Dwight D. Eisenhower, had his staff scrupulously study all the relevant variables, such as weather, terrain disposition of enemy units, whereabout of senior enemy generals, availability of landing crafts, the morale of the troops, etc.

Conversely, another example from the Second World War is the planning by the Germans of the invasion of Norway in 1940. The command of the operation was given to General Nikolaus van Falkenhorst. He later wrote that to learn about Norway, he went to a bookstore and purchased a Fodor's Travel Guide to Norway, so that he could familiarize himself with such key points of interest as major cities, parks, landing strips, highways, demographics, and cultural variables, such as language and money notes.

There is an obvious correlation between analytics and specific knowledge of a subject matter. The literature offers few clues of how to describe these similarities. Perhaps a good distinction would be that analytics is the result of some analysis of the subject matter, whereas knowledge is a very general descriptor of what is known about the subject matter—mostly without an analysis of any substantial type.

Another fact that emerges from the use of analytics is that leaders (and managers) are not obligated to use this instrument of analysis. They would opt to use it mainly if they believed that such use would give them competitive advantage over both their colleagues and adversaries. As history clearly teaches us, there are numerous instances when leaders failed to use analytics, and thus had to pay for their mistake. Successful leaders and managers in their organizations excelled because they had recognized the value of analytics to their work and their accomplishments. Analytics is therefore a valuable asset, at the disposal of insightful leaders or managers.

The Case of the Rothschilds

Although this cliché has been criticized by several authors, there is some truth in the "knowledge is power" statement. The more leaders or managers know about their organizations, their human resources, and the conditions of the marketplace within which they operate, the more successful they will be. For instance, there is the famous example of the banking house of Rothschild. This financial empire was founded in the 1760s in Frankfurt, Germany. The patriarch of the family sent his five sons to the five main capitals of Europe, where they established and managed the bank's branches. The Rothschilds thus had a presence in Naples, Vienna, Paris, London, and Frankfurt. During the Napoleonic wars, the bank had established a network of messengers who communicated with each other across borders by "semaphore" (the use of two flags in certain positions to signify words). This network gave the bankers in London, Paris, and Frankfurt, immediate news of the outcomes of battles anywhere in Europe, so that the bank could purchase in a timely manner bonds of the victors and dispose/sell those of the losers. This was perhaps the first known case of "insider trading."

The Rothschild case clearly demonstrates that knowledge by itself has limited value unless it is obtained in a timely manner. Similarly, analytics is of value only when it is not just relevant, but also timely. Indisputably, the ownership of timely knowledge does indeed endow people and organizations with comparative advantage, which can therefore be translated into pecuniary gains.

In the following chapters I will discuss the cognitive aspects of analytics. That is, how the data collected by the instrument of analytics is entered into a system of synthesis, in which the data is assembled, then distinctly categorized and entered as inputs to how we link the data to the formation of conceptual framework.

A different approach to analytics and its relationship to the outcomes of a given problem—where analytics is used as the instrument of analysis—is described below.

There are three possible scenarios or cases. *Case (a)* is the case where the decision-maker selected the wrong alternative from a set of alternative solutions available to the decision-maker. For example, the decision-maker is considering some form of organizational redesign. The options-for-action which are available to the decision-maker may include: (a) redesign or restructure only one department or unit; (b) redesign or restructure several units; and (c) redesign or restructure the entire organization. The decision-maker selects one alternative. However, if the restructuring involves the entire organization (whereas only one unit had to be redesigned), this choice of alternative would be not only wrong, but also expensive to the organization, in that the cost of applying this wrong option would be added to the cost of implementing the "correct" option, thus making the restructuring economically onerous.

Case (b) is where the alternative was correctly selected, but the implementation of the tools of analytics was wrong. For example, as part of the analysis, the decision-maker employs various statistical methods or tests, such as multiple regression analysis, when the appropriate test should have been a Spearman nonparametric correlation. In this case, the application of the incorrect analytical test leads to the under-measurement or over-measurement of the phenomenon. Either way, the decision-maker is now in possession of an inadequate—perhaps even erroneous—measure.

Case (c) is where analytics is applied to the wrong problem. Thus, the problem could not be resolved, although analytics was used. This case illustrates the use of analytics in vain, whereby the analytics measuring tool had been flawlessly applied—but the original problem has not been solved at all. In some instances, the decision-maker may be able to draw a lesson from this wasted effort. The main lesson may entail the knowledge of where *not* to go, and the scenarios that should *not* be analyzed by the decision-maker.

Because analytics comprises more than one test instrument, the decision-maker has the ability to select an instrument that would best apply to the decision-maker's needs and capabilities to master and manipulate the instrument. This type of alternative action would also limit the decision-maker's range of potential implementation of the test-instrument. Hence, the outcomes or outputs from this problem would also be limited to those that can be applied by the decision-maker without much additional effort.

In summary, business analytics can be described as the manipulation of data within the organization, conducted with the application of selected measurement instruments. This is the quantitative aspect of measuring the selected organizational variables. This reminds me of the immortal words of the Mahatma Gandhi: "When I despair, I remember that all through history the way of truth and love had always won. There have been tyrants and murderers and for a time they seem invincible, but in the end, they always fail…think of it, always" In my own life I had witnessed the unimaginable measure of cruelty of human beings against their brothers and sisters. And I despaired, and I felt a hangman's noose of an ultimate existence in the rabbit's hole of disaster and pain. But, throughout all this, I always knew that, although it was not a dream, this actual nightmare will let go of its grip and disappear with the early rays of the dawn of a new day. The freedom of individuals and nations has always prevailed, no matter how powerful, angry, and inhuman was the attempt to deprive them of the basic elixir of life: their unalienable freedom to exist undisturbed and full of their sense of how to best spend their years on this little planet of ours.

CHAPTER 6

The Power of the Few

> If, according to Von Clausewitz war is a continuation of politics by other means, then peace is the avoidance of war by any other means, and therefore should be pursued by all means. (E. Geisler)

Proposition 1: Managers strive to achieve an acceptable level of conceptualization of their actions with the employment of a small number of variables or elements, which is sufficient to form a useful mental image.

This proposition advances the notion that a few select variables are sufficient to form a mental image of reality but it does not, however, specify what kind of variables, nor whether there is a minimum standard of variables sufficient and necessary for the mental image.

This application of the notion of "power of the few" has both advantages and disadvantages. The key advantage is the need for only a small number of variables for the manager to make an acceptable, elegant, and parsimonious decision. Similarly, this is the application of a small number of variables sufficient to construct a coherent mental image, and the ability to communicate this image to other people. Example of the Power of the Few: How a very small number of people, languages, technologies, cultural events, and the discovery of natural phenomena, have changed the way we live.

E. Geisler, *Beyond Business Analytics*,
https://doi.org/10.1007/978-3-030-43718-3_6

Occam's Razor

This is the story of an English friar who lived in the thirteenth century (1287–1347). William of Occam did not invent the law of parsimony but he heralded it with much vigor and consistency. The Latin definition of this notion reads: "Entia non sunt multiplicandum praeter necessitatem."

A rough translation is that there is no need to have complex explanation when a short one is sufficient. Occam's Razor is generally used to argue that a simple and parsimonious explanation or description is far better than a complex one. If you say something or describe something in a few words, this is better than using multiple words.

The Alphabet

This word is derived from the first two letters of the Greek alphabet: *alpha* and *beta*. An alphabet is a small set of characters or graphs that represent a language. Those characters are also arranged in a given mode, ordering, or sequence. The alphabet thus consists of a small number of characters or letters, which are then combined—per strict rules—into words, then sentences, designed to represent the world and the life of their creators and users. Today there are several major alphabets in use around the world. For example, Latin, Arabic, Hebrew, Indian, Greek, Cyrillic, Runic Chinese, Korean, and Japanese are distinct languages with their unique alphabet.

All these alphabets share common attributes of their design and functionalities. First, they are based on a small number of letters that, by combinatoric analysis, can be converted into a very large number of words. Second, they allow for new words to be incorporated into the lexicon. Thirdly, they seem to be resilient to many cultural and technological developments, and to the influences and pressures of other languages.

This phenomenon of creating a very small number of characters or letters to essentially represent or describe the world of their creators is indeed a magnificent achievement of the human mind and its diverse cultures.

There are several theories of the origin of the alphabet or the *written* language. The widely accepted origin is the dual development of (1) the invention of consonant writing by the Semitic people of the Eastern Mediterranean Sea, perhaps the Phoenicians. This development may have occurred around 1600 BCE (Before Common Era). (2) The second was the invention by the ancient Greeks of characters or letters representing vowels. This occurred between 800 and 700 BCE.

Thus, the important antecedents or the prototypes of the alphabet were the ancient Egyptians' hieroglyphics, and the cuneiform writing of the Sumerians, Babylonians, and Assyrians, and the contributions of the Phoenicians. These were peoples who inhabited lands on the banks of mighty rivers—the Nile and the Tigris-Euphrates. Their geography was conducive to varied commercial activities. Therefore, to satisfy the need for documents and correspondence that enabled them to legally control their commercial activities and to assess the profits and losses of their transactions, they had to come up with some form of written artifact which would allow them to document their commercial and financial interactions and to describe their enterprises. This was a need for business *contracts* which established the legal foundations of the transfer of wealth between generations of a tribe a village, or a city, and between seller and buyer of services and the commercial goods and properties.

Similarly, there was a need to maintain adequate control of the taxes imposed by the rulers on the commercial clans. Because much of the business transactions were conducted across jurisdictions, the commercial people had to keep track of how much they paid each of these different taxation governments.

On the other side, scribes for the rulers and priests of religious organizations with their own taxing capabilities had to document their actual collection of these taxes, so that tax-evaders would be caught and punished—an act also meant to intimidate and to warn other taxpayers into compliance.

Thus, the invention of the alphabet, from the times of Hammurabi to the Egyptians, the Semitic nations, and the Graeco-Roman scribes, had fostered economic and other developments of ancient cities and civilizations.

The formalization of the tax collection activity allowed for increased trust in the tax system and in the good intentions of the tax collectors. There was, after all, written evidence that taxes had been paid, so that any unethical initiatives by tax collectors to establish a "double" or "triple" tax would be impeded by the trusted and unmistakable document, thus avoiding the "he said," "he said" cases of dubious behavior, and the lengthy and highly expensive court proceedings to unravel this problem.

A small number of characters also made it possible for ancient scholars to create documents that preserved their history for centuries, even millennia. Because of the alphabet we know of the lives and epic wars of peoples who used the cuneiform mode of alphabet with only 30 letters. We also know the writings of Homer, describing in great detail the Trojan wars in the Iliad and Odyssey books in about the eighth century BCE. In these epic poems we learned about kings and heroes: Agamemnon, Achilles, and Odysseus. We also learned about the Greek pantheon of gods, interfering in human affairs, and taking sides in the wars between the Greek alliance and the impregnable fortress of Troy.

Much earlier, around 1500 BCE, there occurred the adventure of the Hebrews and their liberation from Egypt, as they trek through the desert to their promised land in Canaan. Their story and the rules imposed on them by Moses are canonized in the Bible. This extraordinary book is a mix of historical accounts and an assembly of religious and civic laws, of standards and norms of behavior, hygiene, health care, and public administration. The ancient Hebrews thus learned how to worship and how to survive as a civic institution in the unforgiving desert. Their entire patrimony was encased in two tablets with ten commandments. The first five instructed them what they *should* do in their relations with God and their fellow-Hebrews. The next set of five commandments laid out what they *must not do* (e.g., do not kill; do not commit adultery; do not steal, etc.).

The magnificent document with its ten commandments is an outstanding example of the way a large volume of information can be forcefully constrained into a single and parsimonious story. In fact, over the centuries, since the appearance of the story of the ten commandments, there have emerged a very large literature on the meaning of this document, and the influence and transformation of the commandments into the Codex of laws of every nation in the western part of Europe and the Americas.

Similarly, other cultures have also managed to create their specialized code of ethic and behavior. For example, the Babylonian king Hammurabi (around 1792–1750 BCE) established a code of 252 laws and their corresponding punishment for those who disobeyed them. About half of the laws in this codex deal with what we call today "contract law." These laws established the compensation to be paid to each litigant profession, as well as laws dealing with family affairs, such as paternity, divorce, and property ownership and distribution, and the punishment of any person breaking any of these laws. This code is written in cuneiform alphabet, which is carved into a stele, or a slab of tall stone whose surface is especially prepared for carving the given message.

Clearly, very few citizens at that time knew how to read, thus they needed the services of those members of their society who were literate, primarily members of the priesthood. Many of these took upon themselves to transcribe the holy scriptures for the use of very few, until the invention by Gutenberg of the printing press, at which time these books became available to any person who could afford the small price for these widely distributed works.

By the simple fact that these ancient rulers, such as Hamurabi, chose small pieces of stone to conserve their message for future generations, they were able to thus allow us to have a glimpse into their thinking, their beliefs, their ethical preferences, and the spirit of the laws that governed their existence.

Not all rulers and cultures were so magnanimous in selecting small monuments to proclaim their legal system. The pharaohs of ancient Egypt built very large structures to house their tombs—in the form of colossal pyramids and other enormous statues as seen in the Valley of the Kings. For example, there is the temple of Queen Hatshepsut (1478–1458 BCE). She reigned alongside her husband Thutmose II, then—upon his death—as regent to her step-son Tutmose III. She brought economic prosperity to her kingdom. Her large and imposing monuments did not last long, because Tutmose III (1479–1425 BCE) who succeeded her, had busily engaged in a campaign to eradicate her memory from the monuments, in order to enhance the influence and future impact of his own dynasty.

Although rulers had routinely erased the memory and achievements of their predecessors, a small set of stele and other monuments for almost all the pharaohs has nevertheless survived for future generations to have a good look at their lives and their achievements. In other words, we do not need to interpret the message of massive temples and structures in order to compose the history of the ruler. Often it is the few small ruins that allow us to reconstruct the past, simply by our ability to read the inscription of a summary of the ruler's life and glory.

In the case of the Egyptian funeral monuments, the phenomenon of parsimony had been maintained. The pharaohs and their talented scribes were able to condense the stories of their lives and their victories on relatively compact surfaces of stele and on the walls of their tombs and other monuments. In some cases, the pharaohs had their achievements carved or painted on the interior of monuments, and they did so even on non-official structures.

In all these cases in antiquity, the principle of the "power of the few" had been applied to the rulers' endeavor in having their name and accomplishments written for centuries and millennia to come.

In fact, the use of hieroglyphs was also a way to employ a limited number of letters, symbols, and characters, although the hieroglyphs contained almost one thousand distinct characters. This number is, of course, some 30–40 times larger than the average of 30 characters in other documents and manuscripts. But, despite its large size, it was also contained in a finite number of characters—more difficult to learn, but applicable nonetheless.

The Hindu-Arabic Numeral System

This numeral system, based on the decimal configuration, was developed in India in about 500 CE (Common Era). The system was further modified in Muslim North Africa. It is believed that an Italian mathematician named Fibonacci (born in 1170 in Pisa, Italy) first used the Arabic numeral system and helped to diffuse its use in Medieval Europe.

This system contains the ten digits (0, 1, 2, 3, 4, 5. 6, 7, 8, 9). Compared with the existing Roman numerals, the Arabic system allowed for much more flexibility with complex computations. The Roman system of letters (representing numbers) was much more cumbersome. Moreover, when diffused worldwide, their use in commercial and financial transactions rapidly replaced all other such systems. Another benefit of this system was the introduction and adoption of the value of zero, and the use of the numeral for zero (0) in other permutations of the Arabic numerals.

The DNA (Deoxyribonucleic Acid)

This compound is the hereditary material in every biological organism, including humans. The DNA is found in the nucleus of almost every cell. It stores the material on the human traits to be passed on to other cells. The DNA stores such information in the form of a code, embedded in four chemical bases: Adenine (A), Guanine (G), Cytosine (C), and Thymine (T). These are known as AGCT.

DNA was first identified by the Swiss scientist Johannes Miescher in 1869. However, the structure of the DNA molecule, in the form of a double helix, was discovered by James Watson and Francis Crick and published in the journal *Nature* (April 25, 1953). The article was two pages long (737–738), but it revolutionized the way the structure of DNA has been suggested at that time.

The DNA plays a crucial and elementary role in genetics. The DNA contains genetic information, which is found in the four nucleotides: AGCT. This arrangement is an incredible feat of nature, whereby an enormously large assembly of genetic information and instructions is contained in the limited setup of nucleotides found in every living cell, which is thus passed along from generation to generation. This is why DNA is added here as an example of the "power of the few."

The Printing Press

This was an invention that merits a place in the list of "the power of the few." It is also considered as one of the human inventions that changed the world: technologically, socially, economically, politically, religiously, scientifically, and ethically.

The printing press was invented (or some say perfected) in 1496 by a German printer named Johannes Gutenberg. He printed the holy Bible, thus making it available to all people at a price that almost everyone could afford—rather than the handwritten version of the Bible, which only the wealthy were able to purchase. Thus, by printing Martin Luther's book, Gutenberg made Martin Luther the first "Best Selling" author in history.

With his printing press, Gutenberg was also instrumental in making the *Renaissance* movement a popular movement, which later helped to leap forward to the *industrial revolution*. The printing press also powered the *scientific revolution*, by publishing and diffusing the works by John Locke, Voltaire, and Jean-Jacques Rousseau. In fact, Francis Bacon wrote in 1620 that three inventions had changed the world: gunpowder, the nautical compass, and the printing press.

The printing press made it possible for any ideas, even fringe ideas, to have a platform, thus reaching many thousands of people worldwide. The printer became an honorable profession. In the Americas, Benjamin Franklin was a proud printer in Philadelphia. Dr Franklin considered printing his first and foremost occupation—in view of his many interests and inventions. The printing press helped catapult public opinion to actual revolution in that, for example, Thomas Paine's *Common Sense* became a popular book and also served as the actual spirit of a growing popular sentiment.

In parallel, the printing press allowed governments to widely distribute laws and regulations—thus replacing the "town crier"—in the form of printed documents. This phenomenon greatly contributed to the explosive growth in government bureaucracies. Hence, a method was found for direct communication between the governed and the rulers. As a side effect, it became a welcomed policy for governments to encourage *literacy* among wide segments of the population.

Without the printing press it would have been very difficult—almost impossible—for fringe ideologies such as Nazism, Fascism, and Communism—to reach wide audiences, thus to convert multitudes of adherents to their philosophy.

On October 31, 1517, history tells us the Catholic priest Martin Luther nailed a piece of paper to the door of the castle church in the town of Wittenberg, Germany. In it, Luther listed 95 opinions that condemned (or "protested") the church's use of "indulgences," by which the church would forgive some sins if the faithful would contribute to the church's projects, principally the renovation of St. Peter's basilica in Rome.

For his protest, in 1521, Martin Luther was excommunicated by Pope Leo X. However, Prince Frederick III (1463–1525), elector of Saxony, defied the papal decision and protected Martin Luther, allowing him to indefinitely stay at his castle, where Luther translated the new testament from Greek to German. This feat, and the invention of the printing press, made it much easier for the German populace to read the Bible for themselves, thus leading to the reform of Catholicism. The Protestant branch of Christianity was born and prospered. As the leader of the reformation, Martin Luther married Katherina von Bora in 1525 and had six children with her until her death in 1546.

The few (95) theses of his revolutionary ideas had exploded into the movement of reformation with its religious, political, economic, and social consequences. After Luther, Europe became the scene of two opposing camps: the Catholics and the Protestants. This led to a series of wars during the sixteenth, seventeenth, and early eighteenth centuries. After the German Peasants' War (1524–1525), there occurred the Thirty Year's War (1615–1648). This state of constant belligerency had decimated Germany, causing the death of almost one-third of the German population. Other such conflicts continued until the Toggenburg War in 1712.

These wars caused millions of victims, dead or wounded, with many thousands of citizens expulsed from their homes, and the devastation of a considerable portion of western Europe. In many ways the effects of these wars are embedded in today's geography, demography, and the cultural tapestry of Europe.

This little machine, the printing press, had changed the nature of an entire continent, for many centuries to come. It facilitated the dissemination of ideas which had led to political and religious revolutions, plus the educational growth of millions of citizens, who were now able to enjoy the pleasure of reading, and consequently dreaming, about far, faraway lands, strange yet thought-provoking philosophies, and about historical heroes and heroines. Moreover, it was imported to other continents (Americas, Africa, Australasia) where it also contributed to a more educated populace, which was now willing to try new ideas, such as freedom, equality in taxation and shared governance, even self-governance, and self-determination. It is hard to imagine the American and the French revolutions without the existence of the printing machine. The magnificent prose of Jean-Jacques Rousseaux in France and Thomas Paine and Thomas Jefferson in the United States had used the printed format to be disseminated among their respective elite populations and thus had forged the philosophical essence of the new nation of the United States and the more equitable and more democratic nation of France. In the United States, such ideas had moved rapidly from the confines of Virginia's taverns to the popular consciousness of the American population from coast to coast. The premises and the notions of democracy and freedom continue to illuminate the American landscape even today.

The Magnetic Compass

The magnetic compass was invented in China, in about 1050 BCE. It works by the means of a magnetic needle, which is allowed to float and freely turn, so it always points to the North pole of the earth's magnetic field. This instrument freed maritime navigators from guessing where is the north, especially in cloudy days and at night—when the stars are invisible.

The compass appeared in Europe in the early years of the fourteenth century. Its usage greatly contributed to mariners taking much more risk, and sailing into areas which, until then, they feared and avoided, leading to more adventurous expeditions well into the Atlantic Ocean, beyond the confines of the Mediterranean Sea.

Thus, a plethora of geographic discoveries had now appeared, and ocean lanes had now been established leading to the intensification of global maritime activity and commerce. The export–import business exploded, fostering a sharp rise in the accumulated wealth of maritime nations such as Spain, Portugal, England, France, and Italy.

The Steam Engine, the Locomotive, and the Railway

A locomotive, pulling dozens of heavy rail cars may look very heavy, but it is really a small cog in the broader phenomenon of a single engine pulling all these heavy cars. This marvelous fact of the "little engine that could" is possible due to the invention of the steam engine. As networks of railroads multiplied and dotted the vast landscape in Europe, Asia, and the Americas, their arrival has fostered the development of towns, factories, military installations, and a transportation system for passengers and cargo. When a generation, after the English engineer George Stephenson applied steam power to locomotives in 1820, railways rapidly spread, and distances within and between countries had collapsed into "how long a trip by rail between London and Glasgow or between New York, Chicago, and San Francisco."

The railways fostered the exploration and the eventual settlement of the American West, the Russian enormous land mass from Vladivostok in the east to Moscow in the west. In the United Kingdom, travel by rail became the glorious achievement of British ingenuity, and the preferred mode of transportation of the British people. As an example, how would Sherlock Holmes conduct his detective achievements without his colleague, Dr. John Watson's all-encompassing knowledge of the elaborate schedules of the British Railways System?

The Use of Nails as Fasteners

This is a case in which indeed the little object called *nail* has been used to fasten materials, thus helping to construct a great variety of structures, furniture, and instruments—for both war and peaceful objectives. This is a classic case of the "power of the few."

The nail as fastener has been in use for several millennia. Nails made of bronze have been found in archeological excavations in Egypt, dating to about 3000 BCE. Metal nails were widely used in ancient Rome, as described in the account of the crucifixion.

The more commonly used nails today are made of brass, aluminum, copper, and steel. The five most common types of nails are

1. *Common*, everyday nail: size varies from one to six inches.
2. *Box* nail: thinner than common nails and available in sizes one to three-and-a-half inches.
3. *Finishing* nail: have a small barrel-shaped head, in sizes one to four inches.
4. *Casing* nail used to attach moldings such as window and door casings.
5. *Roofing* nail: designed to hold in place roofing materials.

Nails are therefore used in all construction, from the little shed in the backyard to the mighty skyscraper.

The Use of Banknotes and Letters of Credit

The earliest known banknotes first appeared in China, around the seventh century CE. This financial instrument is a promissory note, issued by a financial institution, and that can be transacted at face value. The banknote appeared in China because merchants wanted to replace the use of metal coins in their business transactions, and to avoid being the unprotected targets of thieves and road bandits. Later, during the Crusades, when the European nobles needed funds to equip and to supply their small armies for their voyage to Jerusalem, they turned to international entities, such as the Knights Templars. The nobleman would deposit an adequate number of valuables in the local branch of the Templars. These valuables generally included silver and gold artifacts, and the deeds to portions of the nobleman properties. In exchange, he was given a "letter of credit," or a note attesting to his deposits which he could use for expenses on the road to Jerusalem, and upon arriving in the Holy Land and cashing his note at the base of the Templars in the Holy Land.

During the late Crusades, Italian city states, such as Florence, Milan, Genoa, and Venice, who greatly benefitted from the Crusades, by providing the Crusaders with maritime transportation and supplies, became the financial powerhouses in Europe. In fact, the coins issued by the banks in Florence became an international currency, named *florin*. Clearly, there was an issue of *trust* of the public and the merchants in the institutions issuing these notes. In Sweden, for example, the Stockholm Bank separated the notes from the reserves of the bank and, consequently, the bank had to greatly increase the supply of money by printing "paper money," which was not guaranteed by reserves, and this led to the bankruptcy of the bank. In time, commercial banks learned not to issue banknotes without an adequate guarantee.

Nevertheless, the banknote and letters of credit were crucial instruments in the commercial *credit*, thus they revolutionized business activities on a global scale. They fostered an explosive growth in international banking and international commercial transactions. Thus, a unique paper note, inscribed with a promise to pay the bearer, enabled the golden future of imports and exports of goods across seas and oceans. This phenomenon has contributed—more than any other variable– to a dramatic increase in the quality of life of all the trading partners, and of large chunks of the world's population.

The Advent of the Telegraph and the Morse Code

In the early years of the nineteenth century, there was increased activity in the field of physics, electricity, and magnetism. British and American scientists had developed a single-circuit telegraph. This resulted in the establishment of a network of wires across countries and continents. In 1861, the Western Union Company completed the laying of the first American transcontinental line. In 1866 the first intercontinental telegraph line had been laid underwater across the Atlantic Ocean.

This technological feat had enormous social and economic impacts. News could now be exchanged almost instantaneously, and money could now be instantaneously wired, as a business transaction, across land and ocean.

But this was—in our current terminology—the *hardware* of the system. Samuel Morse and Alfred Vail created the Morse Code. This code was based on sets of dots (short marks) and dashes (long marks), allocated to letters by the frequency of their use. Indeed, the most famous message in Morse Code was "Save Our Souls" as: three dots (for S), three dashes (for O), and three dots (for (S): [• • • – – – • • •]).

The Morse Code was a new language, used as routine transmissions by, for example, ships at sea and their headquarters on land, and with other ships. Therefore, a small set of telegraph signals became the lifeline of people at great distances from each other. Without delay, military officers versed in the technology had adopted the code in their routine, as well as in their battle transmissions.

The Advent of Cell Technology and the Internet

The introduction first of the telephone network of land lines within countries and across seas and oceans, and then, led by the American National Science Foundation and the technology giant Motorola, the world witnessed the arrival of the Internet and the cell telephone technology. Ordinary people could now purchase a cellular phone (whose size had come down to that of a pack of cigarettes) and converse with anyone in the world. The quality of communication had also dramatically improved so that a conversation between Chicago and London became as clear as between two houses down the street. Cell towers appeared in every American and then world towns. Aesthetic challenges to the forest of towers from the municipalities quickly died down, as the improved cell communication technology allowed for unhindered and inexpensive telephone links in an enormous network within countries and between them, and within and between cities. The author warmly remembers the day when I was walking on a San Francisco street and, for the first time, calling my wife in a suburb of Chicago by using my cell phone. We conducted a conversation with the clarity of a link as if it were of only a few yards between us.

In mid-1970s, Professor Michael Radnor and I paid a visit to Martin (Marty) Cooper at the Motorola Tower outside Chicago. The purpose of the visit was to interview Marty, as part of a NASA-funded research project, aimed at a better understanding of how inventions are commercialized. Marty was very gracious with his time and proudly told us of his cell technology project. As the "father" of the cell technology, his enthusiasm of his creation was contagious. I began to share with him the vision of cell towers in every town and of the fantastic ability to carry your telephone with you across town, state, and even internationally, and to place calls to whomever and wherever on this globe you desire.

Indeed, four decades later, Marty's dream has come true. The advantages of the cell phone had become so ubiquitous that they had contributed to a richer daily life, and to the extent that people who use cellular phones can hardly imagine what was life before their appearance. These days you can hardly imagine leaving home without a cell phone. In the process, citizens who use this technology had also lost some of their privacy. Cell technology, for example, allows parents to track their young children when they are with their friends, shopping at the mall, or out on a date. It also allows government agencies to track the whereabouts of citizens, as the saying goes: “you can run, but you can’t hide.” This cell technology quickly spread around the word. When my wife Betsy and I visited Israel, we boarded a bus from Tel Aviv to Jerusalem. We noticed that all but one passenger of the full bus was on the cell phone, conducting a conversation.

CHAPTER 7

Beyond Business Analytics and the Pursuit of World Peace

Every so often in the history of the human race there comes a time when the era is defined as "uncertain," "threatening," or a "national nightmare." To paraphrase Charles Dickens: It was a bad time, it was a terrible time, and it was a very frightening time. The United States found itself faced with an economic slowdown and, at the same time, challenged with the horrors of a viral pandemic COVID-19 of the Corona species of virus. All over the country breadlines suddenly appeared and they seemed to multiply, reminiscent of the depression years of the late 1920s and early 1930s. The mood of the populace had acutely deteriorated. Hope has been knocked out of those with a job, and especially the jobless desperately looking for one.

The time when this chapter was written (2021 A.D) was a different time than those that came before it. Nonetheless, it was also a time of marvelous inventions in medicine and other areas of human enterprise. There was a heartwarming cooperation among peoples of all races, national origins, and economic backgrounds, all combined to defeat the horrific infectious disease pandemic. It was also a time when the leading nations on this earth conjured military budgets that far exceeded domestic expenditures that were originally designed to support, feed, and vitalize the middle class and the less fortunate economic classes. It was a time to shine, and a time to fade. It was a time for joy, and a time for sadness. Yes, it was my time. Fortuna perhaps smiled on my compatriots and on

E. Geisler, *Beyond Business Analytics*,
https://doi.org/10.1007/978-3-030-43718-3_7

me, or we had somehow upset her. Anyway, it was an interesting time in the life of our country and in our lives.

I am quoting here from O'Henry (1918) in his book*: Cabbages and Kings*: *from the Walrus and the Carpenter*: "The time has come," the walrus said "to talk of many things, of shoes and ships and sealing wax, and cabbages and kings."

My interpretation of this quote is that O'Henry is a product of his time. The horrors of the First World War had begun to seep into British society. In this war, many of Britain's aristocrats went to fight as officers. Too many of them had died or were terribly wounded alongside their men. In the trenches, the bullets, the bayonets, and the gas thrown at them had a unique attribute of bringing officers and men together, and to an extent, shatter the class divides.

O'Henry suggested that conversations in Britain's *polite society* and in society in general, were not restricted any longer by class lines nor by the protocols of social behavior which dominated the British society until the world war, or as it was called; "The War to End all Wars."

Moreover, in many instances, the friendship between aristocrats and the other classes of the veterans of the war—which was forged in war—had evolved into such joint activities as business partnerships and inter-class marriages, among those who returned from the war.

The veterans from this "war to end all wars' truly believed in an enduring peace. Why, they reasoned, would any person with some understanding, caring, and compassion, support such a horrendous idea as another war? The generation of the 1920s, all over Europe and the United States, wanted a life of pleasure and tranquility, marked by what they called the "art nouveau" in architecture, engineering, and the arts themselves. Their world was simple, although rich with a booming business environment and an explosive upwards of a fantastic stock market. The problems and the suffering of millions of Germans—encumbered with reparations from the first war—and on the other side of the Atlantic, their friends the Americans also witnessed a collapsing economy as they saw their stock markets collapse. In one fall day in October 1929, the world's economies essentially expired, and not one leader and their advisers knew why, let alone how to repair it. The English economist John Maynard Keynes argued for massive government "borrowing" and spending, but this was a notion which ringed like an anathema in the ears of the conservative Europeans, as well as the Americans.

There was, then, total disconnect between "Analytics," which meant the data collected by governments in Europe and the United States on the horrors of the "economic depression"—and the modes and means to overcome it. Unemployment rocketed, and was well-documented as a statistic by the governments. As the Russian dictator Stalin once said: "A single death is a tragedy. A million deaths is a statistic." However, the theories to overcome the depression were isolated in the impenetrable halls of Academia. The world's problem and its possible solutions could not come to the table of resolution. Academics and politicians did not exchange ideas, did not cooperate, and did not work toward a common solution. Therefore, the economic depression had to come to its natural end, while devouring on the way millions of unemployed, impoverished, and hungry citizens.

A similar scenario had occurred in the early decades of the twentieth century. Several physicists in Europe and in the United States had arrived at various solutions to the Physics problem of the day: how to split the atom and safely release the incredible energy it possesses inside. Following Professor Albert Einstein's ideas in his theory of relativity, theoretical physicists had correctly assumed that such "fission" is feasible. Top universities in the United Kingdom, Germany and the United States entered into a "race" to be the first to build a nuclear cell and thus to test and to prove the existence of such power. In the United States, there was a group of scientists who sought refuge from the emerging horrors of the Nazi and Fascist regimes in Germany and Italy, and who now held research positions in various American and British universities. After 1940, when Hitler's troops overran Europe, nuclear scientists from Italy (Enrico Fermi; Bruno Rossi), Denmark (Lise Meitner and Niels Bohr), Hungary (Louis Szilard), Germany, and Poland (Hans Bethe. George Kristiakovski; Victor Weisskopf; Stanislaw Ulam; and Otto Frisch) emigrated to the United States where most of them joined the "Manhattan Project." They helped to accelerate the design and construction of nuclear devices, so that two such bombs were developed and constructed in time to be used against the Imperial Japanese Empire in the cities of Hiroshima and Nagasaki.

It was due to the effort of the indefatigable American General Leslie Groves that this bunch of celebrated nuclear scientists were brought together to a military base at Los Alamos, New Mexico. Under strict military surveillance and secrecy, they feverishly worked to design and build the first nuclear bombs. General Groves managed the administration and secrecy functions of the base, while Professor Robert Oppenheimer, the chief scientist, managed the scientific and technical aspects of the mega-project.

There were very few such superhuman endeavors in recent history. It is worthwhile to list the Berlin airlift of 1948 and the "race to the moon" in the 1960s. Like the "Manhattan Project," these super projects required unparalleled dedication, ample funding, unrelenting support from the highest political echelons in the country, and a committed "brain power" of scientists, engineers, and technical teams, all of whom were willing and ready to take on such projects, and to continue supporting them despite technical and economic difficulties.

On War and the Pursuit of Peace

It has long been established that in the annals of human history the declaration and initiation of war has been easier to start than to end the military hostilities. Wars tend to explode in a self-combustion manner. Like in an internal combustion piston, given the right ingredients in the same place and inevitably combustion occurs. In the case of human events, chaos ensues. War is also easier to spread and to engulf additional participants. Throughout the story of humanity, when populations who had inherently conflicting issues that came in close proximity, there was an explosion that devoured the populations. A comparison can be made with radioactive materials. When held close to a human being, the alpha, beta, and especially gamma radiations which emanate from the radioactive material, will attack the human cells and cause irreparable damage.

In the course of history there have been events which exemplified the quest for peace and the struggle of unique people who became the leaders of the movements to obtain such peace. Among the salient figures of such episodes was Mohandas Karamchand Gandhi. Born in 1869 in Porbandar, in Gujarat, on the west coast of India, he was an attorney trained in England. Gandhi called for non-violent protests ("Satyagraha" meaning in Sanskrit and Hindi: "holding unto truth") aimed at the end of the colonial regime of Great Britain in India. For his non-violent campaign against the British he was lovingly named by his people the Mahatma, or "Great Soul." When the British decided to leave India in 1948, Gandhi tried to reconcile the Hindi majority in India and the Muslim majority both to the east and to the west of the subcontinent, in what they named

Pakistan. The partition of India between the Hindi and Pakistani inhabitants resulted in great movements of populations, and much resentment in both quarters. Gandhi was assassinated in New Delhi on January 30, 1948.

About 8031 miles to the west lies the city of Memphis, in the state of Tennessee, United States. Almost 20 years after Gandhi's assassination, on April 4, 1968, the leader of the civil rights movement in the United States, Dr. Martin Luther King was assassinated in Memphis. Dr. King, like Gandhi before him, advocated non-violence, and the use of peaceful demonstrations against the prevailing discrimination of African Americans in the Southern states of America, as well as throughout the country. History witnessed the killing of two magnificent human beings, simply because they objected to injustice and wished for a more just system of government for their homeland. For Gandhi this meant the end of the Raj and the departure of the British from India, and for Dr. King it was changes in the legislation at the states and federal levels, as well as changes in the attitudes of his fellow citizens toward their neighbors and friends of a different skin color.

Dr. King and the Mahatma Gandhi exemplify the human spirit at its best, when it revolts, without violence, against discrimination of all types and sources. Wherever there is wrong being committed, there are those among us who rise up and protest, until such time when the wrong is corrected or eliminated from our lives. This was the aim of the two civil resisters, in two very different parts of our globe.

Dr. King and the Mahatma also shared other characteristics: first, they had no party affiliation. The Mahatma had worked with the senior officials of the Congress party (such as Nehru and Patel), but did not see the party as his platform to influence the people of India. Second, neither held an elected official position in the government of their country. Third, neither had a dedicated organization under their command, and fourth, both led an uphill battle against a discriminatory regime. Finally, at the height of their campaign's achievement, both had a tragic end at the hand of an assassin.

On the other side of the human experience there is war. Declaring war has always been a less-difficult decision by the military and political leaders of the belligerent country. Its population was more apt to support "going to war" than being mobilized by the peace seekers for the enactment of peaceful projects. These populations were mostly driven by hunger for action, for revenge, or simply for the release of pent-up energy which was, until now, held back by their cautious leaders and their cool-headed advisors. In modern times the declaration of war has become a complex ritual undertaken by the supreme political leadership of the country about to initiate hostilities. This ritual was shared by the supreme military and political decision-makers of the country about to become the recipient of the military destructive power of its agitated adversary. In one example, the leaders of the Imperial Japanese Empire in December 1941 had tried to time their surprise air-attack on the American base in Pearl Harbor with a declaration of war on the United States, to be handed by the Japanese ambassador to the United States, Kishisaburo Nomura, unto the hands of Cordell Hull, the American Secretary of State. The attack was planned to begin *after* the handing of the declaration of war. If the surprise attack would occur before the declaration of war is established, this attack would be considered by the United States and the civilized nations an act of cowardice by the attackers.

However, the Imperial Japanese embassy in Washington was too slow in translating and preparing the 14 points of the Japanese cumbersome declaration. By the time the Japanese ambassadors Nomura and Kurusu had arrived at the State Department, over an hour has passed and cables received by the American government from Hawaii had verified undoubtedly that Pearl Harbor had been bombed by the Imperial Japanese Air Force with hundreds, perhaps thousands of American casualties. When Admiral Isoruku Yamamoto heard of this delay in handing the formal Japanese declaration of war, he is said to have commented: "all we have done was to wake up a sleeping tiger and to fill it with enormous resolve." The next day President Roosevelt asked the American Congress to officially declare war on the Empire of Japan with a moving speech. The American Congress obliged and from that day forward, a state of war existed between the United States and the Empire of Japan until Japan unconditionally capitulated in 1945.

Nevertheless, the American political leaders had to articulate to their constituents the reasons for any policy they will implement that will mean military involvement to a full engagement, thus leading to a global war. The British Prime Minister Winston Churchill, in his orations from the British Parliament and on the British Broadcasting Corporation radio network, told his country that he had nothing to offer them but blood, sweat, and tears. He also articulated the aim of the war, declaring it to be the total capitulation of the enemy. This meant no negotiations with the enemy. Churchill's prose represents, to this date, a classical example of "beyond analytics." After the British government, led by Churchill, had considered the economic, military, and political variables of a total war without even discussing the possibility of a negotiated peace, they took the position of "beyond analytics" whereby they introduced into the decision process on the conduct of the war the extraneous elements of "fighting a brutal regime" and "working to free Europe from the horrors of such a political, racist, and military dark cloud that covered the entire European continent." Winston Churchill's speeches were able to convert these high concepts into simpler notions that were better and easier to understand by the masses of his country. So, when the British Isles were mercilessly attacked by the Luftwaffe on a daily basis, and thousands of British citizens were killed, maimed, or left homeless, these citizens saw their resolve increased. Churchill's prose of their valor and sacrifice continually influenced their sentiment so that they could live with the psychological and the physical horrors of a prolonged state of war.

Similarly, American President Franklin Delano Roosevelt had early on in the conflict decided on a policy of total assistance to Great Britain in its struggle against Fascism and Naziism. He explained it to his people as the United States assuming the global position of "the arsenal of democracy." Its limited role would be to arm and to fully support, with money and materiel, the European democracies in their struggle against the oppressive regimes of Germany and Italy. This program was named "lend-lease." It was designed to supply Great Britain with all it needs as a transaction of "cash and carry." This was aimed at circumventing the Congressional ban on direct help to the European belligerent countries.

In his fireside chat of December 29, 1940, President Roosevelt explained the program, which lasted from 1941 to 1945. He argued that if your neighbor's house is on fire, he needs a water hose to fight the fire. If you had such a water hose you will not ask your neighbor to pay for it now, while his house is burning. As a good neighbor, you will lend it to him with the proviso that he will return it to you in the same condition as given to you, or if consumed by the fire that he will compensate you with the cash equivalent.

Great Britain was out of cash, so Prime Minister Churchill gave the United States—as a collateral for the lend-lease loan—the British bases in the Bahamas, all in the framework of a straightforward commercial real-estate transaction.

Within our understanding of Beyond Business Analytics, Great Britain offered the United States not only a commercial guarantee for the massive loan, but also a slice of the lands of the British Empire. This act meant that there was a *spiritual aspect* in the fact the United Kingdom separated itself from its venerated empire, which they had built for over three centuries, and which was now punctured and where a piece of it was to be given to another country. Yet, Great Britain was undergoing an existential threat, thus necessitating highly unusual means to fund its struggle.

Moreover, it has long been established that it is easier for the political leadership to explain expenditures and a gross national effort—all directed toward the conduct of the war—rather than explain such expenditures for a peaceful endeavor. The war effort is relatively simple: the country must expend such resources in order to survive. If the country resolves not to make such monetary and economic sacrifices, it may end up subjugated to another country, or vanquished and perhaps even destroyed in a war. During the Second World War, the Western Democracies witnessed the subjugation by Germany of such countries as Norway, Denmark, The Netherlands, Belgium, Czechoslovakia,

Eighty years later, on November 7, 2020, Dana Milbank penned an opinion piece in the Washington Post: "Our Long National Nightmare is Over." Milbank gladly welcomed the election of the democratic candidate Joseph Biden. He praised the task of the president-elect as "ousting a demagogue with the loudest megaphone in the land." Such a task was undoubtedly not an easy undertaking.

In addition to the four years of the Trump presidency in which his opponents claimed that he had willingly introduced to the nation a culture of disinformation and falsehoods, the more important and harmful act of his presidency had been the systematic disengagement of the United States from its international participation and from its obligations to key global organizations, and from its leaving the bilateral and multilateral agreements which previous presidents had signed with other world powers.

This action of "leaving" the various global institutions has brought the world ever closer to the perils of possible conflicts. In 2020, the Bulleting of the Atomic Scientists moved the "Doomsday Clock" up to 100 seconds closer to midnight (the presumed end-of-the-world) because of threats from a new bellicose world introduced by the Trump administration and fueled by disregard to possible nuclear conflicts, climate change, and a global state of disinformation. Most of all, the United States has curtailed its funding of various international organizations. On May 19, 2020, Mary Louise Kelly of the National Public Radio has reported an interview with Philip Rucker of the Washington Post regarding President Trump's announcement: "Today, I am instructing my administration to halt funding of the World Health Organization." President Trump had also threatened to cut federal funding to the Center for Disease Control and Prevention (CDC&P). Mr. Rucker commented: "And what we have seen in a pattern in this presidency is that Trump will make these big, bold, bombastic threats in order to gain leverage in the middle of a negotiation or to draw attention to himself, but then rarely actually follows through."

Yet, the pronouncements of the president of the United States on the global scene have already been taken with respect and trust by the leaders of other countries. After all, the United States is the only super-power in today's world—both as an economic giant and as the only remaining military leader. All nations routinely adjust their political and economic positions to those of the United States. Thus, when the leader of the free world changes position or makes a declaration of intent or policy, the world's leaders listen and act appropriately.

However, the November 2020 elections in the United States favored former Vice President Joseph Biden. The new president has made several announcements and he has thus begun to restore the international linkages of the United States in global organizations, and, true to his word, he sharply increased the United States' active participation in world affairs and in world institutions.

It is therefore abundantly clear that when four years earlier the United States had abandoned its leadership position in world organizations, including in defense organizations such as NATO (North Atlantic Treaty Organization), such a withdrawal represented a shift in world's affairs, and a threat to world peace. The plan by President Joseph Biden to reestablish these vital global connections has attenuated some of the fears of world leaders. Nonetheless, history has shown us (as in the case of the League of Nations) that a country's membership in such international institutions is not a guarantee that such country will not engage in hostilities at some point in its future, when the umbrella organization fails to make world peace a permanent state of global affairs.

Although all over the globe level-headed human beings strive, hope, and work for peace, what exactly is this notion of "world peace" and why is it so worthwhile as to make people aspire to it, to struggle for it, and to make it happen at much effort and cost?

The Eight Components of the Notion of "World Peace"

Recently there has been a resurgence of the belief that human beings are "hardwired" to constantly and violently exhibit belligerent behavior which leads to conflicts. This is based on a belief that world peace is an outlier in the human experience. Among the reasons given for such conflict-generating behavior is the need of human beings to acquire scarce resources for the survival of the species. These resources are considered to be few in existence and difficult to get, hence the state of permanent conflict in human relations.

I strongly disagree with this belief. Here is why:

(a) Through mutual agreements: human beings have always dealt with the challenges of acquiring scarce resources for their sustainability and for their survival. In order to accomplish this daunting task, they had to resort, among themselves, to a set of complex promote and enhance their relationships, mutual understanding, cooperation, and mutual agreements, beyond the limitations of familial, tribal, or civilization, aimed at keeping such resources within the community, human beings understood, early on, that, as a community, they have to go beyond their internal rules and procedures and work hard to make such external relationships a success.

(b) Through cooperation: since antiquity there was cooperation within and between tribes and nations. Working together proved to be a better way to marshal one's resources and to make them more productive by complementing one's shortcomings with the resources of the other party. For example, a tribe that controlled a waterway would rather accept a tax or fee for crossing from other tribes, than to engage in violent confrontations every time someone from another tribe showed up to cross the waterway.

(c) Through management: since antiquity human beings opted for the installation and the preference for central authority to store and to distribute limited resources (such as grains) to the highest number of the population—hence the advent of kings and central rulers. This political system allowed for a more centralized, hence more just and more equitable system for distribution and for adjudication in cases of conflict.

(d) Through agreements: since antiquity, in addition to tribal and familial relationships, governments made commercial agreements to conduct their affairs without interruptions and conflicts. This legal arrangement allowed governments to create an umbrella platform into which they could enter a new and more specific agreement. This system allowed for a free flow of commerce, imports and exports of goods and services, and the collection of rents from people on the move (for example: charging fees for crossing bridges and roads built and owned by a certain tribe, a municipality, a county, or a nation, such as the King's Roads).

(e) Through the understanding that peace is better than war: since antiquity, nations and their rulers have realized that peace is a better state of affairs than war. In the minds of many rulers their experience with peace outweighed the costs, pain, and disasters of war. They understood that wars invariably lead to interruptions in agriculture, so that crops would rot in the fields, and food shortages and famine would be disastrous, albeit a common occurrence. We believe that wars in antiquity were conducted away from centers of populations (unless war meant the siege of a fortified city). Hence, although conducted elsewhere, wars nonetheless had some impact on the "home front." Indeed, the home front also did suffer for lack of male workers and for shortages of food and other subsistence and raw materials which had been earmarked for the front lines. In many cases when the enemy laid siege upon a city, hunger, thirst, and disease were the main reasons for the capitulation of the besieged city.

(f) As stated above, there were also destructive psychological effects on the population in the home front. This manifested itself in psychological symptoms such as apprehension, fear of the future, uncertainty, depression, and the deep sentiments of lamenting the absence of the young males. These feelings engendered wounded spirits in the home population. A marvelous example from over two thousand years ago is Homer's saga: the Odyssey. This Greek masterwork narrates the aftermath of the siege of the city of Troy by a league of Greek cities, led by Agamemnon. In this story, Odysseus, king of the city of Ithaca, had excelled himself in the lengthy multi-year war, by inventing the concept of the enormous wooden horse given as a gift by the Greeks to the citizens of Troy. The structure of the horse was too big to enter through the gates

> of Troy, so the trojans left it inside their famously unconquerable walls, after a night of festivities and drinking. Odysseus had hidden many of his soldiers inside the horse. At night, the soldiers came out of the horse and rushed toward the gates, and opened them from inside. Thus, by connivance and trickery, after many years of siege, the Greeks conquered Troy.

Because of his bravura in the war, Odysseus was punished by the Greek Gods. His return voyage to his home kingdom of Ithaca ended up being a very lengthy travel experience of several years. The absence of the glorious king from his city-kingdom has caused much discontent and sorrow among the population of Ithaca, not the least the emotional pain inflicted upon Odysseus' wife Penelope, who was confronted by many suitors, in a constant struggle to protect herself and her kingdom.

In recent times we have also experienced the need to confront the possible Armageddon which may happen when countries with adversarial political, religious, and economic systems had all acquired weapons of mass destruction. This is the confrontational situation called: "Mutual Assured Destruction" or (MAD). Hence, these countries were forced to negotiate and to forge bilateral and multilateral agreements which would prevent the unleashing—by mistake—of a catastrophic and unintended all-engulfing war, that would undoubtedly result in total and utter annihilation of all the parties to the conflict.

Perhaps the most eloquent encapsulation of these components of peace was embedded in the "peace speech" that President John F. Kennedy gave on June 10, 1963, at the graduation ceremony of American University, in Washington, D.C. Kennedy argued that "genuine peace must be the work of many nations as mutual tolerance." He then added the very powerful and conciliatory tone of his speech, as a magnanimous overture to the Soviet Union and its leader, Secretary General Nikita Khrushchev:

> For in the final analysis, our most basic common link is that we all inhabit this small planet, we all breathe the same air, we all cherish our children's future, and we are all mortal.

Therefore, the notion of peace is a complex concept that is virtually imposed on humanity because people all over the globe share not only the earth's resources (such as breathable air) but also the human attribute of caring for your children and of cherishing their future.

10 Steps to World Peace

1. Stamp out exclusion {
2. Establish true equality between men and women { **QUANTATIVE MEASURES**
3. Share wealth fairly {
4. Tackle climate change { (HOW MUCH/MANY?)
5. Control arms sales {

xxxxxxxxxxxxxxxxxxxxxxxxxxxxxxxxxxxxxxxxxxxxxxxxxxxxxxxxxxxxxxxxxxxxxxxxxxxxxxxx

6. Display less hubris; make more policy changes {
7. Protect political space {
8. Fix intergenerational relations { **QUALITATIVE MEASURES**
9. Build an integrated peace movement {
10. Look within { (HOW WELL?)

Some Contributions of the Notion of Peace to Our World

I now propose that the notion of world peace may be structured so as to contain eight components. Consequently, the following eight scenarios may emerge, delineating the contributions of World Peace to the self-preserved global society, economy, and humanity:

1. Peace foments the growth and the acquisition of additional resources, thus increasing the quantity and the usefulness of a country's resources. War, on the other hand, depletes human resources and other assets, all of which could be used for more productive tasks, which will benefit the general population—instead of being squandered for the sake of useless confrontations.
2. Peace foments the relatively free and equitable exchanges of goods, services, and talented people which add to the wealth and the welfare of all the parties involved.
3. When the men of the country are not called to military action, to thus be decimated and mutilated by war, the inevitable growth in

the male population will certainly lead to its more diverse utilization in the marketplace, thus benefitting a plethora of professions and specializations. These will enormously benefit the economy by creating new technological projects and a flourishing of innovations.

4. The maintenance of the ruling class. This scenario may exist because throughout history this class was composed of males trained in knowledge of martial command, and because many of them served in command-and-control positions so that fewer members of this class were killed in battles. Therefore, instead of going to war, they can use these skills to be of service in their own communities by aiding and policing their fellow citizens, thus contributing to the maintenance of harmony and goodwill in their communities.
5. The establishment of commercial treaties with specific clauses for mutual security.
6. The establishment and management of joint projects and enterprises.
7. Peace was never an alien condition for humans. On the contrary, I believe that peace is innate in human ability to cooperate with other humans. If this were not the case, the human race would have exterminated itself several thousand years ago. For their survival, humans are endowed with the capability to discern the need for cooperation and the value of the status of the lack of hostilities in order to overcome the perils in their environment and the changes in conditions surrounding them, including changes in climate and changes in the fauna and flora around them. The fauna and flora were food sources for humans therefore they were crucial for the survival of the human race, and humans became experts in closely monitoring them. At a given point, quite early in our evolution, humans began to domesticate and husband animals for heavy work and for food, and turned to agriculture to grow grains and fruits as a source of vegetable protein and other nutrients, in a clever way to counteract periods of "feast or famine." This innovative event allowed humans to enrich, with agricultural outcomes, their unreliable and their previous people resource-demanding carnivorous diet from hunting. It also allowed humans to form more complex societies which now could be fed regularly, since the introduction of planning into the agricultural effort provided humans with the much-coveted ability to "plan" for periods of famine and to develop mechanisms and processes to successfully store the grain for many

months, even years. In a twist of the mixing of reality and religion, the ancient Egyptians discovered the ability of cats to keep mice and rats at bay, so they could not enter the grain repositories and engorge themselves with the crucial Egyptian commodity. Thus, cats were much revered in the Egyptian pantheon of religious deities.

8. A notable improvement in the spirit of the population may appear in those segments of the population that are happier and that have a very optimistic view of the future. This phenomenon is manifested in a strong belief in a prosperous future, and the willingness of the adult population to increase the size of their families and to invest in longer-term activities, such as education and the training of a standing army. The managing elites of these populations thus encouraged their people to include long-term projects in their portfolio of endeavors and programs. These included expensive multi-year public programs of building magnificent cathedrals, temples, and palaces, and, for the general population they built parks, squares, gardens, and other facilities where the citizens could congregate to worship, conduct commerce, and have beautiful areas designated for their family's enjoyment. A visit to Granada and other former Muslim territories and cities in Spain show with abundant clarity the superior urban planning of the Moors, with their attractive architectures of public gardens and the extraordinary use of flowing water within these gardens.

Indeed, these conditions may have generated a strong sense of willingness in the population to support such activities. For a recent example consider the case whereby the popular spirit was also lifted as the American population witnessed the emergence of a vaccine against the coronavirus. More specifically, during the 13th and 14th of December 2020 the entire United States' population witnessed the televised broadcast of the nationwide shipments of the first vaccine to vaccination centers by FEDEX cargo airplanes and UPS trucks. When the trucks and the airplanes took off for their destinations, there was a widespread national jubilation and the belief in the population that the nation has been able to move forward on the road to vanquish the pandemics.

It is abundantly clear that the eradication of a pandemic does contribute to the pursuit of world peace (as well as to economic growth). It would be impossible to enter into negotiations on achieving world peace, while the pandemic is ravaging the population centers of so many cities and countries worldwide. The first priority of the governments of these nations would definitely be to deal with the task of eradicating the pandemic, and then, and only then, to discuss world affairs with other governments.

Who in society, is pursuing world peace?

1. Heads of State
2. Politicians and office holders
3. Writers, philosophers, academics of all disciplines
4. Journalists, editors, and others working in the communications and telecommunications industries
5. CEOs, captains of industry, senior managers/executives of businesses
6. Civic groups
7. Religious groups and leaders
8. Political parties and their committees and sub-committees
9. Other economic, civic, political, social, environmental, etc., groups and committees.

The mixing of a diversity of people and organizations with different interests and raison d'etre that are actively pursuing world peace is a unique phenomenon whereby so many different organizations vying for the same objective, thus attesting to the strength of the cooperation of disparate organizations for the common good. The entities that pursue world peace are both public and private. They may not openly cooperate in this task, but they nonetheless work in their own manner, which happens to be in unison, under a similar drummer.

Beyond Business Analytics and the Pursuit of World Peace

The theoretical space occupied by the notion of Beyond Business Analytics is the space to be inhabited before we achieve some pursuit of world peace, but *after* we work with the notion of creating analytics (quantitative measures) of the effort that we expended to start the accumulation of these analytics. This is the notion or concept of "Beyond Business Analytics." That is, we have a given effort or a set of activities expended in a given project or program. As we collect the data for this project or program, there is also a benefit for us from such accumulation, because the data allows us to make valid analyses and to come up with value-judgements, so as to make worthwhile or "good" decisions, which are based on actual data.

For example, it was the Russian dictator Joseph Stalin who said: "A single death is tragedy; a million deaths is a statistic." His saying exemplifies the rift between the physical occurrence (what actually happened) and the cognitive reconstruction of the facts (whet we cognitively believe has happened). This cognitive process also applies in the case of evaluation of empirical data, including the evaluation of organizations. The notable examples are the work by Professor Donald Campbell and his associates in the 1970s and 1980s. They provided platforms for the evaluation of social and government programs such as Headstart and similar educational projects.

Historical accounts of large-scale wars have been shown to support the proposition that war or even a military conflict of a lesser scale is easier to start than to end with the establishment of peace. It is also easier to justify and to narrate and describe the events of war, than those of making peace. The conditions or circumstances that seem to promote the occurrence of military scenarios can thus be classified as warlike occurrences. Moreover, declarations of wars have normally encountered a willing and enthusiastic populations. Masses of people would stand and cheer when their national armies would march toward the battlefields. Similarly, upon victory, the victorious armies would return to their capital and march down the main avenues of their cities. Such a recent historical event was the march in Paris, in July of 1944, of troops from the anti-German coalition, upon the liberation of the French capital city from over four years of Nazi occupation.

Another salient example is Barbara Tuchman's masterpiece: "The Guns of August" (1962). She described in detail the events leading to the initial military operations that led to the eruption of the First World War in the summer of 1914. There was a complex interchange of communiques and a maze of activities in the main capitals of Europe: Moscow, Berlin, London, Paris, Rome, Vienna, Warsaw, and Prague. These events led to the mobilization of the armies of the key protagonists. Orders were sent from the capitals to the military chiefs of their armed forces, and those orders could not be rescinded.

The transportation ministries of the soon-to-be belligerent nations went into high alert and high-octane operations, by having trains, wagons, and trucks mobilized to transport troops, materiel, and equipment to the potential battle grounds. This was the shining moments of the Quartermasters of each of the national armies. In London, for example, the first Lord of the Admiralty, Winston Churchill, had ordered the mobilization of the British Royal Navy, as the initial step in the massive preparations for the oncoming war.

Once the first shot was heard and hostilities began, so did the nightmare of the two opposing armies in their maze of trenches, peppered with the inventions of the devil himself: the modern machine gun and the poisonous gas. The trench war would prevail for the next four years and three months. Because of the fact that the two opposing armies were deeply entrenched in their fortifications, they felt like the knights of Europe in the middle ages who had sought refuge behind the walls of their fortresses, their moats, and their archers. Alas, technology arrived with a vengeance. The artillery divisions of the opposing forces had gained added mobility across the battlefields, combined with the growing air power of the combatants and the growing effectiveness of their armored and motorized divisions, capable now of traversing the most difficult and inhospitable terrains. Thus, these technological and tactical improvements had led to a revolution in the use of mobile infantry, transported to the battlefields in trucks and similar motorized means of transport, and taking possession of territory previously bombarded by barrages of artillery and the armored divisions of tanks and half-tracks.

However, military hostilities did not just spring out of nowhere upon the opposing parties. They required careful planning and decision-making by the political leadership. Once the political leadership assumed control of the subject matter, they were also happy to add to their list of responsibilities the economic dimensions of their areas of jurisdiction. This brought about the mixing of financial decision-making and military decision-making. The culmination of such intermingled areas happened during the 1960s and the Vietnam War, when Defense Secretary Robert McNamara applied accounting and economic techniques embedded in the new field of operations research, to the decisions emanating from the Department of Defense.

This brings us to the topic of Beyond Business Analytics and the pursuit of world peace, as well as peace between individual countries in the form of bilateral relations. This aspect of the phenomenon of Beyond Business Analytics can be identified and even measured qualitatively by the actions and decisions made by the protagonists in these relations.

Business-like decisions are made by nations, as well as companies, and all possible combinations of organizations of all sizes and functions in the economy. That is, once the leaders of such organizations conduct an in-house analysis of the strengths and weaknesses of their organizations, the remaining space between such analysis and the ultimate goal or perspective of the organization (to excel or to achieve high levels of performance and productivity) becomes the "beyond" notion.

Simply described, the leaders or managers analyze what they have to offer and what they need in order to move their organization toward the goal or perspective that they desire. This means the space that emerges between the results of the analysis of the organization's strengths and weaknesses, and what is actually needed to reach the desired perspective. In most cases the analysis produces quantitative variables of interest, and beyond these variables the managers look for the relevant and appropriate qualitative variables which will constitute the focus of the concept of Beyond Business Analytics. After a manager answers such quantitative questions as "how much?" and "how many?" there emerge qualitative questions such as "how well?" "how effectively?" and "how successfully?" did the notion being analyzed achieve its goals.

There is seldom a direct and uninterrupted logical line between "how much"? (the resources or the total cost) invested in the endeavor, and "how well?" the organization achieved its goals (to what extent did the organization accomplish what it set out to do). For example, a company may devote large resources to its Research and Development department or division in the development of a new product. Starting with basic research, then moving on to applied research, then development, followed by design and engineering—only to find out that the market is either lukewarm to the new product or unwilling to accept it, regardless of the size and effort of the company's marketing campaign, and even the unique strengths and positive qualities of the product.

Commercial exchange is the lifeline of peaceful relations between countries and between companies. When countries or companies negotiate and conduct business deals of import–export, there is much effort and resources that had been invested in such relations. History has taught us that even when a country declares war on another country, some of its own businesses may decide to continue their commercial exchanges with the other country until such time as bellicose conditions irrevocably prevent the company from continuing its normal relations with the other country. The reasons for such behavior are several. First, such business relations become standard behavior for the company and an important component of its commercial portfolio. Second, there are costs associated with the severance of business relations, such as legal expenses, unsold inventory, and the need to market one's products to new customers. Therefore, companies will try to keep their business relations intact, for as long as possible.

CHAPTER 8

Beyond Business Analytics: How Good Products Made by Good Companies Fail in the Marketplace

This chapter examines the curious phenomenon by which perfectly good products and services fail in the marketplace. That is, these products are carefully planned, with rigorous market research, and made to specifications of quality of the highest order. Yet, when brought into the marketplace, these products fail, to the point where the companies that produced them have to withdraw them from the market, thus absorbing a loss to their bottom line.

As examples of such products, this chapter will examine two such products: the case of the Ford Edsel, as an illustration from the automotive industry, and the Sony Betamax recording device, as an illustration from the consumer electronics sector of the industry.

This chapter also examines the role that Beyond Business Analytics plays in the failure of these products. The chapter will initially show that the unforgiving failure of such good products from good companies is not an isolated incidence. Rather it is found in a wide variety of industries, as it may be compared to an infestation of a virulent disease within many industries and their companies. A key question will be asked in this analysis: why such products fail, and what role, if any, can be played by the method or platform of Beyond Business Analytics to diminish or even eliminate these mysterious failures.

E. Geisler, *Beyond Business Analytics*,
https://doi.org/10.1007/978-3-030-43718-3_8

Examples of Good Products that Failed in the Marketplace

As stated above, the failure of good products from good companies is not an isolated phenomenon. It vigorously applies to all industries. It is also abundantly clear that managerial wisdom and managerial actions have not been able to completely at least mitigate or control this phenomenon, or at best eliminate it.

Following is a list of 25 "worst" cases of the failure of good products in the marketplace. It appears that each scholar or business analyst has a personal list of preferred product failures. Nevertheless, there is somewhat of a sharing of the worst examples among the business analysts and business scholars. Thus, even though this list is my brainchild, many of the proposed companies in this list have also been selected by other analysts for their own lists.

One can therefore say that the identification of failure and even the degree of failure is in the "eye of the beholder," that is, the magnitude of failure is as perceived by the business analyst or business scholar. Moreover, on the other end of the equation, there is little discord among scholars as to the list of good companies. In many cases these "good" or successful companies suffered gravely from the failure of the said products and had to close their doors and abandon their position in the marketplace.

Here is an illustrative list of market failures of good products made by good companies.

1. Napster
2. Sony Betamax
3. Ford Edsel
4. DeLorean Car Company
5. Blackberry
6. Harley Davidson Perfume
7. De Havilland "Comet" passenger jet airplane (first flight in 7/27/1949; Retired in 1997, after 46 years of service)
8. AOL
9. Palm Pilot
10. Smokeless cigarettes
11. Cheetos lip balm
12. New Coke (1985)

13. Netscape
14. Windows 8
15. Myspace
16. Windows Vista (2007)
17. Google Glasses
18. Segway
19. QR Codes
20. Pebble (smart watch)
21. Mapquest (replaced by Google and Apple)
22. Virtual Boy (Nintendo game)
23. TIVO (Original DVR)
24. Kitchen meal entries made by Colgate
25. ET (Extra Terrestrials) video game by Atari.

Another interesting list is that of popular networks of stores, serving the consumers directly via their presence in shopping malls and Main Streets of American and worldwide cities. This is a list of 20 such popular stores, which saw their heydays in the 1990s, but which in 2021 no longer exist.

1. BLOCKBUSTER
2. BORDERS (BOOKS AND MUSIC)
3. CIRCUIT CITY
4. TOYS R US (BANCKRUPT IN 2018)
5. KB TOYS
6. THE LIMITED
7. LIMITED TOO
8. LINENS-N-THINGS
9. RADIO SHACK (BANKRUPT IN 2017)
10. SHARPER IMAGE
11. SPORTS AUTHORITY
12. TOWER RECORDS
13. VIRGIN MEGASTORE
14. WOOLWORTH (FIVE & DIME)
15. STRUCTURE (BECAME EXPRESS MEN IN 2001)
16. GAMESTOP
17. WALDEN BOOKS
18. SAM GOODY (RECORDS/MUSIC)
19. B DALTON (BOOKS)

20. KINNEY SHOES.

Examples of Companies that Failed Internationally

This is a set of companies that operated internationally. They had "everything going for them." Some of these companies continue operations in the United States and Canada, but their at one time ubiquitous presence in international markets is no longer the case.

a. **TARGET**: the American chain of stores of apparel had tried to penetrate the Canadian market. All seemed right, so that an expansion of the chain to the Canadian market seemed to be a natural progression of its strategic plan. The company's losses in this venture amounted to millions of dollars. The company had opened 124 stores at once, and was forced to close all its 133 Canadian stores. The reason was that Target had little time to develop its supply chain outside the United States, therefore it ended up with empty shelves and very little merchandise with which to attract customers.
b. **HOME DEPOT's** involvement in China had failed, primarily because the company did not nurture in the Chinese market the American custom of do-it-yourself renovation of one's home as a hobby. Without the influx of customers, the company lost over $150 million and had to withdraw.
c. **WALMART** in Germany had failed to consider the cultural idiosyncrasies of the German people. The company opened 85 stores in 1997, hoping to repeat its American success story as a discount chain of stores in the largest economy in Europe. However, the company had to struggle with the German restrictive labor laws, tight regulations, and limited business hours when its stores could operate legally. In 2006, after less than a decade, Walmart had to abandon the German market. The cost of the company's German adventure was almost one billion dollars.
d. **STARBUCKS** entered the Australian market in the year 2000. However, the initial hopes for a successful presence in this market had disintegrated within a few years, and in 2008 the company, without warning or a public announcement, closed its 61 stores and left the Australian market. The failure of Starbucks "down under"

was due to: (1) Australians already had an advanced coffee consumption culture; (2) the pace of expansion in the Australian market was too fast, without a clear plan of progressive growth in this market, and (3) the lack of effort by the company to adapt to the Australian ways of consuming beverages. Starbucks simply imposed its standard model which proved to be successful in North America and in Europe, without considering the specific needs and predilections of the Australian consumers.

e. **BEST BUY** in the United Kingdom was a good example of a company whose entry into an international market unfortunately coincided with a downturn in the global and in the British economies. Best Buy had a solid plan in its attempt to penetrate the British market. The company invested $1.3 billion in the British mobile phone company Carphone Warehouse, and it also planned to open 200 stores. However, economic realities forced Best Buy to sharply reduce its expected growth to 100 stores, then to 11 stores, which Best Buy also later decided to close due to disappointing sales figures. Unfortunately for Best Buy, the company decided to undertake its expansion at the height of the worst economic recession that gripped the Western economies. The loss to Best Buy from this failed enterprise was substantial, at over 300 million Dollars. Among the lessons learned by the company's management was their decision to scrap any additional plans of expansion into the international market.

Why Did They Fail?

There is not one overarching reason for the market failure of these good products made and marketed by good companies. Each of these products failed due to combinations of a few factors. These are discussed below.

1. *Timing* of the introduction of the product. Some products were introduced too early, and to a public which was not ready for this kind of product, or the public was waiting for another product to come along, perhaps with better quality or a better price.
2. Some *attributes* of the product did not appeal to the potential users. For example, Sony's Betamax could tape only one hour, whereas the VHS technology of JVS, Sony's competitor, could

tape up to two hours. In addition, JVC entered in agreements with stores that rented out these tapes to the wide population of users, thus creating a market for its VHS tapes. The Betamax product was thus not accepted by these chains of stores.

Another illustrative case is that of QR codes (Quick Response Codes) which are similar to a barcode. Although popular in Europe, the American market did not accept this product because customers found it to be ugly and jarring.

3. The *market was too small* with limited abilities to grow. For example, the case of the Pebble smartwatch is illuminating. Founded by Eric Migicovsky in the Netherlands, the company sold a million watches in 2014. In February 2015 the company introduced the second generation. However, the concept of wearing a computer on one's sleeve did not generate great appeal in the marketplace. It took real "aficionados" to desire such as device and to actually use it. Pebble was also threatened by Apple as a new arrival in the market segment of smartwatches. This is also a case in which first to market did not guarantee continuing dominance in the market (See also the cases of the Blackberry and the Newton described below).
4. The *product itself was defective*, such as the Comet De Havilland aircraft. This type of aircraft had suffered crashes that created an aura of a dangerous, even lethal product.
5. *Competitive pressures* by other companies had impacted the case of Pebble. In 2016 Pebble's rival Fitbit acquired the company for $40 million, and Pebble went out of business.
6. *Replaced by a more advanced, more attractive, or more user-friendly product or technology.* Examples are the blackberry, the Newton, and the Palm Pilot, and how Apple's iPhone substituted them. The story of the PDA (Personal Digital Assistant) stretches for almost two decades. In 2008 the Blackberry Storm was released. These devices, when they were still in the design phase, and up until their release into the marketplace, were at the front edge of innovation. Any revisions that Blackberry introduced into their devices were incremental improvements and they were also used to the fixing of any defects or bugs. Then came Steve Job's Apple. The product took the market by storm. The iPhone was not only a revolutionary product, but also had such features as a camera, which the owners

of Blackberry refused to install. The RIM company and its Blackberry line of PDAs were caught by surprise, and when they began to realize that Apple and the iPhone are taking over the market, it was too late for them to compete with Apple. The iPhone has many features and innovations for which consumers were impatiently waiting. This Apple product was a far cry from the existing competition in the marketplace, thus it had the power to gain a sustained position in the market.

7. *The product itself was not attractive* to potential customers/users because of insecurity (such as the Segway) or because of other attributes of the product. For example, Windows 8 was very business unfriendly. Its applications would not easily shut down, and its layout was very unfriendly to the users.
8. The product was a well-thought product *but its owners failed to properly manage it*. For example, Napster was for music file sharing, and was highly desired by consumers, especially the younger generation. Nevertheless, this product failed because its owners failed to transfer the copyright of the music across the network. Napster was challenged in the courts and in 2001 it had lost the legal battle and was forced to shut down.
9. Some products, such as American-made automobiles, *were designed for "planned obsolescence." The product had a "shelf life" or a "half-life" of a few years, after which the product began to deteriorate*. In the case of the "planned obsolescence" of automobiles made in the United States, other countries understood this mortal deficiency of the American manufacturing system as the supplier of a low-quality product. Thus, several European companies as well as Japanese, and thereafter South Korean firms began to compete with the Americans. The "big three" (Ford, GM, and Chrysler) in the American manufacturing scene were forced to innovate and fiercely compete with their newly arrived Asian and European competitors. The key driver for this action was the oil embargo and the shortages of the 1970s. The primary attribute of the competing cars was the size. American manufacturers had no choice but to follow the example of their competitors and to make smaller cars, thereby diminishing the role in the marketplace of the "gas guzzlers" large cars and trucks they had been used to manufacture and to market for several decades. One American company, American Motors, had to close its doors, whereas

the remaining automakers such as Chrysler, received very large and favorable government loans, which allowed them to continue their operation. Such novel government action of a "bailout," with emergency financial support of the carmakers caused an uproar in several economic and political segments of American society, who objected to government's policy of artificially "picking" the industry winners. Of note, Chrysler, under the efficient leadership of Lee Iacocca, indeed was able to repay the massive loan several years before the deadline.

10. Some senior managers decided to enter a market or to terminate a product in a given market based on a decision-making process which is flawed, because the managers infuse the process with their human biases. As described below, these managers make decisions based on their beliefs, their predilections, and their vision of what would be the impacts of their decision on their firm. There is an ancient Sanskrit saying: "Vinasa Kale Viba Reetha Pudthai" ("When time for your destruction is at hand, you take strange decisions"). This means that under a specific set of circumstances, the manager will make decisions that are influenced by such organizational events. For example, when the firm is about to undergo a review by a parent organization, the managers of the firm will do the best they can to make quick yet influential decisions that will allow the firm to present its best face. Another example is when the firm faces intensive competition. Its managers must quickly adapt and make the changes necessary for the firm to remain active and competitive in its market.

The Phenomenon of Cognitive Dissonance

Decisions to enter a market, to rightly price one's product or service and to leave a market are all made by managers who are human beings that are charged with the difficult task of navigating the organization through the hurdles and the vicissitudes of the turbulent marketplace. As humans they strive for consistency and stability in their environment. They look for harmony, where things fall in place and there is a logic to the behavior of the environment and of their competitors, consumers, regulators, and those firms that collaborate with them. When such consistency and stability are absent, the decision-makers experience the phenomenon of cognitive dissonance. First identified by Leon Festinger in the 1950s, this phenomenon suggests that when stability and consistency are absent, humans become distressed. This sentiment may cause biases in their reasoning and their decision-making. Following a decision that they make, these managers may experience a period of stress, while they question the validity of their decision, and the rationale that led to it. They make decisions that are geared to reducing their stress, rather than decisions that are made specifically to solve organizational problems.

Such bias in the decision-making process and in the behavior of the managers may lead to an overall failure of their product or service in the marketplace, and may even threaten the survival of their firms in the turbulent environment in which they exist. Cognitive Dissonance may lead to changes in their beliefs, their attitudes, and their approach to solving problems in their firms. Such changes may ultimately lead to wrong or premature decisions that are illogical, impractical, and for all practical purposes, inimical to the organization's survival.

The larger the firm, the more this phenomenon may be widespread, thus it may be more difficult to manage. In this case, the Beyond Business Analytics method may be highly beneficial to the firm, because it focuses on the behavior of the decision-maker, rather than solely on the decision itself. If the emphasis is the decision itself, there is no attempt being made to also focus on the business decision-maker. In this case the wrong decision lingers and becomes an integral part of the basic structure of the firm. Consequently, the more this wrong decision lingers, the more difficult it becomes to change it or replace it with a decision based on the human behavior of the decision-maker.

The View of the Press and Academia

When big and successful companies fail, this phenomenon ignites the interest of Academia, the public, and the press. In its edition of April 3, 2017, TIME magazine listed the most successful corporate technology failures. The list of 20 companies includes most of the companies listed in this chapter, such as Betamax, Netscape, Segway, Pebble, Mapquest, and TIVO.

A story about the Sony Betamax was authored by Fuller, Jones and Lukowski on December 6, 2016, in the publication: Applied Communication at UM-Flint. The authors described the events that made Sony the short-lived leader of the industry with their Betamax tapes, until the arrival of JVC's VCR technology and the VHS tapes.

The American press reported this Betamax-VCR phenomenon in a manner that harshly condemned Sony's Betamax product failure, while describing the winning technology of the VCR as a winner in an all-out war with Sony. Clearly, anytime that a giant electronics company, such as Sony, reportedly loses a marketplace battle with a smaller company, the press finds the phenomenon exciting and worthy of complete coverage, as perhaps the story of David versus Goliath. Clearly, we all root for the disadvantaged David.

It is abundantly clear that the case of Sony's Betamax and its failure, represents a classic illustration of a massive technology failure, by a company who "should have known better."

But companies sometimes hold on to a losing course of action, even though they are perfectly aware of other avenues for their planned action. Why, then, do these companies stick to a losing course of action?

Barry Staw and Jerry Ross published a revealing article in the Harvard Business Review in March 1987. The title was: "Knowing When to Pull the Plug." They argued that the following reasons can be offered for the choice of a course of action that calls for the termination of a project or a program in the organization. Staw and Ross start off by describing situations in which some managers "seem almost programmed to follow a dying cause." They continue by listing the evaluation of the project itself. That is, asking questions of the project such as is the project failing because of problems which were known to us, yet we, as managers, failed to take action or to prevent these problems from happening. Secondly, a project which absorbed a large chunk of expenditures is not easily terminated. These expenditures are considered like "lost leader" or "sunk costs," hence there has been too much of an investment in this project, so that regardless of the project's chances of success these costs are not a reason to terminate the project. Thirdly, managers are reluctant to propose terminating a project because of psychological issues. Managers who have a good career track record of managing on-going projects are aware of the potential damage to their inherent reputation in the organization as the manager who failed to effectively manage the project, or even the manager who killed the project. Simultaneously, taking a risk and then ending up a winner, because the project became a successful enterprise is a risk that many managers are willing to take. The other side of the coin is when managers may consider bad news about the project as their own personal failure, irrespective of the role that they played in the execution of their managerial tasks, and their contribution to the success or failure of the project. Thus, managers may continue to pour resources into the losing project, among other reasons, because they wish to prove to themselves and others, that they are running a successful project. Finally, there is an almost "taboo" on any mention of the word "failure."

In this regard, some years ago we conducted a research study of investments in several categories of R&D, such as basic, applied, development, and engineering. We used the methodology of a similar study by the Aston group in the United Kingdom. The methodology called for classifying the R&D projects in the company into two categories: successful and failures. When, however, we interviewed a representative sample of managers in the company, they easily identified those projects of theirs which were successful, but refused to identify even one project that failed. We found ourselves in a conundrum which threatened our methodology and our timeline for the research.

In the midst of our angst, I had an epiphany. Perhaps, I wondered, the differences we are examining are not contextual but linguistic. Thus, armed with this possibility, I then proposed to our team of researchers that we should change the nomenclature, from "projects that *failed*" ("we don't have any of those") to "projects that were *not so successful*" ("we have many of those"). The use of the attribute "failed" or "failure" became informally unacceptable or even forbidden in the corporate culture. One manager in this company explained to me that if R&D indeed called a failed project as having failed, the remainder of the company and particularly senior managers would be reluctant to continue allocating to the R&D function in the company the resources to which "they had been accustomed." Senior management would rationalize changes in funding for the R&D department by declaring that they will not continue funding a "losing department" in the organization. In one case, even one project which happened to be the "brainchild" of the Chief Executive Officer and was also his most favorite project, became a candidate for termination because of poor performance. The managers told us that, with the consent of the CEO, they placed this project "on probation" with the condition that if its performance will not improve in the next 6 months (or show a movement toward improvement) the system that evaluates R&D projects that they had designed and had used in the company for all projects, will indeed be applied to this case, and will probably recommend the termination of the project.

The Role of Beyond Business Analytics

In this particular case of projects that failed, the method of Beyond Business Analytics may serve as a monitoring device for the corporate R&D portfolio, and for and its technological development. This method takes us beyond the variables that describe the project, and into the space of: "what happens next." That is, what are the outputs and the consequences of the failure, to the people involved and to the organization. Has the failure influenced the company's managers to change their long-term policies? Has the failure influenced the company's managers to take action in the short term? Some possible actions include the termination of the R&D project, or at least in putting the said project in a list of projects under review, with possible terminations. In addition, some of the consequences of the failure may be a change in the degree to which corporate managers view such projects and their actual or potential contributions to the firm's performance.

This effect of the notion and the method of Beyond Business Analytics also manifests itself in the steps that the company takes to compose the list of "favorable" projects. A common action by the company is to enter into this list those projects which have a higher degree of probability that they will perform well, versus those projects with a low probability of being good performers in the marketplace. This method defines the performance of the R&D or technological department as a two-step process. The first step is answering the question: "Was the project *technically* successful?" The second step is answering the question: "Was the project *commercially* successful in the marketplace?". That is, a project may be a great success technologically ("we can do it"), but fail in the marketing effort of the company ("we cannot sell it"). This dichotomy of possibilities demands that the manager consider both the possible events.

This also means that the company will select the "winners" before these projects are tested in the marketplace. This is done by surveying managers and asking them to assign probabilities of success (technically as well as commercially) to the projects listed in a master list of the company. Those projects that don't "make the cut" are then candidates for termination. The business managers, in collaboration with the technical managers, decide on the hierarchy of this evaluation instrument, and where the "cutoff" point will be.

The method of Beyond Business Analytics emphasizes the decision space beyond the mere annotation of successful versus failing projects.

Once the variables of the degree to which the projects succeed or fail are established, the application of these variables moves down the road of scrutiny by the Beyond Business Analytics effort. In a way, it forces the organization to consider the effect of implementing the variables they had selected, so that the managers can ask such questions as: "what have we gained from applying these variables?" and "was it worthwhile to apply these variables, in terms of the organization's effort to perform and to survive in the complex and hostile business environment," and "what were the effects on the managers themselves: their performance, their attitudes, and their perceptions of the organization and its performance and growth."

Beyond Business Analytics is also a mechanism by which the organization is made aware of the data or information that it possesses and the data or information that it needs. In case the organization needs some given data or information, it then mobilizes its resources to obtain such data or information. Managers are well aware of the difficulties in compiling the data and information that their organization needs, and then looking for such data or information in the marketplace. Business Analytics is a mode by which the organization procures such data. The effort to identify such needs and to quantify them for data collection is done by the use of selected mechanisms such as those proposed by Michael Porter (market forces) and Robert Kaplan and David Norton (Balanced Scorecard). In general, the mechanisms proposed by Porter and Kaplan and Norton are descriptions of what the information or data dimensions are to be procured by the management of the organization. This step is of utmost importance, because, among other things, it allows the manager to succinctly go after specific information or data which will be useful for the manager's decision-making processes.

Beyond Business Analytics also leads the manager into the space of the qualitative attributes of the outcomes from the manager's application of decision-making techniques. As mentioned above, the manager is now able to ask questions beyond the ubiquitous query: "how many?", "how much?", etc. Now, the questions which may be asked are: "to what end?" "what was the value acquired with these variables?" and, more important, "how well are we doing and how well are we projected to be doing in the future?".

The aforementioned are questions that relate to the evaluative notions of the decision process. With this we embark on a wonderful journey the manager is able to make, into the area of inquiry which goes beyond the data, that is, beyond the qualitative as well as the quantitative data that describe the phenomenon. For example, suppose we are asked to determine the attributes of a certain building. We can come up with several such attributes as height (how many floors), width (what is the area of the street/s the building occupies), and how many units of space are there on each floor. However, these data do not answer such questions we usually have as: "what is the purpose of the building?" (e.g., is it commercial or residential); "why are there n number of floors?" (e.g., what is the purpose of that many or that few floors?) and "what kind of people or firms occupy the spaces in the building?" (e.g., manufacturing firms, versus storage facilities, versus offices).

This kind of data or information also gives us some inroads into the requirements that these firms would have in their use of space in the building. This means that the firms may require special access facilities such as large doors and elevators, or platforms for loading and unloading, as well as facilities for the people with disabilities such as ramps. Here, therefore, we must also take into account the requirements demanded by the Occupational, Safety and Health Administration, which is the federal agency in charge of safety and health in the workplace. OSHA would require specific standards for the attributes of the building, as well, for example, the type of flooring used in the facility that is non-skid type of flooring and non-skid stairs throughout the facility. Another such OSHA requirement would be the use of specific types of paint (e.g., lead-free). The overarching objectives of OSHA's requirements are the safety and health of the workers in the facility. Strict legislation assures the compliance of firms to these safety and health standards.

Beyond Business Analytics therefore takes us into the standards of usage and into the value of the facility under consideration, well beyond just the attributes of the facility (e.g., how big or how wide, or how it is structured or sub-divided). As listed above, it leads us to answers to questions such as what is the *purpose* of the facility? how *effectively* is it being used? and what *added value* does it provide to the owners and to the users of the facility?

Beyond Business Analytics does exactly what its name indicates: it answers *business* questions that have to do with the use and the value of the facility or the business phenomenon under consideration. We thus go beyond the descriptors of the facility to the value or to the commercial contributions that the facility provides. This, of course, applies to any variable that we are evaluating, such as the business firm and the industry to which it belongs, and the economy of a city, state, county, or country, or also to the not-for-profit organization.

The mere analysis of the phenomenon itself or the organization in which it is operating is not sufficient for a good grasp of the phenomenon. The analysis must be expanded to include the business attributes. That is precisely what the Beyond Business Analytics method provides.

In summary, the role of Beyond Business Analytics is to give the analyst and the manager a powerful tool for their understanding of how the phenomenon is occurring, and the behavior that decision-makers in the organizations should exhibit. All this should occur beyond simply the description of the phenomenon and its variables. Therefore, to understand why good products made by good companies fail in the marketplace, one has to expand the limits of the analysis to include the business aspects of this case, and to thus unravel the mystery of good products failing.

In the traditional market analysis, the focus is on the attributes of the marketplace and the consumers. The analyst observes the fluctuations in the behavior of the consumers, thus explaining why a product will be rejected by these consumers, regardless of its good qualities. Topics such as a change in fashion or taste of the consumers is a favorite explanation for the failure of the product (or service). Another is the appearance in the market of a competing product or service. The competition may be in price (offering the product or service at a lower price) or it may be in the attributes of the product or service such as more potential uses; more user-friendly design and operation of the product or service; innovations in the product or service that make it a new and attractive presence in the marketplace; and overcoming the resiliency of the existing product or service to the competing products or services by, for example, the users being accustomed to the product.

This latter phenomenon is also observed in the commercial applications of robots. Some years ago, there was a movement in the technological world to build and use robots for the office and the home, beyond their applications in industry. The prototypes of these robots, in their appearance, invariably resembled people. The reason was the need to create a situation whereby the user is familiar with the appearance of the robot, thus able to be at ease with its presence and its operation. This was particularly the case of the locomotion technology of these robots. They were bipedal, imitating the human legs, and their arms also imitated their human equivalent. Designers of robots confessed that it would be much more effective to build robots that move on wheels or on electromagnetic propulsion, and that have different arms, such as tongs, but no hands or fingers as humans have them.

Good products fail in the marketplace not solely because they are "not good enough," but mainly because of the idiosyncrasy and the eccentricity of the marketplace, which generally are not easily predicted. By the time the innovating company launches its good product with its innovative attributes, the market may have changed and moved on, so that the fashion, the predilection, or the taste of the consumers have also changed, and the new product or service is therefore essentially obsolete, and are unable to catch up with the changing characteristics of the market.

A good example is the case of Henry Ford's insistence on making his cars in the color black. When advised that consumers are desirous to have cars in other colors, Ford is said to have replied that they can have it in any color they want, as long as it is black. The consumers did not heed to Ford's advice and went elsewhere to General Motors and Chrysler for their colorful cars. When Ford was replaced at the helm of the company, the Ford Motor Company was able to join its competitors and offer its customers the kind of product they desired, and in the color they preferred.

But the case of the downturn of the automotive industry was not only in terms of the color of the cars. It was also the case of the size of the cars and trucks manufactured by the Detroit three giant automakers. When Japanese automakers began flooding the American (and worldwide) market with smaller cars, this was in the 1970s, in conjunction with the oil crunch of the era that was brought about by the boycotts of the petroleum producing nations (OPEC), which caused the long lines of consumers at the gas stations in the United States and Europe. American automakers insisted on making big cars, whereas the market had already decided on its preference for smaller, less gas-guzzling cars and trucks. Japanese imports to the United States dramatically increased throughout the 1970s. When, however, Ford and General Motors finally decided to manufacture small cars, they initially lacked the technological sophistication of the Japanese, thus they produced a series of "lemons."

Another marked difference between the Japanese and the American auto makers was the Japanese companies' preference for manufacturing quality vehicles. The Japanese resolutely rejected the American manufacturers' policy of "planned obsolescence," whereby the vehicles made in America had a "sunset" timeframe of a few years, after which the vehicles would essentially start to disintegrate, with selected parts of the engine and transmission simply failing, or even breaking, due to their use over the years. This policy has led to the consumer being forced to buy a new car every few years, or, as soon as the period of warranty of the manufacturer (usually one to three years) has expired, the consumer would be forced to spend thousands of dollars to keep the vehicle running.

In fact, a similar phenomenon also occurred in the area of rubber tiers for automobiles and trucks. The major tire manufacturers for cars and trucks, such as Goodyear, Pirelli, and Firestone, due to increased competition, were forced to improve the quality and the endurance or life-expectancy of their tires. Pirelli, the Italian tire maker was established in 1872, whereas BF Goodrich was established in 1870, primarily as a maker of tires for aircrafts; Goodyear in 1898; Firestone in 1900; Cooper in 1914; Bridgestone was established in Japan in 1931; Michelin was established in France in 1885; Dunlop was established in 1889 as a maker of tires for racing cars. These data show that the competition was worldwide, and the manufacturers which sprang in Europe and Japan, imposed a competitive threat to Goodyear, Firestone, and Cooper. The quality of the tires, heralded by Michelin, Dunlop, and Bridgestone, had forced Goodyear and Firestone to improve the quality of their tires and to abandon the notion of "planned obsolescence."

If American auto executives would have adopted early on the notion of Beyond Business Analytics, perhaps they would have been able to predict the need for certain policies and actions that would have been necessary to compete in the new marketplace, dominated by makers of smaller cars and trucks. Beyond Business Analytics would have allowed them to think beyond the quantitative aspects of their production policies of "planned obsolescence" and their marketing policies that neglected the consumers' predilections and their tastes and desires. In such a scenario, the automakers would have been able to take the human elements of their consumers into account, when making decisions about what type of cars and trucks to make and how, and also when, how, and to whom to market them. Although this analysis is complex—because it takes into account variables from several business phenomena—the analysis is nonetheless very feasible, since the analyst is equipped with the analytical tools of Beyond Business Analytics.

CHAPTER 9

Beyond Business Analytics: How Good Public Organizations Fail in Their Mission

Only those who will risk going too far can possibly find out how far one can go.

The previous chapter examined how and why good private companies fail in the marketplace. This chapter focuses on how and why public organizations fail in their mission. The public sector in the economies of the United States, the United Kingdom, Canada, and the democracies of Europe, Australia, and other nations is a substantial portion of these countries' national expenditures. When defense expenditures are included, the budgets of the public sectors of these countries take up over half of the Gross National Product. As the annual reports of the American National Science Board have consistently shown, the national research and development budgets are expended by both the civilian and the military sectors of the economy. However, a significant portion of these expenditures by the private sector consists of projects that the government procures with civilian laboratories and companies. Some of the larger companies in the United States, such as General Dynamics, General Electric, and Boeing, owed their consistent growth to the defense programs they conduct for the government.

In the history of the United States, there is an exceptional episode that occurred on January 17, 1961 when President Dwight D. Eisenhower, upon leaving the presidency, spoke of the emergence in the country of the threats of what he described as the military-industrial complex.

E. Geisler, *Beyond Business Analytics*,
https://doi.org/10.1007/978-3-030-43718-3_9

He said: “But now we can no longer risk emergency improvisation of national defense; we have been compelled to create a permanent armaments industry of vast proportions. Added to this, three and a half million men and women are directly engaged in the defense establishment. We annually spend on military security more than the net income of all US corporations. This conjunction of an immense military establishment and a large arms industry is new in the American experience. The total influence—economic, political, even spiritual—is felt in every city, every state house, every office of the Federal government. We recognize the imperative need for this development. Yet we must not fail to comprehend its grave implications. Our toil, resources and livelihood are all involved; so is the very structure of our society. In the councils of government, we must guard against the acquisition of unwarranted influence, whether sought or unsought, by the military-industrial complex. The potential for a disastrous rise of misplaced power exists and will persist. We must never let the weight of this combination endanger our liberties or democratic processes. We should take nothing for granted. Only an alert and knowledgeable citizenry can compel the proper meshing of the huge industrial and military machinery of defense with our peaceful methods and goals, so that security and liberty may prosper together. The prospect of domination of the nation’s scholars by Federal employment, project allocations, and the power of money is every present and is gravely to be regarded. Yet, in holding scientific research and discovery in respect, as we should, we must also be alert to the equal opposite danger that public policy could itself become the captive of a scientific-technological elite. It is the task of the statesmanship to mold, to balance, and to integrate these and other forces, new and old, within the principles of our democratic system—ever aiming toward the supreme goals of our free society.”

President Eisenhower had the advantage over other politicians in that he served both the military and the civilian arms of the nation. Therefore, armed with this dual and extensive experience, he unequivocally and forcefully warned the nation of the growing and already fearsome power of the combination and the inter-dependency of the Federal military establishment and the American industrial complex, the latter impatiently waiting for a share of the national budget in the form of projects deem necessary for maintaining a strong national defense. This meant that these companies of the military-industrial complex were charged with the design, testing, engineering, and construction of armaments and weapon systems for the American ground forces, the naval fleets, and the millennia air force. In 1961 there was the initial drive into space, which began with the establishment in 1958 of the National Aeronautics and Space Administration (NASA). The military projects built into the space effort would continue to support this activity well beyond the "putting a man on the moon and bringing his safely back" Apollo program, which was achieved in 1969. In the 1970s, however, the American public had shown symptoms of "space fatigue," to the extent that the allure of the space program had been tarnished, and the budgets for this effort had been curtailed. The planned landing of a man on Mars had to be indefinitely postponed.

These are some instances of other successful projects undertaken by government entities. Let's remember that the main reason for the government's intervention and application of its resources into selected mega-projects (such as the Manhattan Project, the nuclear submarine "Nautilus," and the Apollo program) was because private industry was unable, with its own slack resources, to engage in such long-term and expensive enterprises. Nevertheless, the Department of Defense and NASA had to rely on hundreds of private firms in order to make these projects viable and successful. The agency funded the R&D effort of these firms, as well as the construction of the space rockets, the space capsule, and all other installations designed for the training of astronauts and the launching of the massive rockets that would carry these astronauts to the moon and perhaps further away in our exploration of our galaxy.

However, the history of public funding of other mega-projects and other large-scale projects is strewn with cases where the government failed, and by failing had caused the partial or the complete failure of the mission and in many instances also the lives of the men and women who participated in these enterprises. Examples include the tragic accidents that cost the lives of astronauts when their capsule was destroyed by combustion, and the horrific accidents of the Challenger explosion a short time after its launch. This phenomenon of failures of missions and enterprises was particularly salient in times of war. The military tapestry of affairs is an excellent illustration of what went well and what did not in times of war. This is mainly because:

a. War is a well-defined enterprise, compared with other socio-economic programs. Theoretically it is carefully planned. War planners painfully understand that if one component of the plan fails, it may result in a series of disasters for the remaining components.

b. War is a totally consuming and highly integrative and time-sensitive activity. In war, various components of the armed forces have to work in cooperation, even in unison. If one component fails (for example lack of air cover for advancing ground forces) this may develop into a failure to complete the mission, and in casualties among the troops who counted on air support. Sir Winston Churchill recounts his experiences in the Second World War when the British evacuated over 300 thousand of their soldiers from the French beaches in Dunkirk. The ground troops, waiting for the boats and ships to ferry them back to England, suffered a constant barrage of German airplanes strafing them without opposition. What the ground troops did not see was the constant air battles between the German war planes and the Royal Air Force, which took place above the clouds. Both sides suffered considerable losses in pilots killed and aircraft downed. When the RAF personnel, in their blue uniform, would in the aftermath enter a pub in England, they were met with fury and accusations that they failed to appear and confront the German airplanes. When British Prime Minister Winston Churchill heard of it, he spoke to the nation in an effort to correct the misconception. He then uttered the famous words: "never in the field of human conflict, was so much owed by so many to so few."
c. War is the ultimate sacrifice and the deepest commitment of human beings to a cause. It is, in fact, a matter of life or death. In war all resources are applied, and all human endeavor is uniquely focused and dedicated to one proposition: to win the war.
d. War is a fountainhead of inventions and innovations, because of the need to apply all available talent to win it. Technological developments such as RADAR had their initial successful application in a war. Similarly, aerial photography, precision navigational instrumentation, tanks, submarines and underwater detection, aviation, avionics, and the use of jet technology in aviation, plus the beginning of rocket science, are but some of the innovations from the world wars of the twentieth century that could be and were converted into civilian uses. Perhaps, as some historians suggest, previous wars in Europe, such as the Franco-Prussian wars, did not produce significant innovations, primarily because these wars were limited to a certain region in Europe and to very few nations as combatants. The First World War involved almost every country

in Europe, Asia, Australia, New Zealand, and the Americas. The Second World War involved additional countries and truly encompassed the entire globe in this conflict, except for a few neutral countries such as Portugal, Switzerland, and Sweden.

The annals of military history are also replete with other cases of failures, particularly in the field of military engagements and the supporting activity of military intelligence. Here is a selective list of such military disasters, from antiquity to modern warfare. The interesting aspect of these cases—that ties them together as a unique phenomenon—is that in these cases the losing party was not expected to lose. Although not exactly a scenario of David vs. Goliath, these cases do approximate the fantastic encounter between the little Hebrew shepherd David and the enormous and well-trained Goliath, the hero of the Philistines. In the application of an analysis of military prowess, Goliath would invariably always come on top as the best bet for winning this encounter. In this case of David, the winning qualities of the shepherd boy were agility, innovativeness, and marksmanship. Here are the historical illustrations of dramatic failures that should not have happened.

1. The battle of Marathon in 490 BC: The Persians were vastly superior in every department, yet a small force of Greek combatants was able to utterly destroy the Persian army. Some historians have suggested that the reason for their victory was that the Greeks were defending their native soil, whereas the Persians were fighting a war far away from their homeland. Thus, the motivation of the Greeks far outweighed the incentives of the Persians. Additionally, the Greeks had formed a coalition of city states, and formed a citizen-army. They were also led by two talented and highly motivated leaders, Callimachus and Miltiades, whereas the Persians were led by their king, Darius I, who led an army of about 30 thousand versus the 10 thousand that the Athenians were able to assemble. As the historian Herodotus told us, some 50 years after the battle, the Athenian victory was unequivocal, and elevated the reputation of the Greek city states to that of an almost invincible force.
2. The battle of Cannae in 216 BC: The Carthaginians, led by Hannibal, destroyed 16 Roman legions, an army led by Lucius

Aemilus Paulus, and Gaius Terentius Varo. Over three-quarters of the Roman army ended up dead or captured.

3. The battle of Ilipa in 206 BC: A Roman army of 48 thousand under the command of Scipio Africanus vanquished and destroyed 54,000 Carthaginians
4. The battle of Hastings in 1066 A.D. in which the invading army of Normans, led by William the Conqueror, invaded southern England. This invasion culminated with the Norman victory and with the killing of the Anglo-Saxon king Harold. Consequently, the Normans ruled England for several centuries.
5. The battle of Hattin (1187), in which a force of Crusaders left Jerusalem to engage the Muslim army of the sultan Saladin (1137–1193 CE). The Crusaders were overconfident and fell into a trap prepared for them by Saladin. He lured them into a deserted area and defeated them, to the point where he captured their leaders, Guy, king of Jerusalem and Reginald of Chatillon. Saladin treated his Crusader opponents with much respect, and his reputation in the Christian world had led the poet Dante to refer to him as the "virtuous pagan."
6. The battle of Bannockburn in 1314 A.D. in which King Robert of Scotland led 7000 Scottish warriors to defeat King Edward II's army of over 20 thousand men.
7. The battle of Cajamarca was fought in 1532, in which the Spaniard Francisco Pizarro led 200 soldiers against about 10 thousand Incas. He killed over 2000 of the enemy and even captured the Inca emperor, Atahualpa, without incurring a single battle casualty. This was the end of the Inca rule over the portion of South America which now mostly encompasses the country of Peru.
8. The battle of San Jacinto on April 21, 1836 had led to the Treaty of Velasco. The Spanish general Santa Anna confronted the Texan army under General Sam Houston. In the ensuing battle, the Spanish lost 1400 soldiers versus only 9 Texans. The remainder of their army was captured, including the commanding general Santa Anna. Under the Treaty of Velasco, Santa Anna withdrew all his forces from the Texas territory, with a promise never to return.
9. The charge of the Light Brigade which occurred on October 25, 1854, during the Crimean War. As part of the Battle of Balaclava, the British attacked the positions held by the Russian artillery and they were slaughtered. The poet Alfred Lord Tennyson described

for posterity this futile bravery in his poem "The Charge of the Light Brigade." This event was also made into a movie in 1936, with Errol Flynn playing the role of Major Vickers, who led the charge under orders from Lord Cardigan. At the end of that day, 666 British soldiers charged the Russian positions, with 271 casualties, of which 110 were killed, 129 wounded, and 32 taken prisoner. 375 of their horses were also killed. Here is the poem:

I
Half a league, half a league,
Half a league onward.
All in the valley of Death
Rode the six hundred.
"forwards, the Light Brigade!
Charge for the guns!" he said
Into the *Valley* of Death
Rode the six hundred.

II
"Forward the Light Brigade"
Was there a man dismayed?
Not though the soldier knew
Someone had blundered.
Theirs not to make reply,
Theirs not to reason why,
Theirs but to do and die.
Into the valley of Death
Rode the six hundred.

III
Cannon to right of them,
Cannon to left of them.
Cannon in front of them
Volleyed and thundered;
Stormed at with shot and shell,
Boldly they rode and well,
Into the jaws of Death,
Into the mouth of hell
Rode the six hundred.

IV
Flashed all their sabres bare,
Flashed as they turned in air
Sabring the gunners there,
Charging an army, while
All the world wondered.
Plunged in the battery-smoke
Right through the line they broke;
Cossack and Russian
Reeled from the sabre stroke
Shattered and sundered.
Then they rode back, but not
Not the six hundred.

V
Cannon to right of them,
Cannon to left of them
Cannon behind them
Volleyed and thundered;
Stormed at with shot and shell,
While horse and hero fell,
They that had fought so well
Came through the jaws of Death,
Back from the mouth of hell,
All that was left of them,
Left of six hundred.

VI
When can their glory fade?
O the wild charge they made!
All the world wondered.
Honour the charge they made!
Honour the Light Brigade,
Noble six hundred.

Such honorable adventures in a far, far away land, captured the imagination of the British people and ignited their pride in their race, and also provided an unquestionable justification for the British investments in the empire. The reason this poem is included here in its entirety is because this magnificent event of the charge of the light brigade occurred at the beginning of the British rule of its worldwide dominions and territories. After "losing" the United States, the British monarchy and its ruling class had to "compensate" for this loss by intensifying their adventures in Africa and South Asia (in particular, in South Africa and the Indian subcontinent), thus acquiring several colonies rich in natural resources and that were also crucial in their positions at critical points in the maritime routes.

The English people drew much pleasure from the gallantry of their soldiers and the valor of their leaders. Although the casualties in the episode of the charge of the light brigade were relatively high, this was the price to pay for the establishment and the security of the British Empire. In England, the tales of these adventures, as narrated by Alfred Lord Tennyson, had the receptive ears of many Britons who were starting to move into the cities, as the industrial revolution was about to become the new economic reality. In their dark and confining tenements, the average English peasant—turned into a factory worker—delighted to hear about the prowess of his fellow citizens, and to vicariously experience their incomparable military achievements in these exotic lands far, far away.

In many historical instances, such as those related above, the popular folklore of the peoples involved in these adventures tends to color the events with the mantra of such adjectives as "bravery," "gallantry," "heroism," and "Patriotism." These men and women who ventured far and achieved much are turned into the popular heroes and heroines of the pantheon of national pride. In a way, they replaced the gods and goddesses of ancient Athens and Rome. Unlike the gods, these modern heroes were human beings—just like us—to whom we sing praises and wish to emulate their appearance as well as their deeds and adventures.

For example, we call a long and hard voyage an "Odyssey," and we describe a treacherous act as a "Trojan Horse," in memory of the siege of Troy (around 1250 BC) by the Greek coalition of city states. A similar situation occurred during the American race to the moon in the 1960s and 1970s. The first landing on the moon in 1969 had electrified the world, from New Delhi to Nairobi and from Cairo to the Caribbean islands.

This poem is also included because it sings the praise of a small island in the North Sea which represents a unique phenomenon in the world's history. This small island of the United Kingdom (including England, Scotland, Wales, and Ireland), with the size of 94,525 square miles, is comparable to the American state of Oregon (95,988 square miles). Yet, despite its relatively small size, the United Kingdom had established its domination of the world's maritime routes, and had built a worldwide empire where "the sun never sets."

Perhaps part of a possible explanation for this phenomenon may be the size of the population in the United Kingdom as compared with other countries, and its geographical location. The United Kingdom sits on the receptive end of the "Gulf Stream," thus giving the United Kingdom a temperate climate in winter. The British capital, London, is on the parallel latitude of, for example, Moscow in Russia. Without the Gulf Stream, London and the United Kingdom would be as cold as Moscow, even colder than Canada, maybe by at least 5 degrees Celsius. Thus, the mild, albeit rainy climate in the British Isles had allowed its population to benefit from a highly productive agriculture, and its relative abundance of minerals, such as iron and coal, which are encountered in geographic proximity to each other, had contributed to its leading pioneering role in the industrial revolution.

Beyond Business Analytics allows us to evaluate the historical events beyond the data or information provided to us, such as in the description of battles, how many fought on each side, or what was the geographical locations of the opposing countries, or perhaps what was the size of the economies of the fighting nations. These are all business analytics, describing certain critical aspects of the variables. As we could clearly determine in the examples above, the size of the opposing parties, or the available resources that they commanded, do not necessarily nor completely explain the historical narrative and the outcomes of historical events. We need, therefore, to look beyond the data to more elaborate notions and more complex phenomena. The case of public organizations is a good candidate for this form of analysis.

Some Historical Examples of Failing Public Organizations

The previous section focused on historical episodes which described the failure of one party to a conflict, when this party was initially considered the potential winner. This section will offer selected examples of public organizations which were also candidates for success, yet dramatically failed in their mission. These cases of failure can be explained with the four basic reasons for the failure: (1) **negligence** of the commanding generals or the emperor himself to study the forthcoming campaign and to collect sufficient analytics about the terrain where the battles will be fought, the characteristics of the opposing army, and the attributes and known behavior in tactics and strategies of the officer or nobility in command of the opposing army. (2) **over-confidence** of the commanding elite that their strategy and battle tactics will prevail, and that their plans will succeed in vanquishing the enemy's forces. (3) **over-reliance** on too few analytics, such as the state of the roads in the enemy's territory, the disposition of enemy troops, including his reserves, and the availability of food and shelter if the invading army is forced to live off the land. For example, in the Second World War the allies conducted exhaustive studies of the French terrain and roads in the Normandy countryside, where the allied armored divisions, in the campaign of "Overlord" and coming from the beach heads in Normandy, could navigate the terrain without fear of being stuck in the mud. And (4) **lack of professionalism and expertise to conduct analytics of the campaign and its variables (such as terrain, enemy troops, enemy command, the enemy's strategies and tactics of conducting war, such as frontal attacks versus guerrilla warfare and the study of weather)**.

a. Napoleon's invasion of Russia is an excellent example of engaging his Grand Armee in a massive campaign without sufficient analytics. This led to a dismal situation of faulty logistics; inadequate supply lines; poor discipline and high discontent of the soldiers; diseases due to the lack of adequate clothing and adequate nutrition, and the relentless impacts of the inclement Russian weather. With analytics all these variables could have been studied, predicted, and acted upon. The French campaign started in June 1812, but failed to be complete before the setting of the Russian winter in November and December of 1812. During their retreat from Russian territory, the French were constantly attacked by the Russians. The remaining French soldiers who returned to France were but a shadow of the enormous army with which Napoleon carried out the invasion.
b. The battle of the bulge during the Second World War exemplifies a "last ditch" counteroffensive of the German armed forces. The German armored divisions were concealed from Allied observation flights in the dense forest of the Ardennes. Allied command believed that the thick forest would not allow heavy armored vehicles to navigate through them. Thus, when in the winter of 1944/1945 German armor appeared from the dense forests, it caught the allies by complete surprise. The defense strategy of the allies did not

foresee any such possibility, that masses of tanks would suddenly emerge from the forests of the Ardennes. Regardless of the superior intelligence services of the allied armies, there was no warning from the intelligence staff nor from the planning staff of the allied headquarters that a possible attack was possible from the supposedly impassable Ardennes mountains. The allies were able to regroup and amass their superior armored and air forces to ultimately defeat the German offensive.

c. The Battle of Bannockburn: In 1314 the Scottish king Robert I with a small army of about 7000 men encountered the English army of King Edward II, which numbered over 20,000 soldiers. The Scotts defeated the much larger English contingent and captured or killed many English nobles, while King Edward was able to flee the battle field.
d. The famous case in 1589 of the Spanish Armada of King Phillip II and its defeat in the English Channel by the smaller fleet of Queen Elizabeth I: The much smaller yet more maneuverable English ships were able to prevent the Armada from taking hold of the Channel. Upon retreat from the battlefield, the Spanish encountered storms which destroyed about half of their ships and their forces.

The lessons learned by both sides were: (1) the value of concealment and of a surprise attack as a viable tactic which is powerful enough to throw the opposing armies into at least a temporary halt and reassessment of the battle field's situation; (2) every geographic formation may be used by the enemy to conceal its formations; and (3) although a smaller force is able, by a surprise attack, to temporarily dominate the battlefield, in the end the superior force of the enemy (in combatants and materiel) shall be victorious. Another good example of the above is the surprise attack of the Japanese Imperial Navy on Pearl Harbor on December 7, 1941. The initial advantage of the Japanese forces disintegrated within a year, when American naval and air forces obliterated much of the Japanese naval forces in the battle of Midway. From that day on, the American naval and air forces had grown exponentially in the number and quality of surface and underwater vessels, in naval aviation, military technology, and military tactics.

Some Historical Examples of Failing Countries or Nations

The four examples listed above focused on historical instances of selective military or civilian organizations that failed because of their involvement with their country's failed policies that had resulted in the country's defeats in its relations with their national foes. In contrast, this section focuses on the failure of *entire* nations to successfully challenge its enemies and thus to survive, or merely continue their existence without growth and in some instances by losing a leadership position in their environments.

In this regard, two scholars come to mind. The first is Barbara Tuchman. In her magnificent book: "The March of Folly," Professor Tuchman described four historical incidents in which the outcome led to the radical transformation or the demise of one of the parties to the conflict. She referred to the government leaders in these conflicts as suffering from "woodenheadedness." In many instances, these leaders followed a policy which was erroneous and led to failures and disasters. Although these leaders understood the folly of their decisions, they nevertheless continued in this position, to the ultimate defeat, even collapse, of their countries. In part, the adherence of these leaders to a losing course of action can be explained in three ways: (1) they expended many resources to reach this point and are reluctant to give up their position, albeit a losing one, (2) they were unwilling to admit that they acted in error, thus to expose their folly to their countrymen and women, and (3) they lacked a "plan B" because they could not imagine a situation in which they would fail. This was due, perhaps to over-confidence blended with human arrogance. They knew the risks, and they knew that the decision they were about to make is erroneous, bordering on folly, yet they decided to do it anyway; because they could.

Professor Tuchman also discussed the following historical incidents: the Trojan horse, the Protestant secession, the American revolution, and the American involvement in Vietnam. Although in each of the cases there was an alternative solution available to the decision-makers and a solution which was known to them, the decision-makers "stuck to their guns" and refused to change their position.

Professor Arnold Toynbee is the second example. In his book: "The Study of History," Toynbee believed that history can be understood only when the historian observes the birth, the growth, and the fall or demise of a civilization. In this view, the unit of analysis in historical perspective is the civilization. Since the beginning of the history of humankind, Toynbee identified twenty-three civilizations, of which half of these have disappeared, and the remaining seven civilizations are essentially frozen in time. This leaves the Western Civilization fueled by Christianity, which is still evolving, growing, and providing immense benefits to its followers and to the remainder of humankind. Such a "successful" civilization also dominates its region, and in some instances makes advances toward the existence and the assets of other civilizations.

According to Toynbee, when a civilization collapses, so do the nations that compose it. The failing nations may not entirely disappear, and they may be integrated into the new emerging civilization. The Roman empire substituted the Greek cities, and when it collapsed, other nations in Europe, many as we know them today, emerged to take its place. Toynbee's thesis has been criticized by many historians, particularly on the basis of a counter-thesis that some nations tend to re-emerge in the image and the format of their past, such as the Jews of their Diaspora who, after two millennia, had reconstituted their ancient homeland in the land between the River Jordan and the Mediterranean Sea, in which their ancient homeland once existed.

In selected historical events, such a reconstitution of the geographical map of countries had occurred by design, through the systematic recharting of the map by victors of wars. For example, after the First World War, the League of Nations and the victors, led by Great Britain and France, reconfigured the map of Europe. Their representatives made some minor adjustments to the map, such as the declaration of the free ports of Gdansk and Memel. They recreated the boundaries of Poland and Czechoslovakia, and they also dealt with the colonies in Asia and Africa, which were the territories of Great Britain, France, Belgium, and Italy.

Beyond such historical trends, the rise and fall of civilizations also produced cultural contributions in many areas of human endeavor. These contributions fall within the space of "beyond analytics." In many cases they may be "larger than life," in the sense that a small country may generate cultural and other contributions beyond its size. Examples are the Greek coalition of cities, the Roman Empire, France, Italy, Germany, the British Empire, and the United States. If we assess cultural prowess by, for example, the indicator of Nobel prize winners, then Germany, Great Britain, and the United States lead the rest of the world. The same is true when we analyze the origins of technological achievements in transportation, agriculture, industrial might, military equipment, strategies, and tactics; the management of municipalities, states, and country governments, and the applications of technological innovations and the sciences, we find these same countries globally in leading positions. Almost all major scientific and technological discoveries in the nineteenth and twentieth centuries came from Germany, Great Britain, and the United States.

Historians who follow Toynbee have also argued that the downfall of states and empires begins with the decline of their institutions: cultural, political, economic, religious, and social. A good example is the Roman military, which has changed its policy during the times of the Empire, by allowing non-Roman citizens to gain positions of influence in the Roman army. In time, this policy has led to a cadre of officers who lacked the fealty, the unreserved degree of loyalty to Rome, and the untarnished patriotism of the original officer corps, which was composed, in many instances, of the sons of the founding families of the Roman republic.

Another viewpoint and a different unit of analysis is the study of start-up companies, and why they succeed or fail. Tom Eisenmann published a revealing article in the Harvard Business Review in May–June 2021. He suggested that it's not a secret that more than two-thirds of startups fail, but he asked: why so many did fail so disappointedly. He went on to argue that there are four reasons for such a phenomenon. First these firms fail to define their problems to the extent that a solution can be offered. Second, even when they define the problem, they fail to develop a viable solution. Third, there is a lack of solution validation, and fourth, they fail to maintain balance. They may have started with a promising idea, but failed in the process to make it a lasting reality.

Beyond Business Analytics may also serve as a method with which managers and analysts of such situations—as the four listed above—may analyze the entire phenomenon, including the attributes of the situation and the meaning of such attributes to the assessment of the situation. This method is thus able to give the managers and their stakeholders a rational, comprehensive, and satisfactory explanation of how and why these firms will eventually fail. The contribution of Beyond Business Analytics to such an explanation is that this form of evaluation ventures to move the analysis beyond the facts and the quantitative and even qualitative descriptors of the firm's situation. This move takes the evaluator to the space of the behavioral aspects of the decision-making process and the decision-maker and evaluator himself/herself. The analysis is thus extended from *what is* the decision being made to *who makes* the decision and what are their attributes. Within such an extended analysis we also find the potential answers to such questions as: *Cui Bono* (who benefits from the analysis) and *why* is this analysis being conducted.

The Fall of the Aztec Empire

The following are some salient examples of the failure of entire countries or nations to the point where they practically disappeared from the annals of history. The first was the fall and subsequent disappearance of the Aztec Empire. In 1519 Hernan Cortes set sail to Mexico, in command of 500 men and 11 ships. He reached Mexico in February 1519, at the port of Tabasco. His next stop was Veracruz, where he sunk his ships, except one ship which he sent back to Spain. Without their ships his men had no choice but to remain in the new world and were thus highly motivated to fight with Cortes against the Aztecs. Thus, in November 1519 Cortes entered Tenochtitlan, near what is today the metropolitan center of Mexico City. The native king Montezuma was killed. Although the Spaniards had to retreat during their first battle with the natives, Cortes returned to fight the Aztecs and he was the victor in the battle of Otumba on July 7, 1520. By August 13, 1521 he controlled Tenochtitlan and this meant the end of the Aztec empire.

Although they were vastly outnumbered, the Spaniards had one big military advantage over the Aztecs. They had domesticated horses which are very versatile "beasts of burden," trained for hauling heavy cargo and for attacks on the battlefields. However, in order to fully utilize the horse for military purposes and for hauling (in teams) large cargo over distances there was a need for carts, which the Spaniards possessed and utilized for transport and for military uses. The Spaniards could thus transport people and cargo over long distances, whereas the Aztecs were relatively sedentary, confined to marching on foot, so that they had to operate within their limited geographical confines. Therefore, although Cortes lacked many advantages of numbers of soldiers and adequate knowledge of the terrain, all vis-à-vis the Aztecs, he had the technological advantage of rapid movement over distances and in the inhospitable terrain.

The Fall of the Inca Empire

Some 4252 kilometers south of Mexico City, another Spanish "Conquistador" (conqueror) was Francisco Pizarro. His destiny in the New World coincided with the reign of Atahualpa, the 13th and the last emperor of the Inca empire, in what is today the territories in the countries of Peru and Ecuador. The Inca people, numbering at that time 12 million, had erected a magnificent empire, with its capital high up on the Andes mountains and in the western coast on the shores of the Pacific Ocean. The Inca designed and built outstanding public works and sophisticated agricultural and irrigation systems.

Pizarro landed in the western coast of South America with a force of 180 armed men. With this puny army he intended to conquer the Inca empire. Pizarro became fascinated with legends and stories he heard of the amazing wealth of a country in the south, with the name of "Biru" or Peru, perhaps named after a river by the name of Vire. Pizarro returned to Spain to obtain the backing of emperor Charles V. The emperor agreed, and further decided that Pizarro will receive the lion's share of the profits from this planned adventure. Thus, armed with the Spanish emperor's backing, Pizarro returned to Peru. Upon his return, Pizarro executed Atahualpa, and had conquered the Inca capital Cuzco. In 1535 Pizarro went to the coast of the Pacific Ocean and there he founded the city of Lima, in order to greatly improve the maritime line with Panama, which at that time was the main Spanish colony in Mid-America.

Pizarro was later assassinated by Diego Monzo, the son of Diego Almagro, formerly the governor of Chile. Almagro came to Lima to demand his share of the Inca treasure, and in a battle with Pizarro's half-brother Hernando, he lost the conflict and was executed. In June 1541, his son Monzo and his friends killed Pizarro while he was dining in his palace in Lima.

The outcome of these events was the decision by the Spanish emperor to assign a viceroy to Peru. The first was Andres Hurtado de Mendoza who decisively dealt with the situation, upon his return to Peru in 1558. The arrival of the viceroy signaled the end of the independent state of the Inca, and it was then incorporated as a colony of the Spanish Crown. Thus, in a few decades since the Spaniards' arrival, the empire of the Inca had ceased to exist, never again to re-emerge as an independent entity. In summary, twelve million Incas effectively handed their empire to a few hundred Spaniards, thus ending their independence as a prosperous country.

Although the Inca were an advanced civilization, they did not invent the use of the wheel. In order to ferry people and cargo on carts, there is a need for three variables to occur simultaneously. First, the is a need for flat terrain. The carts or chariots initially appeared in Egypt and Mesopotamia, both inhabiting flat surfaces, on the shores of magnificent rivers. Second, there is a need for the invention of the wheel, which will make the carts a feasible mode of transportation. Thirdly, there is a need for "beasts of burden," such as oxen or horses. The Inca did not possess any of these, partly because they inhabited a mountainous terrain, and the only animals they possessed were the llama, which, with their delicate legs and back were unsuitable for the ferrying of people or heavy cargo. Therefore, the Inca did not see the urgent need to invent the wheel and their modes of transportation remained limited to the llamas. These facts had magnified the Spanish advantages of menacing contingents of horses and carts, never before seen by the Inca. The Inca had considered the Spaniards, with their shining armor, their "killing sticks" of rifles, and their horses, to be the long-awaited Gods, that the Inca religious priests had predicted. Atahualpa and his advisors expected benevolent and friendly gods, but to their amazement and utter disappointment, the invaders turned out to be a race of cruel and avaricious warriors.

Why Nations Fail

In 2013, Acemoglu and Robinson published their insightful book titled: "Why Nations Fail: The Origins of Power, Prosperity, and Poverty." The authors covered in 480 pages the rise and fall of a plethora of nations. They were looking for the common cause for these nations' successes and failures, the one or more variables that will act as causes for this behavior and for the growth or decline trajectory of these nations.

For example, in their Chapter 13, "why nations fail today" they proposed that nations fail today "…because their extractive economic institutions do not create the incentives needed for people to save, invest, and innovate. Extractive political institutions support these economic institutions by cementing the power of those who benefit from the extraction. Extractive and political institutions, though their details vary under different circumstances, are always at the root of this failure. In many cases, for example, as we will see in Argentina, Colombia, and Egypt, this failure takes the form of lack of sufficient economic activity, because the politicians are just too happy to extract resources or quash any type of independent economic activity that threaten themselves and the economic elite" (p. 372).

An illustration of a salient reason or cause for the failure, sometime even collapse of nations which the authors did not discuss in their seminal book, is the social or political mantra of the regime. The state, in this case, imposes its social, political, or religious beliefs on its population. When the citizens are not in agreement with their government, they will act to change the regime. A good example is the "spring" of Eastern Europe in the 1980s and 1990s, when countries such as Poland, Czechoslovakia, and East Germany decided to gain independence from the Soviet domination of Eastern Europe. These countries decided to adopt a more capitalistic regime, and to abandon the socialist nature of their economies and their political makeup. Another example is the collapse of the Persian monarchy in Iran, after twenty centuries of ruling the country. In its place the Islamic leaders in Iran established a religious regime. The Shah was forced into exile. In this example, an initial movement of exiled extremist Islamic scholars who became dissatisfied with the regime they had previously supported, had exploded into a national movement strong enough to foster the uprising of the Iranian people who then unseated their monarchy, as the French, for example, had done in their revolution against the Bourbon monarchy almost two centuries before.

Another seminal and fascinating analysis of why nations fail is Jared Diamond's book: "Collapse: How Societies Choose to Fail or Succeed" (Penguin Books, 2011). The author argued that societies make disastrous decisions because: (1) they lack a road map to success; (2) they fail to anticipate future events; (3) they fail to perceive the unfavorable situations they encounter; (4) they act with rational bad behavior; and (5) they have disastrous and defeatist values. In essence, these nations fail to anticipate future problems and when they are challenged by these problems, they solve them with "reasoning by false analogy." Diamond proceeded to give an example of such reasoning in the way in which the French military prepared its forces, after the First World War, to face, if needed, the next war with Germany. Unfortunately, the French military assumed that the next war will be fought in a manner largely identical to the First World War. They failed to take into account the developments in technology, transportation, control of the air, and military strategies, which occurred since the end of the First World War. The French relied on static fortifications (the famed "Maginot Line") but the German military, within days, had proven the total inadequacy of stationary defenses against a mobile army with its highly mobile armored divisions and highly mobile artillery and infantry, all in close radio communication, and the coordinated action with its air force. Within days, to the astonishment of the French and the entire world, the German divisions overran the French fortifications and in less than two weeks, essentially unopposed, they conquered the entire country.

It is therefore abundantly clear that Acemoglu and Robinson, as well as Diamond, made the argument that regimes as well as entire countries had failed because of reasons that were almost entirely within the control of the rulers. They failed because their governments are unable to analyze and to understand the situation in which they encounter themselves and their organizations, as well as to predict the intentions and actions of their rivals. They also lacked what we today call: updated overall military and specific battlefield intelligence.

The search for a better understanding of one's rival, competitor, or enemy, has been an activity rooted in the long history of the human race. The Biblical narrative of Moses, Joshua, and the Israelites is a revealing example. Before embarking on his campaign against the peoples who inhabited Canaan, the land between the Jordan River and the Mediterranean Sea, Moses needed to gain some knowledge of the enemy. He was obeying the words of the Lord: "Send men to explore Canaan, which I am giving to the Israelites. Send one leader from each of their ancestors' tribes." Among these assigned spies was Joshua, son of Nun, from the large tribe of Ephraim. Moses had specific orders for these spies: "Go through the Negev and then into the mountain region. See what the land is like and whether the people living there are strong or weak, few or many. Is the land they live in good or bad? Do their cities have walls around them or not? Is the soil rich or poor? Does the land have trees or not? Do your best to bring back some fruit from the land." The spies returned with fruit from the explored land, and their report to Moses was a glowing description of the coveted land: "We went to the land where you sent us. It really is a land flowing with milk and honey. Here is some of its fruit. But the people who live there are strong, and the cities have walls and are very large." They also added the now famous words: "The land we explored is one that devours those who live there...all the people we saw are very tall… We felt as small as grasshoppers, and that's how we must have looked to them." Thus, in spite of the negative reports from his spies, Moses, and later Joshua, decided to invade Canaan. Joshua did not believe in the inflated stories of giants ("Nephilim") who seem to inhabit the land. Before attacking Jericho, the large city on the border of Canaan, and the first fortified city he was planning to attack, Joshua sent his own spies. They spent time at Rahav's restaurant/bar/hotel/house of ill-repute establishment, and she helped them gather information about the city of Jericho, its walls, and its defenders, and then escape back to their camp.

Another salient example of the role that knowledge of one's rival plays in the success of a military campaign is John Keegan's book: "Intelligence in War: Knowledge of the Enemy from Napoleon to Al-Qaeda". The author describes the role of knowledge generated by the intelligence departments of the military in the ultimate success in the war. He describes, for example, the success of the allies in the Second World War, which, in part, could be attributed to their superior intelligence of the enemy's intentions and strategies. In part, this accomplishment was due to the team who broke the German naval code. British Prime Minister Winston Churchill was especially proud and supportive of his decoders of the German Enigma machines, with which all commands of the German naval forces was routinely transmitted. Located in the town of Bletchley Park, outside London, these decoders included Alan Turing, a mathematician who contributed to the emergence of the modern computers. Other famed decoders were: Gordon Welchman, Bill Tutte, Dily Knox, and Nigel de Grey.

In the First World War, the case of Mata Hari became a household name, and a title given, since then, to almost every woman spy. She was born in 1876 with the name of Margaretha Zelle. In 1905 she came to Paris and assumed the professional name of Mata Hari (meaning "eye of the day" in the Malay language).

On October 15, 1917 she was put to death by a French firing squad, after she was found guilty of spying for Germany during the First World War. Her life is a mixed story of professional dancing and of being a hostess in her house to many French and British officers. The charges levied against her by the British and the Belgians were never fully substantiated. Throughout her short life she entertained many lovers, from the political and military elites of France and Britain, but none came to her defense.

To this date it is unclear how serious was the intelligence, if any, that she was accused of giving to the Germans. Her case was more that of a beautiful woman spy, a fact that ignited the interest of the public. It was never specified, let alone proven in the accusations against her, what type of intelligence she allegedly handed to the Germans, nor how such an act had threatened the security of France, Great Britain, and their allies.

The case of Mata Hari did not end up with the failing of a country, nor with its fall and disappearance from the annals of history. There may have been some damage to the security of France and its allies, but perhaps the most powerful negative impact was the fact that this case became public, and that it exposed the weaknesses of the French and the British intelligence services, for allowing a beautiful spy to threaten the existence of these services. Usually, it takes months, perhaps years, for a security agency to be rehabilitated and to regain its high standing in the country.

Beyond Business Analytics is a method by which such accusations may be examined and their impacts can be assessed by the evaluator. Such an analysis would require filling in some data into the space of the analytics (type, quantity, and quality of intelligence) and beyond analytics, which considers the space of what were the impacts and the consequences of this transfer, if any, on the organization from which this intelligence had been generated.

Beyond Business Analytics and the Outcomes of Historical Events

In his book: "Intelligence in War," John Keegan had argued that in the Second World War, although the allies had broken the ENIGMA code of the German navy, and thus they knew precisely the positions in the Atlantic Ocean of Admiral Doenitz's submarine fleet, and when they were ordered to attack the merchant convoys, which were England's pipeline to the Western hemisphere, from which it received from the United States and Canada its foodstuff, armaments, and other crucial material so as to continue prosecuting the war. The codebreakers at Bletchley Park had broken the German ENIGMA code, but they kept this fact an absolute secret known to very few in the British military and political elite (with the codename ULTRA). The British intelligence agencies had worked out a complicated system of deception, buy which they explained their attacks on the German submarines as a product or such factors as air reconnaissance, human spies within the German military, and sheer luck, when British destroyers would presumably and by chance, come across the German submarines. The deception was a success, and only decades after the war, when the British released to the public the story of Bletchley Park and the breaking of ENIGMA, the public was allowed to know the details of this deception.

Nevertheless, despite the cases in history in which intelligence played a crucial part in the successful outcome of battles, it was the battlefield exchange of military forces in a war that engulfed both sides of the conflict, that was responsible for the success or failure of the belligerents. To use a cliché: enemy intelligence of the enemy, its dispositions, its forces, and its quality of fighting may have been a necessary condition to win a battle, but it was not a sufficient condition.

In another example, the American navy had won the Battle of Midway in the Summer of 1942, not because it had broken the Japanese naval code, but because, despite its inferiority in numbers and quality of vessels, the American admirals Nimitz and Spruance were able to apply naval tactics which caught the enemy by surprise, and also because of sheer luck, when their enemy made several crucial tactical errors in judgment, and in its prosecution of the naval battles, and also. when the American fighter pilots were able to locate, by chance, in the vastness of the Pacific Ocean, the Japanese fleet as it happened to be in the midst of re-arming its airplanes. The Japanese carriers were loaded with aircraft getting ready for another mission. When the American bombers had arrived, the Japanese fleet was caught completely by surprise, had no aerial cover to speak of, and had its carriers loaded like "sitting ducks."

A similar scenario is found in the naval engagements of the Second World War in the Atlantic Ocean of the German submarines and the convoys of the allies on route to the beleaguered British Isles. As described above in the case of the ENIGMA machine and the allies' foreknowledge of the dispositions of the German submarine "wolf packs" in the North Atlantic, in the final analysis the Battle of the Atlantic was won due to the superiority of the Allies' naval power which, after Pearl Harbor and the United States entering the war, was greatly enhanced by the ever-growing might of the American naval forces. After December 7, 1941, the American industrial outputs of naval vessels, aviation, ground forces, and other military equipment and materiel had grown exponentially. In terms of Analytics, the numbers were in favor of the allies, and with America in the fight, sooner or later the victory would be achieved. But, as the notion of beyond analytics shows, even with such superior forces, the war dragged on for another three-and-a-half years. Just having the quantitative or qualitative superiority does not, by itself, make the organization a "sure winner." There are several other various factors in play, such as changes in circumstances; human errors; human excellence in planning and execution; and unforeseen events which by themselves may not be a cause for alarm, but their combined impacts may be a true "game changer."

The confluence of these seemingly unrelated events, and the fact that the American naval commanders were able to exploit them—by design or by luck—made the victory at Midway a reality. The Imperial Japanese Navy had never recovered from its Midway loss of prestige and from the fact that the bulk of its aircraft carriers was decimated in that battle. The threat from the Imperial Japanese Navy to Hawaii and to possibly the American West Coast had been neutralized. To paraphrase Sir Winston Churchill, the battle of Midway was not the end of the war in the Pacific, but it was the beginning of the end. From that summer day in 1942, it was the American military in pursuit of the Japanese armed forces, for three more years, until the surrender of Japan in 1945, in Tokyo Bay.

Thus, the ability of organizations to exploit favorable events, and to bring their plans to fruition, are the core of the notion of beyond analytics. This notion may be extended to business, military, political, social, and any other type of sector and organization. It is also abundantly clear that in both cases of private as well as public organizations, the role of managers is crucial to the attainment of the objectives of the organization and, as discussed above, managers or commanders (in the case of the military) have the wherewithal to succeed or fail in their mission. These abilities or characteristics of managers and their successful exploitation of these events are the core of the notion of "Beyond Business Analytics." Clearly, not all of the objectives and missions of public organizations are successfully met and exploited by their managers. The literature is replete with cases of grave mistakes made by these managers. The main difference between private and public organizations is that in the private sector such mistakes, miscalculations, or simply negligence are uncovered relatively quickly and the firm takes action to solve these problems and replace the managers in charge of the negative situation. Public organizations are slower than their private counterparts in uncovering such mistakes, blunders, and miscalculations, and in handling them with relative effectiveness.

Thus, analytics may be a contributor to the outcome of events, but it is not the only, and certainly not even the principal factor which impacts such outcomes. Being in possession of information is not a sufficient variable in the workings of private as well as public organizations. It behooves on Beyond Business Analytics to take over this task and to cover the space beyond the mere quantitative aspects of the event or phenomenon, which thus becomes: Beyond Business Analytics.

CHAPTER 10

The Road Ahead

This book merely "scratched the surface" of this new theoretical space I call: "Beyond Business Analytics." This space comes into being after the quantitative and qualitative variables are collected by the organization, so that there is an abundance of data and information. There is a point in this process where the focus of the narrative reverts to notions of higher-level concepts, such as the pursuit of happiness and the pursuit of world peace.

The theoretical space of "Beyond Business Analytics" is perhaps the precursor of an area of organizational research in which we explore the behavioral dimensions of what happens beyond the space of business analytics. As described in the chapters above, this means that we describe, albeit in general terms, how we start to manipulate the elements of business analytics in order to arrive at higher-level notions.

Yet, this is only the beginning of this new area of research. Once we bring to life the behavioral aspects of analytics, we are in a position that allows us to relate this new area to how people and organizations make decisions and how they apply these decisions to their routine existence. They do so by linking these inputs to their decision processes, so that their decisions are the result of the conversion of decision elements to their behavioral syntheses.

E. Geisler, *Beyond Business Analytics*,
https://doi.org/10.1007/978-3-030-43718-3_10

The road ahead in this new area of research includes the application of Beyond Business Analytics to the many areas or disciplines of business. Examples include manufacturing, transportation, healthcare delivery, international exchanges, and select applications in the areas of the military, as well as various and sundry areas of public activities.

In our road ahead, the key questions we ask after we collect and obtain business analytics are: what do we do with these data and this information? To what uses do we put these data? What were the fundamental reasons or motivators why we embarked on this information-collection endeavors? and finally: when we embarked on such data collection, did we already have in mind the framework and the rationale for the use and application of the data?

If the answers are yes to all these questions, it is therefore abundantly clear that we and our organizations have a robust planning activity, whereby the collection of business data is an integral part of the routine manipulation of information in the organization. Clearly, this situation is the most beneficial to the organizational and to its members. It allows them to improve the quality of their decision-making processes, as well as to better plan and control their activities.

Thus, organizations and individual researchers should strive to collect and manipulate business data and therefore to process them as business analytics, so that they will be in a position to affect their effective dealing with the space of Beyond Business Analytics in their everyday activities as a successful organization.

So, the road ahead in research and practice is to explore these questions, both individually and as a group of related queries. Our basic aim is to improve our understanding of the space of "Beyond Business Analytics": how the dimensions of this space behave, and how the dimensions of this space converge to form higher-order notions. Since humans communicate more efficiently via the exchange of notions or concepts, it is evident that Beyond Business Analytics can be of much assistance in developing such notions, thus to contribute immensely to human communication.

Bibliography

Selected Bibliography

Abdikalyk, K., Z. Abitzhanova, et al. 2016. Concept as the Main Research Object of Cognitive Linguistics. *International Journal of Environmental & Science Education* 11 (10): 3167–3178.

Acemoglu, D., and J. Robinson. 2012. *Why Nations Fail*. New York: Currency-Crown Publishing Group.

Agor, W. 1986. The Logic of Intuition: How Top Executives Make Important Decisions. *Organizational Dynamics* 14 (3): 5–18.

Anderson, P. 2002. *The Origins of Postmodernity*. London, UK: Verso Publishers.

Argote, L., and P. Ingram. 2000. Knowledge Transfer: A Basis for Competitive Advantage in Firms. *Organizational Behavior and Human Decision Processes* 82 (1): 150–169.

Aydiner, A., S. Tatoglu, E. Bayraktar, S. Zaim, and D. Delen. 2019. Business Analytics and Firm Performance: The Mediating Role of Business Process Performance. *Journal of Business Research* 96: 228–237.

Bahrami, M., B. Bozkaya, and S. Balcisoy. 2020. Using Behavioral Analytics to Predict Customer Invoice Payment. *Big Data* 8 (1): 25–37.

Baker, L.S., S.W. Atlas, and C. Afendulis. 2008. Expanded Use of Imaging Technology and the Challenge of Measuring Values. *Health Affairs* 27 (6): 1467–1478.

Bakri, A., et al. 2012. Malaysian Computer Science Publications: A Citation Study. Brunei International Conference on Engineering and Technology, 159–170.

E. Geisler, *Beyond Business Analytics*,
https://doi.org/10.1007/978-3-030-43718-3

Bamden, J. 2006. Artificial Intelligence, Figurative Language and Cognitive Linguistics. In *Cognitive Linguistics: Current Applications and Future Perspectives*, ed. G. Kristiansen et al. Berlin, Germany: De Gruyter Mouton.

Bannister, B., and R. Griffith. 1986. Applying a Causal Analytic Framework to the Mobley, Horner and Hollingsworth (1978) Turnover Model: A Useful Reexamination. *Journal of Management* 12 (3): 433–443.

Barczewski, S., et al. 2015. *Britain Since 1688: A Nation in the World*. New York: CRC Press.

Barney, J. 1991. Firm Resources and Sustained Competitive Advantage. *Journal of Management* 17: 99–120.

Barreto, E. 2021. The Time of the Uprooted: The Real Nowhere Man. *Academic Letters*, Article 529.

Beller, M., and A. Barnett. 2009. Applying a Causal Analytical Framework to the Mobley, Horner, and Hollingworth (1978) Turnover Model: A Useful Reexamination. *Journal of Management* 12 (3): 433–443.

Bhandari, R., M. Singer, and H. Van der Scheer. 2014. *Using Marketing Analytics to Drive Superior Growth*. New York: McKinsey and Company.

Bingham, N., and H. Byrne. 2021. *Archival Strategies for Contemporary Collecting in a World of Big Data: Challenges and Opportunities with Curating the UK Web Archive. Big Data & Society*, January–June, pp. 1–6.

Blok, A., and M.A. Pederson. 2014. Complementary Social Science Quali-Quantitative Experiments in a Big Data World. *Big Data & Society*, 5: 1–6.

Bloom, N. 2007. Uncertainty and the Dynamics of R&D. *American Economic Review* 97 (2): 250–255.

Boavida, N., A. Moniz, and M. Laranja. 2016. The Process of Construction of Evidence: An Analysis of the Use of Indicators in Two Decisions of Innovation Policy. In *21st International Conference on Science and Technology*, 150–167, Sept 14–16, Valencia, Spain.

Bollier, D. 2010. *The Promise and Peril of Big Data*. Aspen, CO: The Aspen Institute.

Bonacich, P. 1987. Power and Centrality: A Family of Measures. *American Journal of Sociology* 92 (5): 1170–1182.

Borgman, C. 1999. The User's Mental Model for an Information Retrieval System: An Experiment on a Prototype Online Catalog. *International Journal of Human-Computer Studies* 51 (2): 435–452.

Borner, K., and A. Scharnhorst. 2009. Visual Conceptualizations and Models of Science. *Journal of Informetrics* 3 (3): 161–172.

Borzacchini, L. 2021. Metaphysical Traces from a Radically Historicist Philosophy of Mathematics and Logic. *Academia Letters*, Article 668.

Boudreau, J. 2015. Predictive Analytics for Human Capital: Think Outside the Line. *CFO*, April 27.

Braiman, C., et al. 2018. Cortical Response to the Natural Speech Envelope Correlates with Neuroimaging Evidence of Cognition in Severe Brain Injury. *Current Biology* 28 (December 3): 1–7.

Braunstein, D. 1974. Beyond Leavitt's 'Narrow' Analytic Manager. *Interfaces* 4 (4): 28–31.

Brown, D. 2021. *The Art of Business Wars*. New York: Harper Business.

Brown, S., D. Gandhi, L. Herring, and A. Puri. 2019. The Analytics Academy: Bridging the Gap Between Human and Artificial Intelligence. *McKinsey Quarterly*, September, pp. 1–9

Bruger, N. 2018. *The Archived Web: Doing History in the Digital Age*. Cambridge, MA: MIT Press.

Bugajska, A. 2021. The Future of Utopia in the Posthuman World. *Academic Letters*. https://doi.org/10.20935/AL155.

Bukowitz, W., and R. Williams. 2000. *The Knowledge Management Field Book*. London: Prentice-Hall.

Burckhardt, J. 1990. *The Civilization of the Renaissance in Italy*. New York: Penguin Classics.

Burrows, L., and M. Savage. 2014. After the Crisis? Big Data and the Methodological Challenges of Empirical Sociology. *Big Data & Society*, April–June, pp. 1–6.

Campbell, D., and J. Stanley. 1963. *Experimental and Quasi-Experimental Designs for Research*. New York: Houghton Mifflin Company.

Chadegani, A., et al. 2013. A Comparison Between Two Main Academic Literature Collections: Web of Science and Scopus Databases. *Asian Social Science* 9 (5): 18–26.

Chamorro-Premuzik, T. 2019. *Why So Many Incompetent Men Become Leaders and How to Fix It*. Boston, MA: Harvard Business Review Press.

Charan, R. 2015. *The Attacker's Advantage: Turning Uncertainty into Breakthrough Opportunities*. New York: Public Affairs.

Chase, W., and H. Simon. 1973. Perception in Chess. *Cognitive Psychology* 4: 55–81.

Chen, C., et al. 2005. Mapping Scientometrics (1981–2001). In *Proceedings of the American Society for Information Science and Technology*, November, pp. 25–34.

Chen, K., and J. Guan. 2011. A Bibliometric Investigation of Research Performance in Emerging Nanobiopharmaceuticals. *Journal of Informetrics* 5 (3): 233–247.

Chen, H., R. Chiang, and V. Storey. 2012. Business Intelligence and Analytics: From Big Date to Big Impact. *MIS Quarterly* 36 (4): 1165–1188.

Chong, D., and J. Druckman. 2007. Framing Theory. *Annual Review of Political Science* 10 (2): 103–126.

Churchland, P. 2019. *Conscience: The Origins of Moral Intuition*. New York: W. W. Norton & Company.

Coker, C. 2008. *Ethics and War in the 21st Century*. Abington, VA: Routledge Publishers.

Collins, J., and W. Lazier. 1992. *Beyond Entrepreneurship*. New York: Prentice Hall.

Collins, J., and B. Lazier. 2020. *Beyond 2.0: Turning Your Business into an Enduring Great Company*. New York: Penguin Random House.

Conboy, K., P. Mikalef, D. Dennehy, and J. Krogstie. 2020. Using Business Analytics to Enhance Dynamic Capabilities in Operations Research: A Case Analysis and Research Agenda. *European Journal of Operational Research* 281 (3): 656–672.

Connor, K. 2012. Taming the Data Tidal Wave. *Analytics Magazine*, September–October, pp. 21–24.

Cook, T., and D. Stanley. 1979. *Quasi-Experimentation: Design and Analysis Issues for Field Settings*. Boston, MA: Houghton Mifflin Company.

Cornwell, B. 2014. *Waterloo: The History of Four Days, Three Armies, and Three Battles*. New York: Harper.

Coulson, S., and C. Canovas. 2014. Understanding Timeline: Conceptual Metaphor and Conceptual Integration. *Cognitive Semiotics* 5 (1–2): 198–219.

Court, D. 2015. Getting Big Impact from Big Data. *McKinsey Quarterly*, January. http://www.mckinsey.com/insights/business_technology/getting_big_impact_from_big_data. Accessed 13 July 2015.

Czarnitzks, D., and A. Toole. 2011. Patent Protection, Market Uncertainty, and R&D Investment. *Review of Economics and Statistics* 93 (1): 147–159.

Dahl, R. 1963. *Modern Political Analysis*. Englewood Cliffs: Prentice-Hall.

Dane, E., and M. Pratt. 2007. Exploring Intuition and Its Role in Managerial Decision-Making. *Academy of Management Review* 32 (1): 33–54.

Davenport, T. 2013. *The Rise of Analytics 3:0: How to Compete in the Data Economy*. Portland: International Institute for Analytics.

Davenport, T. 2014. *Advanced Analytics and Big Data Adoption Report*. Portland: International Institute for Analytics.

Davenport, T., and J. Harris. 2007. *Competing on Analytics: The New Science of Winning*. Boston: Harvard Business School Press.

Davenport, T., J. Harris, and R. Morrison. 2010. *Analytics at Work, Smarter Decisions, Better Results*. Cambridge, MA: Harvard Business Review Press.

Davenport, T., et al. 2013. *Managing with Analytics at Procter & Gamble*. Boston: Harvard Business School Publishing.

Davenport, T., et al. 2015. *CAO, CDO or Both: The Evolving Roles in Data and Analytics Leadership, Executive Summary*. Portland: Enterprise Research Service, International Institute for Analytics.

Dean, J., and M. Sharfman. 1996. Does Decision Process Matter? A Study of Strategic Decision-Making Effectiveness. *Academy of Management Journal* 39: 368–392.

DeLangue, B., S. Puntoni, and R. Larrick. 2017. Liner Thinking in a Non-linear World. *Harvard Business Review*, May–June, pp. 130–139

Delen, D., and S. Ram. 2018. Research Challenges and Opportunities in Business Analytics. *Journal of Business Analytics* 1 (1): 2–12.

Dennet, D. 2017. *From Bacteria to Bach and Back: The Evolution of Minds*. New York: W. W. Norton Company.

D'Eredita, M., and C. Barreto. 2006. How Does Tacit Knowledge Proliferate? An Episode-Based Perspective. *Organization Studies* 27 (12): 1821–1841.

Dimensional Insight. 2020. *6 Ways Analytics Can Help With*. Burlington, MA.

Drosou, M., H. Jagdish, E. Pitoura, and J. Stoyanovich. 2017. Diversity in Big Data: A Review. *Big Data* 5 (2): 73–84.

Drucker, P. 1988. The Coming of the New Organization. *Harvard Business Review*, 1: 45–53.

Druckman, J. 2001. Evaluating Framing Effects. *Journal of Economic Psychology* 22 (1): 91–101.

Durbach, I. 2019. Scenario Planning in the Analytic Hierarchy Process. *Futures & Foresight Science* 1 (2): 1–12.

Durbach, I., R. Lahdelma, and P. Salminin. 2014. The Analytic Hierarchy Process with Stochastic Judgements. *European Journal of Operational Research* 238 (2): 552–559.

The Economist. 2021. The Warner-Discovery Deal and the Future of Streaming, May 18.

Eisenmann, T. 2021. Why Start-Ups Fail? *Harvard Business Review*, May–June

Ericsson, K., and H. Simon. 1980. Verbal Reports as Data. *Psychological Review* 87: 215–251.

Ertiningsih, D., S. Bhulai, and F. Spieksma. 2018. A Novel Use of Value Iteration for Deriving Bounds for Threshold and Switching Curve Optimal Policies. *Naval Review of Logistics* 65 (4): 638–659.

Etner, J., M. Jeleva, and J. Tallon. 2012. Decision Theory Under Ambiguity. *Journal of Economic Surveys* 26 (2): 234–270.

Evans, G., W. Biles, and Ki-Hwan Bae. 2019. *Analytics, Operations, and Strategic Decision Making in the Public Sector*. IGI Global: Hershey, PA.

Fabiszak, M. 2007. *A Conceptual Metaphor Approach to War Discourse and Implications*. Poland Poznan: Adam Mickiewicz University Press.

Fauconnier, G., and M. Turner. 2002. *The Way We Think: Conceptual Blending and the Mind's Hidden Complexities*. New York: Basic Books.

Ferrer-Serrano, M., M. Pilar-Latorre-Martinez, and L. Fuentelsaz. 2021. The European Research Landscape Under the Horizon 2020 Lenses: The Interaction Between Science Centers, Public Institutions, and Industry. *The Journal of Technology Transfer* 46: 828–853.

Festinger, L. 1957. *A Theory of Cognitive Dissonance*. Evanston, IL: Peterson Publishers.

Fortuna, N. 2018. Beyond Analytics. *MHI Solutions*, March 23.

Fox, C., and A. Tversky. 1995. Ambiguity Aversion and Comparative Ignorance. *Quarterly Journal of Economics* 110 (3): 585–604.

Fox, C., and A. Tversky. 1998. A Belief-Based Account of Decision Under Uncertainty. *Management Science* 44 (7): 879–895.

Franks, B. 2012. *Taming the Big Data Tidal Wave*. New York: Wiley.

Frenken, K., and J. Hoekman. 2014. Spatial Scientometrics and Scholarly Impact: A Review of Recent Studies, Tools, and Methods. In *Measuring Scholarly Impact: Methods and Practice*, ed. Y. Ding, R. Rousseau, and D. Wolfram. New York: Springer.

Fusaroli, R., and S. Morgagni. 2014. Introduction: Thirty Years After. *Cognitive Semiotics* 5 (1–2): 1–290.

Galef, J. 2021. *The Scout Mindset: Why Some People See Things Clearly and Others Don't*. New York: Penguin Random House.

Gantz, J., et al. 2014. *The Digital Universe of Opportunities: Rich Data and the Increasing Value of the Internet of Things*, 7th ed. Milipitas: IDC Corporation.

Gao, S., R. Alhaij, R. Rokne, and J. Guan. 2011. Mining Sequential Patterns with Extensible Knowledge Representation. *Intelligent Data Analysis* 15 (6): 889–911.

Geeraerts, D., and H. Cuyckens. 2007. *Cognitive Linguistics*. New York: Oxford University Press.

Geisler, E. 1979. An Empirical Study of a Proposed System for Monitoring Organizational Change in a Federal R&D Laboratory. Unpublished dissertation, Evanston, Illinois, Northwestern University.

Geisler, E. 1997. *Managing the Aftermath of Radical Corporate Change: Reengineering, Restructuring and Reinvention*. Westport, CT: Quorum Books.

Geisler, E. 2000. *The Metrics of Science and Technology*. Westport: Quorum Books.

Geisler, E. 2001. Organizational Change Phenomena, Managerial Cognition and Archival Measures: Reconceptualization and New Empirical Evidence. Working Paper, Illinois Institute of Technology.

Geisler, E. 2002a. On the Ubiquitous Inadequacy of Co-Variation Design in Strategy Research. *International Journal of Technology Management* 23 (6): 558–577.

Geisler, E. 2002b. Indexing Transition Indicators of Medical Technology: Evaluation by Comparing Process and C-Variation Methodologies. Presented at the Hawaii International Conference on Systems Sciences (HICSS), January 7–10.

Geisler, E. 2006. A Taxonomy and Proposed Codification of Knowledge and Knowledge Systems in Organizations. *Knowledge and Process Management* 13 (4): 285–296.

Geisler, E. 2013. Beyond Analytics: The Special Case How Technology Managers Translate Big Data into Actionable Decisions. In *Proceedings of the PICMET (Portland International Conference on the Management of Engineering and Technology) Conference*, Aug 3–5, San Jose, CA.

Geisler, E., and R. Kostoff. 1999. Strategic Management and Implementation of Textual Data Mining in Government Organizations. *Technology Analysis & Strategic Management* 11 (4): 493–525.

Geisler, E., and B. Ritter. 2003. Differences in Additive Complexity Between Biological Evolution and the Progress of Knowledge. *Emergence* 5 (2): 42–55.

Gholizadeh, H., et al. 2014. Relationship Among Economic growth, Internet Usage and Publication Productivity: Comparison Among ASEAN and World's Best Countries. *Modern Applied Science* 8 (2): 160–170.

Ghosh, B., and J. Scott. 2011. Antecedents and Catalysts for Developing a Healthcare Analytic Capability. *Communications of the Association for Information Systems* 29 (22): 395–410.

Gibbs, R. 2013. Why Do Some People Dislike Conceptual Metaphor Theory? *Cognitive Semiotics* 5 (1–2): 14–36.

Godin, B. 2006. On the Origins of Bibliometrics. *Scientometrics* 68 (1): 109–133.

Goel, R., and M. Nelson. 2020. How Do Firms Use Innovations to Hedge Against Economic and Political Uncertainty? Evidence from a Large Sample of Nations. *The Journal of Technology Transfer* 46: 407–430.

Gonthier, C. 2020. Charting the Diversity of Strategic Processes in Visuspatial Short-Term Memory. *Perspectives on Psychological Science* 16 (2): 294–318.

Gregg, B., J. Heller, J. Perrey, and J. Tsai. 2018. *The Most Perfect Union: Unlocking the Next Wave of Growth by Unifying Creativity and Analytics*. New York: McKinsey and Company.

Halper, F., and K. Krishnan. 2013. *TDWI Big Data Maturity Model Guide*. The Data Warehouse Institute.

Hammer, M. 1996. *Beyond Engineering*. New York: Harper Business Publishers.

Hand, D. 2004. *Measurement Theory and Practice: The World Through Quantification*. Chichester, UK: Wiley.

Hand, D. 2018. Who Told You That? Data Provenance, False Facts, and Separating the Liars from the Truth-Tellers. *Significance* 15: 8–9.

Harris, M., and B. Thayler. 2019. Tying Performance Metrics to Strategy Has Become an Acceptable Best Practice Over the Past Few Decades. *Harvard Business Review*, September October, pp. 64–69

Higgins, E. 1992. Achieving 'Shared Reality' in the Communication Game: A Social Action that Creates Meaning. *Journal of Language and Social Psychology* 11 (2): 101–131.

Horner, P. 2018. Analytics Extravaganza. *Informs/Analytics Magazine*, November–December, p. 2

House, P., and R. Shull. 1988. *Rush to Policy: Using Analytics Techniques in Public Sector Decision-Making*. London, UK: Routledge.

Hubbard, D. 2014. *How to Measure Anything: Finding the Value of "Intangibles" in Business*, 3rd ed. Hoboken: Wiley.

Hult, M., and Sven-Ake Lennung. 1980. Towards a Definition of Action Research: A Note and Bibliography. *Journal of Management Studies* 17 (2): 241–250.

Hummel, P., M. Braun, M. Tretter, and P. Dabrock. 2021. *Data Sovereignty: A Review. Big Data & Society*, January-June, pp. 1–17.

IBM Press Release. 2012. Using Analytics, Santam Saves $2.4 Million in Fraudulent Claims, May 9.

Isabella, L. 1990. Evolving Interpretations as a Change Unfolds: How Managers Construe Key Organizational Events. *Academy of Management Journal* 33 (1): 7–41.

Iturbe-Ormaetxe, I., et al. 2011. Framing Effects in Public Good: Prospect Theory and Experimental Evidence. *Games and Economic Behavior* 72 (2): 439–447.

Jenkins, M., and G. Johnson. 1997. Linking Management Cognition and Organizational Performance: A Preliminary Investigation Using Causal Maps. *British Journal of Management* 8 (2): 77–90.

Johnson, E., J. Hershey, J. Meszaros, and H. Kunreuther. 1993. Framing Probability Distortions and Insurance Decisions. *Journal of Risk and Uncertainty* 7 (1): 35–51.

Kachelmeier, S., and M. Shehata. 1992. Examining Risk Preferences Under High Monetary Incentives: Experimental Evidence from the People's Republic of China. *American Economic Review* 82 (5): 1120–1141.

Kahneman, D., and A. Tversky. 1973. On the Psychology of Prediction. *Psychological Review* 80 (4): 237–251.

Kahneman, D., and A. Tversky. 1979. Prospect Theory: An Analysis of Decisions Under Risk. *Econometrica* 47 (2): 263–292.

Kahneman, D., P. Slovic, and A. Tuersky (eds.). 1982. *Judgement Under Uncertainty: Heuristics and Biases*. London: Cambridge University Press.

Kamien, M., and N. Schwartz. 1982. *Market Structure and Innovation*. Cambridge, UK: Cambridge University Press.

Kaplan, S. 2011. Research in Cognition and Strategy: Reflection on Two Decades of Program and a Look to the Future. *Journal of Management Studies* 48 (3): 665–695.

Kaplan, R., and D. Norton. 1996. *The Balanced Scorecard*. Boston, MA: Harvard Business School Press.

Kaplan, R. and D. Norton. 2007. Using the Balanced Scorecard as a Strategic Management Tool. *Harvard Business Review*, July–August.

Karlan, D., and J. Apppel. 2016. *Failing in the Field: What We Can Learn When Field Research Goes Wrong*. Princeton, NJ: Princeton University Press.

Karp, T. 2005. Unpacking the Mysteries of Change: Mental Modeling. *Journal of Change Management* 5 (1): 87–96.

Karthik, P.M. 2021. *Chess Intuition Versus Calculation: Understanding What You Need*. Monee, IL.

Kaufman, M., and J. Kirsch. 2014. *Advanced Analytics: The Hurwitz Victory Index Report*. Needham: Hurwitz & Associates.

Keegan, J. 1988. *The Price of Admiralty: The Evolution of Naval Warfare*. New York: Penguin Books.

Keen, P. 1978. *Decision Support Systems: An Organizational Perspective*. Reading, PA: Addison-Wesley.

Klimant, P., M. Tieber, and H. Risku. 2018. Introduction to the Thematic Section: Expertise and Behavior: Aspects of Cognitive Translation Studies. *Hermes Journal of Language and Communication in Business* 57 (1): 7–9.

Kiron, D., R. Shockley, N. Kruschwitz, G. Finch, and M. Haydock. 2010. *Analytics: The Widening Divide: How Companies are Achieving Competitive Advantage Through Analytics*. New York: IBM Institute for Business Value.

Kostoff, R. 2012. Text Mining for Science and Technology: A Review—Part I-Characterization/Scientometrics. *Journal of Scientometrics Research* 1 (1): 11–21.

Kostoff, R., and E. Geisler. 1999. Strategic Management and Implementation of Textural Data Mining in Government Organizations. *Technology Analysis & Strategic Management* 11 (4): 493–525.

Kraemer, K., and J. King. 1986. Computing and Public Organizations. *Public Administration Review* 46 (November): 488–496.

Kramer, A., J. Guillory, and J. Hancock. 2014. Experimental Evidence of Massive-Scale Emotional Contagion Through Social Networks. *PNAS* 111: 8788–8790.

Kraus, M., S. Feuerrigel, and A. Oztekin. 2020. Deep Learning in Business Analytics and Operations Research: Models, Applications, an Managerial Implications. *European Journal of Operational Research* 281 (3): 628–641.

Kristoffersen, E., P. Mikalef, F. Blomsma, and J. Li. 2021. Towards a Business Analytics Capability for the Circular Economy. *Technological Forecasting & Social Change* 171.

Kuehnhanss, C., B. Heyndels, and K. Hilken. 2015. Choice in Politics: Equivalency Framing in Economic Policy Decisions and the Influence of Expertise. *European Journal of Political Economy* 40 (B): 360–374.

Kuhn, T. 1962. *The Structure of Scientific Revolutions*. Chicago, IL: University of Chicago Press.

Labbe, P., et al. 2019. *Intelligence with Qlik Sense*. Birmingham, UK: Packt Publishing.

Laibson, D., and R. Zeckhauser. 1998. Amos Tversky and the Ascent of Behavioral Economics. *Journal of Risk and Uncertainty* 16: 7–47.

Lanning, A., and G. Meklaus. 2021. Beyond COVID-10: Four Ways AI is Shaping the Future of Healthcare. *Healthcare Innovation*, May 18.

Laurson, G.H.N., and J. Thorlund. 2010. *Business Analytics for Managers: Taking Business Intelligence Beyond Reporting*. New York: Wiley.

LaValle, S., M. Hopkins, E. Lessor, R. Schockley, and N. Kruschwitz. 2010. *Analytics: The New Path to Value: How the Smartest Organizations are Embedding Analytics to Transform Insights into Action*. IBM Institute for Business Value.

Leavitt, H. 1975a. Beyond the Analytic Manager. *California Management Review* 17 (3): 5–12.

Leavitt, H. 1975b. Beyond the Analytic Manager: Part II. *California Management Review* 17 (4): 11–21.

LeCarre, J. 1963. *The Spy Who Came in from the Cold*. New York: Penguin Books.

Lee, D. 2005. *Cognitive Linguistics: An Introduction*. New York: Oxford University Press.

Lee, C. 2011. Bounded Rationality and the Emergence of Simplicity Amidst Complexity. *Journal of Economic Surveys* 25 (3): 507–526.

Lehtiniermi, T., and M. Ruckenstein. 2019. The Social Imagineries of Data Activism. *Big Data & Society*, January–June, pp. 1–12

Leventhal, R. 2020. Health Systems Greatly Underutilize Analytics, Report Finds. *Healthcare Innovation*, January 14.

Levine, J., L. Resnick, and E. Higgins. 1993. Social Foundations of Cognition. *Annual Review of Psychology* 44 (4): 484–612.

Lewis, M., C. Andriopoulos, and W. Smith. 2014. Paradoxical Leadership to Enable Strategic Agility. *California Management Review* 56 (3): 58–77.

Leydesdorff, L. 1998. Theories of Citation? *Scientometrics* 43 (1): 5–25.

L'Huillier, G., and S. Maldonado. 2011. Future Trends in Business Analytics and Optimization. *Intelligent Data Analysis* 15 (6): 1001–1017.

Li, Z., and D. Hensher. 2011. Prospect Theoretic Contributions in Understanding Traveler Behavior: A Review and Some Comments. *Transport Reviews* 31 (1): 97–115.

Liberatore, M., and W. Luo. 2010. The Analytics Movement: Implications for Operations Research. *Interfaces* 40 (4): 313–324.

Liu, X., A. Montgomery, and K. Srinivasan. 2018. Analyzing Bank Overdraft Fees with Big Data. *Marketing Science* 37 (6): 855–882.

Lodish, L., and C. Mela. 2007. If Brands are Built Over Years, Why Are They Managed Over Quarters? *Harvard Business Review*, July–August.

Luscher, L., and M. Lewis. 2008. Organizational Change and Managerial Sense-making: Working Through a Paradox. *Academy of Management Journal* 51 (2): 221–240.

Madtiavan, R., and P. Grover. 1998. From Embedded Knowledge to Embodied Knowledge: New Product Development as Knowledge Management. *Journal of Marketing* 62 (4): 1–12.

Maoqing, L., N. Fard, and K. Sadeghzadeh. 2017. Large-Scale Spectral Clustering for Managing Big Data in Healthcare Operations. *International Journal of Big Data Intelligence* 4 (3): 195–207.

March, J. 1991. Exploration and Exploitation in Organizational Learning. *Organization Science* 2 (1): 71–87.

Marr, B. 2017. *Data Strategy: How to Profit from a World of Big Data, Analytics, and the Internet of Things*. London, UK: Kogan Page.

Martin, G., et al. 2017. Institutional Complexity and Individual Responses: Delineating the Boundaries of Partial Autonomy. *Organization Studies* 38 (1): 103–127.

Massingham, P. 2019. *Knowledge Management: Theory in Practice*. Thousand Oaks, CA: Sage Publications.

McCarthy, B., C. McShea, and M. Roth. 2018. Rebooting Analytics Leadership: Time to Move Beyond the Math. McKinsey & Company, NewYork, November 2018.

McKinsey Global Institute. 2016. *The Age of Analytics: Competing in a Data-Driven World*. Burlington, MA.

McKinsey & Company. 2016. *How Companies are Using Big Data and Analytics*. Burlington, MA.

Meissner, P., O. Siboney, and T. Wulf. 2015. Are You Ready to Decide? *McKinsey Quarterly*, April, pp. 1–4.

Mendoza, F., and A. Baicchi. 2005. Cognitive Linguistics: Internal Dynamics and Interdisciplinary Interaction. In *Cognitive Linguistics Research*, ed. R. Dirven, R. Langacker, and J. Taylor. Berlin: Mouton de Gruyter Publishers.

Minelli, M., M. Chambers, and A. Dhiraj. 2013. *Big Data Big Analytics: Emerging Business Intelligence and Analytic Trends for Today's Businesses*. New York: Wiley.

Mingers, J., and L. Leydesdorff. 2019. A Review of Theory and Practice in Scientometrics. *European Journal of Operational Research* (in press).

Mintzberg, H., B. Alstrand, and J. Lampel. 2010. *Management? It's Not What You Think*. New Work: ANACOM.

Mohammadi, E. 2012. Knowledge Mapping of the Iranian Nanoscience and Technology: A Text Mining Approach. *Scientometrics* 19 (3): 593–608.

Morgan, G. 1986. *Images of Organizations*. Thousand Oaks, CA: Sage Publications.

Mulla, K. 2011. Mapping of the International Journal of Information Science and Management (2003–2009): A Citation Study. *International Journal of Information Science and Management* 9 (1): 1–17.

Neiberg, M. 2016. *The Path to War: How the First World War Created Modern America*. New York: Oxford University Press.

Nisbett, R.E., and L. Ross. 1980. *Human Inferences: Strategies and Shortcomings of Social Judgment*. Englewood Cliffs: Prentice-Hall.

Nutt, P. 1990. Strategic Decision-Making by Top Executives and Middle Managers with Data and Process Dominant Stages. *Journal of Management Studies* 27 (2): 173–194.

Pang, W., and A. Rochwerger. 2021. Choosing an Organizational Structure for your AI Team. *Upside Data Business*, May 18.

Pederson, L., and T. Ritter. 2021. The 4 Types of Leadership. *California Management Review* 63 (2).

Pepper, G., and G. Larson. 2006. Overcoming Information Communication Technology Problems in a Post-Acquisition Organization. *Organization Dynamics* 35 (2): 160–163.

Petrovich, E. 2016. From Little Philosophy to Big Philosophy: Some Problems in the Applications of Traditional Historical-Philosophical Notions to the Evolution of Contemporary Philosophy. In *2016 Symposium of the Swiss Philosophical Society, University of Geneva, Geneva, Switzerland*, Sept 15–17.

Petrovich, E. 2018. Accumulation of Knowledge in Para-Scientific Areas: The Case of Analytic Philosophy. *Scientometrics* 116 (2): 1123–1151.

Plomp, R. 1990. The Significance of the Number of Highly Cited Papers as an Indicator of Scientific Prolificacy. *Scientometrics* 19 (3–4): 185–197.

Polyrack, R. 2018. *The New Mind Readers: What Neuroimaging Can and Cannot Reveal About Our Thoughts*. Princeton, NJ: Princeton University Press.

Popper, K. 2005. *The Logic of Scientific Discovery*. New York: Routledge Oxford Analytica.

Rahmen, J. 2018. Determining Cognitive Distance Between Publication Portfolios of Evaluators and Evaluees in Research Evaluation: A Exploration of Informetric Methods. Doctoral Dissertation, Faculty of Social Sciences, University of Antwerp, Belgium.

Raynor, M. 2007. *The Strategy Paradox: Why Committing to Success Leads to Failure*. New York: Crown Business.

Reiter, N., and B. List. 2013. An Analytics Maturity Model: How Analytically Mature Is Your Organization and How Can It Do Better. *Analytics*, Nov–Dec. http://www.analytics-magazine.org/november-december2013/904-informs-analytics-maturity-model?format=pfd. Accessed 8 July 2015.

Reuter, E. 2021. To Compete, Walmart Had to Acquire a Telehealth Business. *MedCity News*, May 7.
Rockart, J., and C. Bullen. 1986. *The Rise of Managerial Computing: The Best of the Center for Information Systems Research*. Homewood: Irwin Publishers.
Rockart, J., and D. DeLong. 1988. *Executive Support Systems: The Emergence of Top Management Computer User*. Homewood: Irwin Publishers.
Rose, P. 2021. Speculative Philosophy and the Tyranny of the Practical. *Academia Letters*, 168
Rothman, J. 2020. The Equality Conundrum. *The New Yorker*, January.
Rotolo, D., I. Rafols, M. Hopkins, and L. Leydesdorff. 2017. Strategic Intelligence on Emerging Technologies: Scientometric Overlay Mapping. *Journal of the Association or Information Science and Technology* 68 (1): 214–233.
Rubenstein, A., and C. Haberstroh. 1960. *Some Theories of Organization*. Homewood, IL: Richard D. Irwin.
Rubenstein, A., and E. Geisler. 1991. Factors Influencing the Adoption and Use of Intelligent Systems in Professional Service Organizations. Paper presented at PICMET 1991. International Conference, Oct 27–31, Portland, Oregon.
Rubenstein, A., E. Geisler, M. Glaser, et al. 1992. Preliminary Design Features of a Series of Intelligent Support Machines for Professional Knowledge Workers. Paper prepared for IAMOT, 1992 and Management of Technology III, ed. T. Khalil and B. Bayraktar.
Ryan, V. 2015. Mastering Predictive Analytics. *CFO*, July 30.
Ryan, V. 2016. Special Report: The Promise of Predictive Analytics. *CFO*, October 16.
Saunders, C. 1981. Management Information Systems, Communications and Department Power: An Integral Model. *Academy of Management Review* 6 (3): 431–442.
Scheepers, M., et al. 2011. A Mental Model for Successful Inter-Disciplinary Collaboration in Curriculum Innovation for Information Literacy. *South African Journal of Libraries and Information Science* 77 (1): 169–178.
Schroeck, M., R. Scockley, J. Smart, D. Romero-Morales, and P. Tufano. 2012. Analytics: The Real-World Use of Big Data: How Innovative Enterprises Extract Value from Uncertain Data. Business Report, IBM Institute for Business Value.
Schwaninger, M. 2000. Managing Complexity: The Path Toward Intelligent Organizations. *Systemic Practice and Action Research* 13 (2): 207–241.
Schwarz, J. 2017. *How CEOs and CHROS Can Connect People to Business Strategy*. Cambridge, MA: Harvard Business Review Analytic Services Report.
Shadish, W., T. Cook, and D. Campbell. 2002. *Experimental and Quasi-Experimental Designs for Generalized Causal Inferences*. Boston, MA: Houghton Mifflin Company.

Shapero, A. 1977. What Management Says and What Managers Do. *Interfaces* 7 (2): 106–108.

Siegel, E. 2013. Predictive Analytics. *Analytics Magazine*, July/August, pp. 38–43.

Simon, H. 1952. Comments on the Theory of Organizations. *American Political Science Review* 46 (4): 1130–1139.

Simon, H. 1976. *Administrative Behavior: A Study of Decision-Making Processes in Administrative Organizations*, 3rd ed. New York: Free Press.

Smalltree, H., and W. Eckerson. 2015. How, Where, and Why Big Data are Delivering Value. June Tech Target Benchmark Report.

Smith, A. 2016. 5 Reasons Why People Stick to Their Beliefs, No Matter What. *Psychology Today*, March 28

Spohrer, M. 2013. Murphy's Law in Action: The Formation of the Film Production Network of Paul Lazarus Barbarosa (1982)-An Actor-Network-Theory Case Study. *International Journal of Actor-Network Theory and Technological Innovation* 5 (1): 19–39.

Stickles, E., O. David, E. Dodge, and J. Hong. 2016. Formalizing Contemporary Conceptual Metaphor Theory: A Structured Repository for Metaphor Analysis. *Construction and Frames* 8 (2): 166–213.

Suen, C., and L. Qin (eds.). 2021. *Book Series on Language Processing, Pattern Recognition, and Intelligent Systems*. Singapore: World Scientific Publishers.

Suha, A., and M. Dashti. 2021. The Use of the Telegram Application as an Information Sharing Tool. *Journal of Information & Knowledge Management* 20 (2).

Talia, D. 2019. *Big Data and the Computable Society*. Singapore: World Scientific Publishers.

Taran, Y., M. Boer, and P. Lindgren. 2015. A Business Model Innovation Typology. *Decision Sciences* 46 (2): 301–331.

Taylor, L., R. Schroeder, and E. Meyer. 2014. Emerging Practices and Perspectives on Big Data Analysis in Economics: Bigger and Better or More of the Same? *Big Data & Society*, July–December, pp. 1–10.

Terry, K. 2012. Analytics: The Nervous System of IT-Enabled Healthcare: Strategies for Managing Sophisticated Analytic Tools in the Healthcare Industry. Institute for Health Technology Transformation, White Paper.

Timmermans, S., and A. Mauck. 2005. The Promises and Pitfalls of Evidence-Based Medicine. *Health Affairs* 24 (1): 18–28.

Toynbee, A. 1948. *A Study of History*. New York: Oxford University Press.

Tuchman, B. 1985. *The March of Folly: From Troy to Vietnam*. New York: Random House.

Turing, A. 1950. Computing Machinery and Intelligence. *Mind* 49 (4): 433–446.

Tversky, A., and D. Kahneman. 1983. Extensional Versus Intuitive Reasoning: The Conjunction Fallacy in Probability Judgement. *Psychological Review* 90 (4): 293–315.

Tversky, A., and D. Kahneman. 1992. Advances in Prospect Theory: Cumulative Representation of Uncertainty. *Journal of Risk and Uncertainty* 5 (3): 297–323.

Ungerer, F., and H. Schmid. 2006. *An Introduction to Cognitive Linguistics*, 2nd ed. Harlow, UK: Addison Wesley.

Valdya, O., and S. Kumar. 2006. Analytic Hierarchy Process: An Overview of Applications. *European Journal of Operational Research* 169 (1): 1–29.

Van de Kaa, E. 2010. Applicability of an Extended Prospect Theory to Travel Behavior Research: A Meta-Analysis. *Transport Reviews* 30 (6): 771–804.

Vis, B., and D. Kuijpers. 2018. Prospect Theory and Foreign Policy Decision-Making: Underexposed Issues, Advancements, and Ways Forward. *Contemporary Security Policy* 39 (4): 575–589.

Walsh, B. 2013. The NSA's Big Data Problem. *Time Magazine*, June 24, pp. 24–25.

Wang, H. 1986. *Beyond Analytic Philosophy: Doing Justice to What We Know*. Cambridge, MA: MIT Press.

Ward-Perkins, B. 2005. *The Fall of Rome and the End of Civilization*. Oxford, UK: Oxford University Press.

Watkins, H. 2020. The Morality of War. *Perspectives on Psychological Science* 15 (2): 231–249.

Weber, M. 1971. The Interpretation of Social Reality, ed. J.E. Eldridge. New York: Scribner.

Weick, K. 1995. *Sensemaking in Organizations*. Thousand Oaks, CA: Sage Publications.

West, D., T. Zaidatun, et al. 2018. Learning Analytics Experience Among Academics in Australia and Malaysia: A Comparison. *Australasian Journal of Educational Technology* 34 (3): 122–139.

Willison, K. 2021. Dual Process Models in Sociology: Reflections and Potential. *Academic Letters*, Article 201.

Woody, T. 2012. Automakers, Tech Companies Mining Electric Car Big Data to Plot Industry's Future. *Forbes*, June 18

Wouters, P. 1999. The Citation Culture. Doctoral Thesis, University of Amsterdam.

Wouters, P., and E. Noyons. 2014. Context Counts: Pathways to Master Big and Little Data. In *Proceedings of the Science and Technology Indicators Conference*, Leiden, The Netherlands, University of Leiden Press.

Wouters, P., et al. 2015. The Metric Tide: Literature Review (Supplementary Report I to the Independent Review) of the Role of Metrics in Research Assessment and Management, HEFCE.

Yigit, A., and D. Kanbach. 2021. The Importance of Artificial Intelligence in Strategic Management: A Systematic Literature Review. *International Journal of Strategic Management* 21 (1): 5–40.

Zabelina, D., D. O'Leary, N. Pornpattanangul, R. Nusslock, and M. Beeman. 2015. Creativity and Sensory Gating Indexed by the P-50: Selective Versus Leaky Sensory Gating in Divergent Thinkers and Creative Achievers. *Neuropsychologia* 69 (2): 77–84.

Zhu, S., D. Dalal, and J. Mathieu. 2021. Team Decision Making: The Dynamic Effects of Team Decision Style Composition and Performance Via Decision Strategy. *Journal of Management* 47 (5): 1281–1304.

Ziff, Davis. 2016. Big Data, Little Data, and Everything in Between—IBM SPSS Solutions Help You Bring Analytics to Everyone. White Paper, San Francisco, CA.

Zill, M., and E. Bassecoulard. 2008. Challenges for Scientometric Indicators: Data Demining, Knowledge-Flow Measurements and Diversity Issues. *Ethics in Science and Environmental Politics* 8 (1): 49–60.

Zimmerman, F. 2021. Population Health Science: Fulfilling the Mission of Public Health. *Milbank Quarterly* 99 (1): 9–23.

Additional Bibliography

Agor, W. 1986. The Logic of Intuition: How Top Executives Make Important Decisions. *Organizational Dynamics* 14 (3): 5–18.

Bannister, B., and R. Griffith. 1986. Applying a Causal Analytic Framework to the Mobley, Horner and Hollingsworth (1978) Turnover Model: A Useful Reexamination. *Journal of Management* 12 (3): 433–443.

Beller, M.J., and A. Barnett. 2009. Next Generation Business Analytics. Lightship Partners LLC. Retrieved 2009-06-20.

Borgman, C. 1999. The User's Mental Model for an Information Retrieval System: An Experiment on a Prototype Online Catalog. *International Journal of Human-Computer Studies* 51 (2): 435–452.

Burrows, L., and M. Savage. 2014. *After the Crisis? Big Data and the Methodological Challenges of Empirical Sociology. Big Data & Society*. April–June, pp. 1–6.

Braunstein, D. 1974. Beyond Leavitt's 'Narrow' Analytic Manager. *Interfaces* 4 (4): 28–31.

Chen, C.L., and Chun-Yang Zhang. 2014. Data-Intensive Applications, Challenges, Techniques and Technologies: A Survey on Big Data. *Information Sciences* 275: 314–347.

Chen, H., R. Chiang, and V. Storey. 2012. Business Intelligence and Analytics: From Big Data to Big Impact. *MIS Quarterly* 36 (4): 1165–1188.

Cosentino, T. 2015. Data Preparation Is Essential for Predictive Analytics. Perspectives, Ventana Research.

Court, D. 2015. Getting Big Impact from Big Data. *McKinsey Quarterly*, January.

Dahl, R. 1963. *Modern Political Analysis*. Englewood Cliffs, NJ: Prentice-Hall.

Davenport, T. 2014a. *Advanced Analytics and Big Data Adoption Report*. Portland, OR: International Institute for Analytics.

Davenport, T. 2014b. *Big Data at Work: Dispelling the Myths, Uncovering the Opportunities*. Cambridge, MA: Harvard Business Review Press.

Davenport, T., and J. Harris. 2007. *Competing on Analytics: The New Science of Winning*. Boston, MA: Harvard Business School Press.

Davenport, T., J. Harris, and R. Morrison. 2010. *Analytics at Work, Smarter Decisions, Better Results*. Cambridge, MA: Harvard Business Review Press.

Davenport, T., M. Iansiti, and A. Sereis. 2013. *Managing with Analytics at Procter and Gamble*. Boston, MA: Harvard Business School Publishing.

Drucker, P. 1988. The Coming of the New Organization. *Harvard Business Review*, January–February, pp. 45–53.

Elgendy, N., and A. Elragal. 2016. Big Data Analytics in Support of the Decision Making Process. *Procedia Computer Science* 100: 1071–1084.

Etner, J., M. Jeleva, and J. Tallon. 2012. Decision Theory Under Ambiguity. *Journal of Economic Surveys* 26 (2): 234–270.

Fauconnier, G., and M. Turner. 2002. *The Way We Think: Conceptual Blending and The Mind's Hidden Complexities. Basic Books*. New York: Basic Books.

Ferguson, K. 2013. *Measuring the Universe: The Historical Quest to Quantify Space*. San Francisco: Transworld Digital.

Fox, C., and A. Tversky. 1995. Ambiguity Aversion and Comparative Ignorance. *Quarterly Journal of Economics* 110 (3): 585–604.

Fox, C., and A. Tversky. 1998. A Belief-Based Account of Decision Under Uncertainty. *Management Science* 44 (7): 879–895.

Gao, S., R. Alhaij, R. Rokne, and J. Guan. 2011. Mining Sequential Patterns with Extensible Knowledge Representation. *Intelligent Data Analysis* 15 (6): 889–911.

Geisler, E. 1979. An Empirical Study of a Proposed System for Monitoring Organizational Change in a Federal R&D Laboratory. Unpublished dissertation, Northwestern University, Evanston, IL.

Geisler, E. 1997. *Managing the Aftermath of Radical Corporate Change: Reengineering*. Greenwood, CT: Praeger Publishers.

Geisler, E. 2000. *The Metrics of Science and Technology*. Westport, CT: Quorum Books.

Geisler, E. 2002. On the Ubiquitous Inadequacy of Co-Variation Design in Strategy Research. *International Journal of Technology Management* 23 (6): 558–577.

Geisler, E. 2013. Beyond Analytics: The Special Case. How Technology Managers Translate Big Data into Actionable Decisions. In *Proceedings of the PICMET (Portland International Conference on the Management of Engineering and Technology) Conference*, Aug 3–5, San Jose, CA.

Geisler, E., and R. Kostoff. 1999. Strategic Management and Implementation of Textual Data Mining in Government Organizations. *Technology Analysis & Strategic Management* 11 (4): 493–525.

Ghosh, B., and J. Scott. 2011. Antecedents and Catalysts for Developing a Healthcare Analytic Capability. *Communications of the Association for Information Systems* 29 (22): 395–410.

Gibbon, E. 1978. *The Decline and Fall of the Roman Empire*. New York: Dutton.

Hammer, M. 1996. *Beyond Engineering*. New York, NY: Harper Business Publishers.

Hubbard, D. 2014. *How to Measure Anything: Finding the Value of "Intangibles" in Business*, 3rd ed. Hoboken, NJ: Wiley.

Hult, M., and Sven-Ake Lennung. 1980. Towards a Definition of Action Research: A Note and Bibliography. *Journal of Management Studies* 17 (2): 241–250.

Horner, P. 2018. Analytics Extravaganza. *Informs/Analytics Magazine*, November–December, p. 2.

Janssen, M., H. van der Voort, and A. Wahyudi. 2017. Factors Influencing Big Data Decision-Making Quality. *Journal of Business Research* 70 (C): 338–345.

Jenkins, M., and G. Johnson. 1997. Linking Management Cognition and Organizational Performance: A Preliminary Investigation Using Causal Maps. *British Journal of Management* 8 (2): 77–90.

Kahneman, D., and A. Tversky. 1973. On the Psychology of Prediction. *Psychological Review* 80 (4): 237–251.

Kaufman, M., and D. Kirsch. 2014. *Advanced Analytics: The Hurwitz Victory Index Report*. Needham, MA: Hurwitz & Associates.

Kiron, D., R.B. Ferguson, and P.K. Prentice. 2013. *From Value to Vision: Reimaging the Possible with Data Analytics*. MIT Sloan Management Review, Research Report. Government Organizations. *Technology Analysis & Strategic Management* 11 (4): 493–525.

Kiron, D., R. Shockley, N. Kruschwitz, G. Finch, and M. Haydock. 2010. *Analytics: The Widening Divide: How Companies Are Achieving Competitive Advantage Through Analytics*. IBM Institute for Business Value.

Kraemer, K., and J. King. 1986. Computing and Public Organizations. *Public Administration Review* 46 (November): 488–496.

Laurson, G.H.N., and J. Thorlund. 2010. *Business Analytics for Managers: Taking Business Intelligence Beyond Reporting*. New York, NY: Wiley.

Leavitt, H. 1975. Beyond the Analytic Manager. *California Management Review* 17 (3): 5–12.

L'Huillier, G., and S. Maldonado. 2011. Future Trends in Business Analytics and Optimization. *Intelligent Data Analysis* 15 (6): 1001–1017.

Liedtka, J., and T. Ogilvie. 2011. *Designing for Growth: A Design Thinking Tool Kit for Managers*. New York: Columbia Business School Publishing.

Madtiavan, R., and P. Grover. 1998. From Embedded Knowledge to Embodied Knowledge: New Product Development as Knowledge Management. *Journal of Marketing* 62 (4): 1–12.

Nutt, P. 1990. Strategic Decision-Making by Top Executives and Middle Managers with Data and Process Dominant Stages. *Journal of Management Studies* 27 (2): 173–194.

Polydrack, R. 2018. *The New Mind Readers: What Neuroimaging Can and Cannot Reveal About Our Thoughts*. Princeton, NJ: Princeton University Press.

Popper, K. 1959. *The Logic of Scientific Discovery*. Great Britain: TJ International Ltd, Padstow, Cornwall.

Rockart, J., and D. DeLong. 1988. *Executive Support Systems: The Emergence of Top Management Computer User*. Homewood, IL: Irwin Publishers.

Schlesinger, A.M. 1965. *A Thousand Days: John F. Kennedy in the White House*. Boston, MA: Houghton Mifflin.

Schroeck, M., R. Shockley, J. Smart, D. Romero-Morales, and P. Tufano. 2012. *Analytics: The Real World Use of Big Data. How Innovative Enterprises Extract Value from Uncertain Data*. New York: IBM Institute for Business Value.

Siegel, E. 2013. Predictive Analytics. *Analytics Magazine*, July/August, pp. 38–43.

Simon, H. 1955. A Behavioral Model of Rational Choice. *Quarterly Journal of Economics* 59 (2): 99–118.

Simon, H. 1982. *Models of Bounded Rationality*. Cambridge, MA: MIT Press.

Taylor, L., R. Schroeder, and E. Meyer. 2014. Emerging Practices and Perspectives on Big Data Analysis in Economics: Bigger and Better or More of the Same? *Big Data & Society*, July–December, pp. 1–10.

Toynbee, A. *A Study of History, Vol. I-III (1934), Vol. IV-VI 1939), Vol. VII-X (1954), Vol. XI (1959), Vol. XII (1961)*. Oxford: Oxford University Press.

Ulvila, J.W., and R.V. Brown. 1982. Decision Analysis Comes of Age. *Harvard Business Review* 60 (5): 130–141.

Wang, G., A. Gunasekaran, E.W. Ngai, and T. Papadopoulos. 2016. Big Data Analytics in Logistics and Supply Chain Management: Certain Investigations for Research and Applications. *International Journal of Production Economics* 176: 98–110.

Zwolenski, M., and L. Weatherill. 2014. The Digital Universe: Rich Data and the Increasing Value of the Internet of Things. *Journal of Telecommunications and the Digital Economy* 2 (3): 47.1–47.9.

The manufacturer's authorised representative in the EU is Springer Nature Customer Service Centre GmbH, Europaplatz 3, 69115 Heidelberg, Germany. If you have any concerns regarding our products, please contact ProductSafety@springernature.com

Printed and bound by CPI Group (UK) Ltd, Croydon, CR0 4YY
22/09/2026
02221054-0004